£2.00

UNIVERSITY OF CAMBRIDGE
DEPARTMENT OF APPLIED ECONOMICS

MONOGRAPH 19

TAKE-OVERS

THEIR RELEVANCE TO THE STOCK MARKET
AND THE THEORY OF THE FIRM

UNIVERSITY OF CAMBRIDGE
DEPARTMENT OF APPLIED ECONOMICS

MONOGRAPHS

This series consists of investigations conducted by members of the Department's staff and others working in direct collaboration with the Department.

The Department of Applied Economics assumes no responsibility for the views expressed in the Monographs published under its auspices.

The following Monographs are still in print.

1. The Measurement of Production Movements
by C. F. CARTER, W. B. REDDAWAY *and* RICHARD STONE
4. The Analysis of Family Budgets
by S. J. PRAIS *and* H. S. HOUTHAKKER (*Reissue*)
5. The Lognormal Distribution
by J. AITCHISON *and* J. A. C. BROWN
6. Productivity and Technical Change   *by* W. E. G. SALTER
Second edition, with Addendum by W. B. REDDAWAY
7. The Ownership of Major Consumer Durables   *by* J. S. CRAMER
8. British Economic Growth, 1688–1959
by PHYLLIS DEANE *and* W. A. COLE (*Second edition*)
10. The Economics of Capital Utilisation   *by* R. MARRIS
11. Priority Patterns and the Demand for Household
Durable Goods   *by* F. G. PYATT
12. The Growth of Television Ownership in the
United Kingdom   *by* A. D. BAIN
13. The British Patent System   1. Administration   *by* KLAUS BOEHM
14. The Wealth of the Nation *by* JACK REVELL
15. Planning, Programming and Input-Output Models
Selected Papers on Indian Planning   by A. GHOSH
16. Biproportional Matrices and Input–Output Change
by MICHAEL BACHARACH
17. Abstract of British Historical Statistics
by B. R. MITCHELL *in collaboration with* PHYLLIS DEANE
18. Second Abstract of British Historical Statistics
by B. R. MITCHELL *and* H. G. JONES
19. Take-overs: their Relevance to the Stock Market and the
Theory of the Firm   *by* AJIT SINGH

TAKE-OVERS

THEIR RELEVANCE TO THE STOCK MARKET
AND THE THEORY OF THE FIRM

AJIT SINGH

University Lecturer in Economics and
Fellow of Queens' College, Cambridge

CAMBRIDGE

AT THE UNIVERSITY PRESS

1971

Published by the Syndics of the Cambridge University Press
Bentley House, 200 Euston Road, London NW1 2DB
American Branch: 32 East 57th Street, New York, N.Y.10022

© Cambridge University Press 1971

Library of Congress Catalogue Card Number: 79-160098

ISBN: 0 521 08245 5

Printed in Great Britain
at the University Printing House, Cambridge
(Brooke Crutchley, University Printer)

CONTENTS

TABLES

viii   **Tables**

FIGURES

PREFACE

This study is a sequel to the analysis of the economic characteristics of U.K. quoted industrial firms presented in A. Singh and G. Whittington, *Growth, Profitability and Valuation* (Cambridge University Press, 1968). That book contained an interfirm investigation of *surviving* firms (firms which existed throughout the period 1948–60, or over two shorter periods 1948–54 and 1954–60) in selected industrial groups.

The present study is primarily concerned with firms which did not survive: in particular, with those which died through merger or take-over (the latter being by far the most important cause of disappearance of firms which are quoted on the stock market). It analyses the economic and financial characteristics of taken over firms and compares them with those of firms not taken over. It also compares the records of the taken-over (acquired) and the acquiring firms, as well as those of the acquiring and the non-acquiring ones. A shorter time period (1954–60) is covered than in the earlier study, but the analysis is extended to a larger number of industrial groups.

I first became interested in take-overs several years ago, when I spent a year in Cambridge in 1963 and wrote a preliminary paper on the subject. In the summer of 1964 I presented at Berkeley a revised version of this paper, which was essentially an attempt at testing Robin Marris's theory of take-over bids. I returned to Cambridge at the end of that year, but the work on take-overs was interrupted while *Growth, Profitability and Valuation* was completed. A study of surviving firms took precedence over an examination of those which did not survive – it is a moot point whether this is a correct order of priorities.

It is only in the past two years or so that I have been able to resume empirical research on take-overs. However, as a result of the course of lectures I have been giving on the theory of the firm, my conception of the problem of take-overs has changed considerably since I first worked on it. I have come to realize that the question, 'What kind of firm on the stock market is taken-over?' is of much broader relevance than any particular theory of take-over bids. The following pages give ample demonstration of this changed outlook which I can only hope is a change for the better.

An empirical work of this kind is inevitably the product of the co-operation of several individuals and organisations. It is a pleasure to acknowledge my indebtedness to the Department of Applied Economics where the research project was carried out, and which in addition to providing an encouraging atmosphere for this research, also supplied computing, programming and secretarial assistance. I should especially like to thank H. T. Burley and Joyce Wheeler for help with programming and Joan Morrison and Leslie Cameron for their computational assistance.

Another organisation whose cooperation was essential for the successful completion of this project was the Board of Trade. It is with pleasure that I recall the courtesy and helpfulness of the Board's officials.

The basic data on share prices were obtained from Moodies cards and I should like to thank Moodies Services Ltd for promptly dealing with various queries and for permission to use their files. For the last two years, the research has been financed by a generous grant from the Social Science Research Council. The Esmée Fairbairn Foundation financed the earlier crucial stages of the larger project on company finance at the Department of Applied Economics, which provided the main body of data for this book.

Of the several people who have offered comments or read various portions of the manuscript, I should like especially to thank A. B. Atkinson, D. G. Champernowne, J. L. Eatwell, K. D. George, W. B. Reddaway, R. E. Rowthorn, G. Whittington and A. J. B. Wood. I am particularly indebted to W. B. Reddaway for reading the entire manuscript, for much useful advice and for saving me from some embarrassing errors. An earlier version of this book was submitted as a doctoral dissertation at the University of California, Berkeley, and I am grateful to Dale W. Jorgenson and K. Roland Artle for many constructive comments. None of the above-mentioned individuals or organisations are, of course, implicated in any way by any errors which may remain, or by the conclusions of the study; these are the author's responsibility alone.

Finally, my thanks are due to the editorial officers of Cambridge University Press for the immense pains they have taken with the manuscript.

Cambridge, June 1970   AJIT SINGH

CONVENTIONS AND DEFINITIONS

1. Readers may like to note that in the following chapters the words 'take-over' and 'acquisition' are used interchangeably, as are the words 'company' and 'firm'.

2. The *formal* definitions of 'take-over' and 'merger' used in this study are as follows:

Take-over When a firm A acquires more than 50% of the equity of firm B, B is deemed to have been taken over by A.

Merger A merger between two firms A and B is deemed to occur when these two firms amalgamate to form a new legal entity (say) C.

For an economic interpretation of these definitions, and in particular for the economic significance of the distinction between 'take-over' and 'merger', the reader is referred to chapter 2.

1. TAKE-OVERS, THE STOCK MARKET AND THE THEORY OF THE FIRM

INTRODUCTION

Acquisitions and mergers have been an integral part of the development of capitalist economies and as a result there exists a vast body of literature on these subjects both in the U.S. and in the U.K. Most of the studies are, however, descriptive and non-theoretical in nature. As Jesse W. Markham put it in his survey of the literature on mergers in the United States up to the early 1950s: 'The paths of economic theory and merger literature have rarely crossed.'[†] Even when the paths have crossed, economists have been overwhelmingly concerned with the relationship of mergers and amalgamations to changes in market structure, and their consequences for the allocation of resources.[‡] The relationship between overall merger activity and certain macroeconomic variables has also received attention in the context of the study of merger movements.[§] However, until recently, the subject of take-overs and mergers has been studied relatively little from the point of view of their implications for the *behaviour* of the individual firm.

The present study considers take-overs from this viewpoint. Essentially, it tries to answer the following kinds of questions. In the environment of an advanced capitalist economy, characterised by well organised stock markets and relatively dispersed ownership of shares, what kinds of firms are taken over? What are the important characteristics of the taken-over firm, and how are these characteristics different from those of firms which are not taken over? For firms quoted on the stock market, is it possible to generalise and suggest that the possession of certain definite economic and financial characteristics may make a firm more likely to be taken over?

[†] Jesse W. Markham, 'Survey of the evidence and findings on mergers', in *Business Concentration and Price Policy*, Conference of the Universities–National Bureau Committee for Economic Research, Princeton, 1955, p. 143.

[‡] See for example, G. J. Stigler, 'Monopoly and oligopoly by merger', *American Economic Review*, Supplement, May 1950, pp. 23–34. For an interesting recent study, see J. J. McGowan, 'The effects of alternative merger policies on size distribution of firms', *Yale Economic Essays*, Fall 1965. For the U.K., see for instance P. L. Cook and R. Cohen, *Effects of Mergers*, London, 1958.

[§] Cf. J. Fred Weston, *The Role of Mergers in the Growth of Large Firms*, Berkeley, 1953, pp. 77–84 and R. Nelson, *Merger Movements in American Industry, 1895–1956*, Princeton, 1959, pp. 106–26.

Apart from the fact that such questions are obviously interesting in their own right, there are at least two major reasons why economists should be interested in an enquiry of this kind. First, a study of the comparative characteristics of taken-over (or merged) firms is important for an understanding of the mechanism by which the stock market is supposed to perform some of its principal economic tasks. Secondly, the subject is important because it has a very significant bearing on the current controversy on the theory of the firm; in fact, in an important way, it lies at the heart of the debate between the proponents of the neoclassical theory of the firm on the one hand, and those of the new theories of the firm, such as Robin Marris, Oliver Williamson and W. J. Baumol, on the other. We shall elaborate on these two points in turn in the next two sections.

1.1   TAKE-OVERS AND THE STOCK MARKET

The most important economic function of the stock market – where titles to ownership in the form of securities are traded – is generally thought to be an allocative one: to allocate the capital resources of the community to their most profitable uses. In its ideal form, an active stock market, operating in an economy where there is wide dispersal of share ownership, provides the mechanism whereby the money savings of individuals and other economic units are pooled together and then allocated to those producing units where they are expected to find their most profitable use. If private profitability is assumed to be an indicator of 'efficiency' in the normal calculus of a capitalist economy, a perfect stock market (with equilibrium prices based on accurate forecasting of future profits) would bring about an efficient allocation of the available savings.† However, what is not always appreciated is that, apart from the task of 'efficient' allocation of new investment resources *in this particular sense*, another important function which the stock market may reasonably be expected to perform is to ensure that the *existing* assets of firms are also most profitably utilised.

The pricing of securities is the principal device by which the stock market performs its allocative functions. By assigning higher prices to the securities of the firms with higher prospective earnings per unit of resources, and relatively lower prices to those of firms with low prospective profitability, the market can ensure that the more 'efficient'

† As is well known, provided there is no divergence between social and private costs and valuations, provided competitive equilibrium prices rule in all markets, and provided the income distribution is socially desired, allocation of capital resources on the basis of private profitability would meet the criterion of 'social efficiency' in the sense of conventional welfare economics. Such conditions, however, are very far from being met in the real world; therefore, the word 'efficiency' used here carries no such connotation.

firms have cheaper access to investment funds and are therefore able to make greater use of them. For 'efficient' allocation of investment resources through the stock market it is thus necessary that equilibrium prices rule and that relative share prices accurately reflect the relative earnings prospects of the various firms.†

Although there are differing views on this question, there is a good deal of evidence that the prices yielded by stock markets in the real world are very far from such an ideal. This evidence indicates that apart from the inevitable ignorance of the future, share prices are much influenced by unequal availability of information, speculation, and by many other market imperfections, and that the capital market typically exhibits substantial disequilibrium.‡ There are, for example, large differences in the observed rates of return on company shares, which persist over fairly long periods of time (10 or more years) and which cannot be accounted for by differences in their relative riskiness. These differences can reasonably be explained only on the hypothesis of market disequilibrium and/or market imperfections.§

It is not the purpose of this study to discuss either the above evidence or other ramifications of this issue. However, what *is* relevant to this study is the question how, even if the market yields an ideal or a reasonably good configuration of prices, it ensures that the existing assets of the firms whose securities are traded on the market are efficiently used. How does it discipline the less 'efficient' managements, who may make low, but not necessarily negative, profits? Presumably, one method by which it can do so is again through its normal pricing process, mentioned above, which would assign relatively lower share prices, per unit of assets, to firms with poor profitability prospects (under existing management) and *vice versa*. To the extent that the market judges the profitability prospects of a firm by its past profitability record,‖ the prices assigned to the shares of firms with poor performance would act as a deterrent to their managements. This would make it more difficult and in the limiting cases impossible for such firms to grow by raising new funds on the market.

† Cf. W. J. Baumol, *The Stock Market and Economic Efficiency*, New York, 1965, pp. 35–7.
‡ See for instance, M. Nerlove, 'Factors affecting differences among rates of return on investments in individual common stocks', *Review of Economics and Statistics*, August 1968, pp. 312–31; Otto Eckstein, 'A survey of the theory of public expenditure criteria, reply', in *Public Finance: Needs, Sources and Utilization*, Conference of the Universities–National Bureau Committee for Economic Research, Princeton, 1961, p. 493; M. J. Farrell, 'On the structure of the capital market', *Economic Journal*, December 1962, pp. 830–44. See also Baumol [1965], pp. 39–46, where the evidence on random walk behaviour of share prices and its implications for the allocative efficiency of the stock market are discussed.
§ Nerlove [1968].
‖ There is in fact evidence that the future profitability of a firm is fairly highly correlated with its past profitability. See A. Singh and G. Whittington, *Growth, Profitability and Valuation*, Cambridge, 1968, pp. 133–44.

There are, however, some important limitations to the efficacy of such a disciplinary device. Firstly, a large number of firms in the economy, including many of the large manufacturing firms, make relatively little use of the market for raising new funds. For a number of institutional and other reasons which need not detain us here,† these firms not only raise a very small proportion of their investment resources from the market (relying largely on a self-finance), but also make very infrequent use of it. For example, Gordon Donaldson, in a study of the financing of 20 large U.S. manufacturing corporations over the period 1939–58, found that over the entire 20-year period, '7 of the 20 companies generated internally *more than 100 per cent* of their long-term capital requirements. Five more generated over 95 per cent. Another five were in the 80–95 per cent range. Only 3 fell below 80 per cent...With respect to the frequency of outside financing, 3 of the 20 companies did not go to the long-term capital market at all. Of the remainder, 16 borrowed, 3 of them only once, 5 only twice. Five companies issued preferred stock, 4, common. Only 2 issued common more than once. Only 4 made really intensive use of the capital market.'‡ Donaldson concluded from these figures: 'Thus it may be said of the majority [of companies in the sample] that during the period, either by chance or by design, they were able to conduct their business fundamentally independently of the capital market and with funds over which the management had free and independent jurisdiction.'§

In spite of the fact that larger companies in the U.K. make greater use of the capital market than Donaldson's figures would suggest is the case in the U.S., there are still a number of quoted manufacturing firms which rely almost entirely on self-finance and for which finance from the market is of negligible importance.‖ These firms are clearly able to survive despite the discipline of the stock-market pricing process, although it could still be argued that their growth would be limited relative to the firms which do make use of external finance. It is *a priori* possible to maintain that the firms which do not use external finance may appear not to 'need' it because they limit their growth to what they can finance internally – just because external finance would be expensive. Whether, and how far, this is in fact the

---

† For example, transaction costs, the relative (to retentions) uncertainty of new issue finance, management desire to avoid stock-market discipline, etc. Cf. Farrell [1962], p. 841; Baumol [1965], pp. 71–6.

‡ Gordon Donaldson, *Corporate Debt Capacity*, Boston, 1961. Donaldson's empirical findings are more conveniently summarised in Baumol [1965], p. 69, which is the source of the quotation in the text.

§ Donaldson [1961], p. 39.

‖ Over the period 1954–60, half the quoted firms in the four industries studied by Singh and Whittington generated internally 100% or more of their long-term finance. Cf. Singh and Whittington [1968], pp. 39–45.

case is an interesting empirical question which could repay investigation.

Secondly and more significantly, perhaps, many of the firms which do go to the stock market to meet their investment requirements may *also* be in a position to evade the discipline of the pricing process. This is particularly so in the case of large firms, with widely held shares, in which there is a divorce of ownership from control. In principle, it is possible for the (salaried) managers of such a firm, if they so desire,† to raise finance on the stock market even if the past record of the firm has not been good, its share prices are consequently lower than they should be, and its prospective expansion is relatively unprofitable. The existing individual shareholders of the firm, being dispersed and unorganised, may not be in a position to resist this expansion, in spite of the fact that this would entail the issue of debentures or a dilution of their equity by the sale of shares at a price which is above par, but below the present price of their shares.

Such an extreme situation of managerial ascendency and shareholder impotence would only be possible, however, if no other disciplinary device existed on the stock market apart from the pricing of shares and the (consequent) terms at which external finance is made available to the firms. This is clearly not the case, since even firms in which the shareholders are unable to exercise authority or those which rely entirely on self-finance have to reckon with the threat of a take-over bid. J. E. Meade sums up the argument on this point as follows:‡ 'A company which sacrifices profit either to an easy life or to unprofitable growth makes itself liable to a take-over bid. Suppose that the management of a large concern has become slack in the sense that it is not effectively selling the product for which consumers are prepared to pay most or it is not cutting its costs of production most efficiently; or suppose that the management of the concern is sacrificing profit to growth by using funds to finance the company's growth, even though this is a relatively unprofitable form of business. In such circumstances the replacement of the management by one which is more efficient or profit-minded could increase the market value of the company's shares. It may well be true that the ordinary shareholders dispersed throughout society will not in fact be able to get together to enforce such a change. But a generous bid for the company's shares on the part of some other large company or institution may enable a majority of the shares to be acquired by a single institutional owner which can enforce the change of management, increase thereby the value of the company's shares and thus reap a large benefit. Experience suggests that large

† On managerial motivation and the related issues, see the discussion of the next section.
‡ J. E. Meade, 'Is "the new industrial state" inevitable', *Economic Journal*, June 1968, p. 387.

companies are in fact threatened with this fate if they fail to be suf-
ficiently profit-minded.'

Take-over bids – or the threat of them – thus constitute an important
disciplinary device by which a well organised stock market can perform
one of its major tasks: to ensure efficient utilisation of existing assets,
or, to use Baumol's expressive phrase, to serve as the 'guardian of
efficiency' of the operations of the individual firm.† It is therefore important to study empirically the nature of this disciplining mechanism,
and to discover whether the 'experience' to which Meade refers is a
valid characterisation of reality. By carefully analysing the records of
firms which are the subjects of take-overs, and by comparing them with
the records of firms which are not taken over, it may be possible to
throw some light on these questions.

1.2   TAKE-OVERS AND THE THEORY OF THE FIRM
(a)   Economic natural selection

The assumption of profit maximisation, which is central to the neoclassical theory of the firm and to the rest of neoclassical analysis, has
been the subject of a great deal of criticism from a number of different
quarters. Several economists, over a number of years, have argued that
firms may not be engaged in a single-minded pursuit of profits. Recently,
it has been forcefully argued that in a modern corporation, characterised
by a divorce of ownership from control, the 'salaried' managers will
be less interested in maximising the profits (or stock-market valuation)‡

† Baumol [1965], p. 67. It is surprising that in this connection Baumol does not mention take-
over bids as a *direct* means by which the stock market can perform this task. Instead he
discusses the 'indirect and subtle sanctions which grant fully effective powers of regulation
to the exchange'. He goes on to say (p. 80): 'The evidence on these matters is impres-
sionistic at best. The sceptic may describe it as no more than a collection of anecdotes...
Yet one is left with the strong impression that the basic empirical allegation is correct:
that it is a rare management which is willing to despise and ignore the market's valuation
of its company'. Although the significance of the sociological and other factors which
Baumol mentions is not to be underestimated, it is important to discover the effectiveness
of the market's ability to impose direct sanctions against 'inefficient' firms.
‡ When there are perfect markets and complete certainty, it is trivial to show that profit
maximisation is equivalent to maximising the stock-market valuation of the firm. However,
it has been suggested by Tintner and Papandreou that, when time and uncertainty are in-
troduced, the profit maximisation construct becomes 'an empirically irrelevant tautology'.
(Cf. A. G. Papandreou, 'Some basic problems in the theory of the firm' in B. F. Haley (ed.),
A Survey of Contemporary Economics, vol. II, Homewood, Ill., 1952 and the references to
G. Tintner's papers cited therein.)
In a well known paper (*American Economic Review*, June 1958), it has been shown by
Modigliani and Miller that, provided there is a perfect capital market, profit maximisation
unambiguously implies maximisation of the stock-market value of the firm, even under
conditions of uncertainty. It should be noted, however, that Modigliani and Miller's
argument requires not only a perfect capital market, but also the existence of equilibrium
prices in the capital market, which, if uncertainty is introduced, requires additional
assumptions.

of the firm, than they will be in maximising its rate of growth. This is
in part because the level of managerial salaries, as well as other goals
which the managers are supposed to seek (such as power, prestige etc.),
are related more to the size of the firm than to its profitability: in part,
it is due to the fact that the market for managers is imperfect and
managerial promotion usually takes place through bureaucratic and
political processes within the corporation, rather than through the
market. For all these reasons and many others it is suggested that the
managers are more likely to seek to increase the size of the firm they
work for than to maximise its profitability, in so far as these two objectives
conflict.†

Other writers have argued that, as far as the modern corporation is
concerned, it is no longer possible to talk about any single, all-embracing
fixed 'goal' of the firm, be it profit maximisation or growth maximisation. The present-day corporation is viewed as a bureaucratic organisation, whose goals are neither predetermined nor given, and whose
decisions are not automatically translated into practice. It is said to
possess a diversified and complex internal structure, encompassing
many social groupings, such as top executives, middle managers, shareholders, professional and technical staff, etc., whose interests differ and
(in the case of some of the groups at least) may not include profit maximisation. The interaction of the personal goals, motivations and aspirations
of these diverse groupings, it is suggested, determines at any time the
overall objectives which an organisation may set for itself, and the way
in which these objectives will be carried out.‡

However, the neoclassical position is that in spite of these alleged
changes in the nature of the corporation and its internal structure, it
is still valid for economists to postulate profit maximisation in their
models of the firm. This position has been defended on a number of

---

† This is a summary of the argument developed and documented by R. L. Marris in his
The Economic Theory of 'Managerial' Capitalism, London, 1964, pp. 46–109. See, however, the
work of W. G. Lewellen (*Executive Compensation in Large Corporations*, New York, 1968)
which casts doubt on the notion of purely 'salaried' managers. The question of possible
conflict between growth and profit maximisation is discussed at length in Marris [1964],
pp. 225–65. On this particular point, see also R. L. Marris, 'Profitability and growth
in the individual firm', *Business Ratios*, Spring 1967.
    For other formal models, in which the firm is supposed to maximise a dimension other
than profitability, see O. Williamson, *The Economics of Discretionary Behavior: Managerial
Objectives in a Theory of the Firm*, Englewood Cliffs, 1964 and W. J. Baumol, *Business
Behavior, Value and Growth*, New York, 1959, as well as Baumol's 'On the theory of the expansion of the firm', *American Economic Review*, December 1962.
‡ This is the gist of the argument advanced by some sociologists and the writers of the
behavioural school. See, for example, R. J. Monsen, Jr., and A. Downs, 'A theory of large
managerial firms', *Journal of Political Economy*, June 1965, pp. 221–36, and the references
contained therein; R. M. Cyert and J. G. March, *A Behavioral Theory of the Firm*, Englewood Cliffs, 1963. See also F. Machlup, 'Theories of the firm: marginalist, behavioral,
managerial', *American Economic Review*, March 1967, pp. 1–33.

grounds;† one of the more powerful arguments in its defence is the
notion of 'economic natural selection', due to A. Alchian, M. Friedman,
G. Becker and others.‡ It is argued that the facts about separation of
ownership and control, or the notion of the firm as a bureaucracy, or
the reference to the social relationships within it, are unimportant from
an economic point of view. The external environment of the firm,
mainly in the form of forces of competition, leave it little room for
manoeuvre. The firm is compelled to maximise profits for the sake of
sheer survival, whatever the inclinations of managers and other groups
in the corporation. In Friedman's words:§ 'The process of "natural
selection" thus helps to validate the maximisation of returns hypothesis –
or rather, given natural selection, the acceptance of the hypothesis can
be based largely on the judgement that it summarises appropriately
the conditions for survival.'

In reply to Friedman, Sidney Winter has carefully shown that
economic natural selection does not imply the survival of profit-
maximising firms, and the disappearance of the non-maximisers, in
every state of the world.‖ For example, in certain states of the world
involving oligopolistic competition, 'barriers' to entry, cost advantages
to large scale, etc., it is easy to show that the 'satisficers' (those who
seek satisfactory rather than optimum solutions) or firms pursuing other
goals (such as growth) are more likely to survive than the profit-maximis-
ing firms. In general, whether or not natural selection validates the maximisation of returns hypothesis depends crucially on the state of product
markets, technical conditions of production, the organisational forms
that are present, the financial strength of the existing firms and so on.

In the real world, where, for example, oligopolistic conditions and
high barriers to entry prevail in several important sectors of the
economy,¶ the force of economic 'natural selection', as an *a priori*

† In addition to the selection argument given below, another main line of defence has been
that the assumption of profit maximisation is not susceptible to direct test; that, even if it
were, the empirical validity of the assumptions of a theory is not particularly important in
assessing its usefulness; and that, in any case, in terms of the validity of its predictions, the
traditional theory performs adequately and better than any alternative models. There is
a vast and controversial literature on this subject. See, for example, M. Friedman, *Essays
in Positive Economics*, Chicago, 1953, pp. 3–43; T. C. Koopmans, *Three Essays on the State
of Economic Science*, New York, 1957, pp. 132–46. See also the contributions of H. Simon,
P. Samuelson and others on the methodological issues involved, in *American Economic
Review*, Papers and Proceedings, May 1963, pp. 204–37.
‡ A. A. Alchian, 'Uncertainty, evolution, and economic theory', *Journal of Political Economy*,
June 1950, pp. 211–21; Friedman [1953]; G. S. Becker, 'Irrational behavior and economic
theory', *Journal of Political Economy*, February 1962, pp. 1–13.
§ Friedman [1953], p. 22. A similar position is asserted by H. Johnson, 'The economic
approach to social questions', *Economica*, February 1968.
‖ S. G. Winter, Jr., 'Economic "natural selection" and the theory of the firm', *Yale
Economic Essays*, Spring 1964, pp. 225–72.
¶ See for example, J. Bain, *Barriers to New Competition*, Cambridge, Mass., 1956.

argument in favour of the neoclassical postulate, is thereby greatly diminished. In recognition of this, the argument has recently been recast in terms of competition in the capital market. It is suggested that even if the product markets are not perfect, competition in the capital market will ensure that only those who maximise (monopoly) profits survive. As A. Alchian and R. Kessel have put it,† 'despite the absence of competition in product markets, those who can most profitably utilise monopoly power will acquire control over them: competition in the capital markets will allocate monopoly rights to those who can use them most profitably. Therefore, so long as free capital markets are available, the absence of competition in product markets does not imply a different quality of management in monopolistic as compared with competitive enterprises.'

Indeed, if the capital market functioned in the way suggested – so that all firms which did not make the largest possible profits, given their resources, were acquired by profit maximisers – the neoclassical postulate (of profit maximisation) would be perfectly acceptable, even in the absence of perfect competition in product markets.‡

However, in opposition to the neoclassical economists, J. K. Galbraith and Robin Marris have argued that the selection process in the capital market does not in fact work in this manner. Marris asserts that over time the process of selection will drive out those who maximise profits and leave those who maximise growth.§ The basis for this assertion appears to be his belief that the rise of the management-controlled large corporation to a dominant position in the economy has fundamentally altered the nature of the economic environment and hence the dynamics of the selection process. As a result of this change, it is nowadays the firms which do not strive for maximum growth, or which 'sacrifice' growth to profits, which are more likely to be taken over. In a similar vein, J. K. Galbraith has suggested that 'the danger of involuntary take-over is negligible in the management calculations of the large firm and diminishes with growth and dispersal of stock ownership'.‖

† A. A. Alchian and R. A. Kessel, 'Competition, monopoly, and the pursuit of pecuniary gain', in *Aspects of Labor Economics*, Conference of the Universities–National Bureau Committee for Economic Research, Princeton, 1962, p. 160. A similar argument is put forward in J. G. Manne, 'Mergers and the market for corporate control', *Journal of Political Economy*, 1965, pp. 110–20.

‡ This argument implies *inter alia* that the market possesses full and detailed knowledge of the activities and potentialities of each firm: only if this is the case can any discrepancy between the achieved profitability of a firm and its possible profitability under another management be removed by market action.

§ R. L. Marris, 'Galbraith, Solow and the truth about corporations', *The Public Interest*, Spring 1968, p. 44. See also Marris' review of J. K. Galbraith's *The New Industrial State*, in *American Economic Review*, 1968, p. 242, n. 4.

‖ J. K. Galbraith, 'A review of a review', *The Public Interest*, Fall 1967, p. 114.

In view of these conflicting assertions, it is important to discover what precisely is the nature of the 'selection mechanism' in the capital market. Among the firms which have a quotation on the stock market, what kinds survive and which do not? In view of the fact that take-over is by far most important cause of disappearance of quoted firms (for example, as will be shown in the next chapter, of the industrial firms quoted on the U.K. stock exchanges which 'died' during the period 1954–60, more than 75 % were the victims of take-over), it is important to examine the nature of the companies taken over. This may tell us something about the nature of the selection mechanism and reveal some facts which have a bearing on the controversy in this important area of economic theory.

(b)   Take-overs and new theories of the firm

In the last few years Robin Marris, W. J. Baumol and Oliver William-son, among others, have put forward alternative models of the firm based on behavioural assumptions other than that firms aim to maximise their profits (or their stock-market valuation). Marris' work is par-ticularly relevant to the present study, for not only does the threat of take-overs play an important part in his model, but he also claims to have put forward for the first time a theory of take-over bids.†

It is probably true that until the publication of Marris' *The Economic Theory of 'Managerial' Capitalism*, there did not exist in the literature a formal theory of take-overs – in the sense of a unified explanation of what kind of firm is acquired. The literature did contain, however, a number of scattered suggestions with regard to the motives for acquisi-tions.‡ Though different writers put primary emphasis on different motivating factors, the more important reasons usually given for acquisitions may be summarised as follows:§

 (i)   desire to achieve production economies of large-scale and multi-unit operations;
 (ii) possibility of achieving distribution and advertising economies;
 (iii) financial advantages of large size;
 (iv) strategic control of patents;
 (v)   acquisition of financial resources;
 (vi) response to legal and institutional environment;
 (vii) tax advantages;

---

† Marris [1964], pp. 20, 29–40.

‡ The word 'motives' is used here in the sense of stimuli for take-over activity, as distinct from the overall objectives of the firm, such as profit maximisation, growth maximisation, etc.

§ Weston [1953], pp. 85–6, J. Bain, 'The theory of oligopoly: discussion', *American Economic Review*, Papers and Proceedings, May 1950, pp. 64–6.

(viii) gains from sale of securities;

(ix) gains of promoters;

(x) desire to limit competition, etc.

In Marris' theory of take-overs, all the above-mentioned factors can be subsumed into and conceptualised in terms of a single variable, the 'valuation ratio'. The valuation ratio, v, at any point of time, is defined as:

$$v = \frac{\text{stock-market value of a firm's equity capital}}{\text{book value of its net equity assets}} \dagger$$

If assets were valued in company balance sheets at replacement cost, the denominator of the above expression, with the usual assumptions, could be regarded as a reflection of the value of the economic resources employed by the firm. The numerator on the other hand reflects the stock market's valuation of the earning power of these resources under the existing management, i.e. it reflects the value of the firm as a going concern under the present management. Under certain 'golden age' conditions, it is possible for the valuation ratios of all firms to be equal to unity. However, in the real world of uncertainty, rapidly changing conditions and various imperfections, this ratio will almost certainly be different from unity for most firms.

Marris suggests that, corresponding to the market's valuation ratio (v_{im}) of any firm i, there also exists some other firm (person) j's subjective valuation ratio (v_{ij}), reflecting j's valuation of i if it were to acquire i. The 'theory' of take-over bids then simply asserts that, other things being equal, the firm i is likely to be taken over by firm j if j's valuation ratio for i is higher than the market's and any other firms' valuation ratio for i. The theory is evidently expounded in the context of growth and investment opportunities of larger managerial firms. Firm j's valuation ratio for firm i would normally be higher than the market's only if it expects (by providing better management organisation or by pursuing different financial policies) to obtain a higher rate of return than the market expects to be achieved by the existing management.

This 'theory' of take-overs is indeed simple, but unfortunately it is not easily testable. One of the two main variables (v_{ij}) cannot be observed,

---

† Marris [1964], pp. 22–9. For empirical measurements of the 'valuation ratio' for U.K. quoted industrial firms, see Singh and Whittington [1968], pp. 53–61. The concept of the valuation ratio, although that name is not used for it, is also discussed and empirically measured in the literature on the theory of finance. See, for example, W. Gutman, 'Book value–market value patterns', in E. M. Lerner (ed.), *Readings in Financial Analysis and Investment Management*, Homewood, Illinois, 1963; S. Cottle and T. Whitman, *Corporate Earning Power and Market Valuation, 1935–55*, Durham, N. Carolina, 1959.

For the use of the 'valuation ratio' in a different area of economic theory, see N. Kaldor, 'Marginal productivity and the macroeconomic theories of distribution', *Review of Economic Studies*, 1966, pp. 309–19.

though v_{im} is empirically measurable at any point of time. Although it is possible by making some additional (not altogether implausible) assumptions to derive empirically testable propositions from this theory,† it does not provide a useful framework of analysis for our present purposes since it looks at the problem from the point of view of the acquiring firm rather than from that of the one acquired and there may be a multitude of potential acquirers for any particular firm.

However, the notion of a *threat* of take-over, as embodied in Marris' model of the growth of the firm, is more interesting and has richer empirical content. This threat is expressed in terms of a constraint on the firm's market valuation ratio. In this model, the managers of the firm aim to maximise its rate of growth, subject to the constraint that they do not wish the firm to be taken over. It is suggested by Marris that the lower a firm's valuation ratio, the more likely it is to be taken over. This is a very interesting and an important proposition, which can be tested by making a suitable comparison of the valuation ratios of firms which are acquired and those of firms which are not the subject of take-over.

(c)   *Summing up*

At this point, we shall sum up the discussion of the last two sections, which has ranged over a number of inter-connected issues. In section 1.1 we showed that take-overs are an essential mechanism by which the stock market can perform one of its major tasks – to ensure that the existing assets of firms are properly utilised. If such a mechanism is effective to any degree, then even firms which do not usually go to the market to raise new funds, or which are effectively controlled by 'salaried' managers whose goals may be different from those of the shareholders, will be subject to that degree to *direct* market discipline. And if the take-over mechanism works perfectly, then by definition no non-profit-maximisers will survive.

This conclusion, as we saw in section 1.2 (a) above, is relevant to the controversy over the central behavioural assumption of profit maximisation in the neoclassical theory of the firm. If there is a perfect capital market – perfect both in terms of the valuation of company securities and in terms of the take-over mechanism referred to above – then profit maximisation would seem to be the correct behavioural assumption to make, regardless of what the internal structure of the firm is, and whether or not there are elements of monopoly in the product markets.

Given oligopolistic conditions in many of the product markets in which the large modern corporation typically operates, an essential difference between the neoclassical theory and the new theories of the

† Cf. A. Singh, 'Preliminary notes on a theory of take-overs', unpublished paper, Cambridge, 1963.

firm thus turns on the degree of efficacy of the capital-market discipline. In the limiting case, when this discipline is perfect, the neoclassical theory and Marris' theory, for instance, will yield the same predictions.†

In view of the fact that relatively few of the companies with a quotation on the stock market disappear through liquidation or means other than take-over, the *direct* expression of the capital-market discipline, particularly for the managerially controlled firms, is embodied very largely, if not entirely, in the take-over mechanism.‡ We know that in the real world this mechanism is unlikely to be perfect in the sense described above. However, the empirical question is how imperfect it is: is it only 'slightly' imperfect or 'very' imperfect? An empirical study of taken-over firms, and a comparison of the characteristics of such firms with those of firms which are not taken over, is likely to shed some light on this question, which, as shown above, is relevant both to a study of the efficiency of the stock market and to the current controversy on the theory of the firm. It must, however, be stressed that such a study will not do any more than that: it is unlikely to *settle* the controversy on these important economic issues for the simple reason that we are considering here only one of the ways – albeit a very important direct way – through which the stock-market discipline can work. There undoubtedly exist other sanctions – particularly the indirect, social ones – through which the market can in principle discipline recalcitrant firms, whether or not the take-over mechanism is effective.§ It is however only the latter which is the subject of this study.

1.3. THE PURPOSE AND SCOPE OF THE STUDY

The following chapters are essentially an empirical study of the taken-over (and the relatively very small number of merged ||) firms which were quoted on the stock markets, and which were engaged in manufacturing industry in the U.K., over the period 1954–60. The principal purpose of the empirical analysis is to investigate the nature and the

---

† Cf. Marris [1968], p. 44, and R. Solow, 'The truth further refined: a comment on Marris', *The Public Interest*, Spring 1968, pp. 49–50. See chapter 6 below for further discussion of this point.

‡ In a recent paper, 'Capitalism and the corporation', *Economica*, November 1969, B. Hindley makes a similar point: 'In principle, the market in corporate control is the only external constraint upon the managerial exploitation of the owners. In so far as other constraints are important, they are largely dependent on the existence of a market in corporate control.' (p. 431).

§ See n. †, p. 6, above, where Baumol's reference to these indirect channels is discussed. See also chapter 6 below.

|| For the economic significance of the distinction between take-over and merger, see section 2.2 below.

extent of the discipline which take-overs (or their threat) represent for firms quoted on the stock market. The economic significance of this question – in relation to the theory of the firm and stock-market efficiency – has been indicated in the previous two sections.

In order to dispel any misunderstanding, it is necessary to emphasise the rather limited scope of the present investigation. The previous economic studies of acquisitions and mergers, as noted earlier, have usually been concerned with other aspects of the subject, e.g. the effect on market structure, industrial concentration, etc. Although some of the information provided in this book may have a bearing on these and other issues, such problems receive little systematic attention here.

The present study restricts itself to those empirical questions which are directly related to the issues of stock-market discipline and to certain other aspects of stock-market efficiency. With this objective in mind, the *comparative* economic and financial characteristics of the taken-over firms are systematically analysed and in particular the following empirical questions are discussed in varying degrees of detail. First, given the economic and financial records of firms which are quoted on the stock market, to what extent, if at all, is it possible to discriminate (*a*) between the taken-over and the surviving firms, (*b*) between the acquiring and the acquired firms and (*c*) between the acquiring and the non-acquiring firms? Secondly, if discrimination is possible, what are the most important distinguishing characteristics of the relevant groups of firms? The analysis is done on an inter-firm cross-sectional basis and both the short-term (one- and two-year) and the long-term (three- and six-year) records of firms are considered. Ten basic variables are used to indicate the record of each firm: four measures of the rate of return (pre-tax rate of return on net assets, post-tax rate of return on equity assets, dividend return, and 'productive' rate of return), three variables to indicate the firm's financial policy choices (liquidity ratio, gearing ratio and retention ratio), plus valuation ratio, growth and size. It will become clear in the chapters which follow (especially chapters 6 and 7) that the results of the empirical analysis, apart from their intrinsic interest, bear directly on the economic issues mentioned above.

1.4   THE DATA USED

This study is based on three main kinds and sources of information. First, and by far the most important, are the standardised accounting data on quoted industrial firms prepared by the Board of Trade. These data include more than seventy standardised items of quantitative information for each company for each year, relating to the company's profit and loss account, its balance sheet and its sources and uses of funds statement. Secondly, information on share prices and stock-market valuation of the firms has been used; the data were obtained from Moodies Cards, supplied by Moodies Services (U.K.), and from the Stock Exchange Yearbooks. Thirdly, the identities of the taken-over companies and the date of take-over for each company have been established by means of data obtained from the Board of Trade index of quoted companies and the Board's files on acquisitions.

The first two sources of information, i.e. the accounting data and the data on share prices, were also used in A. Singh and G. Whitting-ton, *Growth, Profitability and Valuation* (Cambridge, 1968), where full details of both were given and their main limitations discussed. It is not necessary to repeat that account in full here and the interested reader is referred to pages 213–37 of that book. A brief description is, however, given below in chapter 3, which also discusses the more important questions of the *relevance* and *suitability* of the information provided by these data for the problems analysed in this study. The third kind of information mentioned above is used and described in chapter 2.

Time period studied

As was pointed out in section 1.3, most of the empirical analysis of the following chapters is confined to quoted industrial firms (in the U.K.) over the period 1954–60. The choice of this particular period was dictated by three considerations. First, it saw a historically un-precedented spate of mergers and take-overs, which is still continuing and which is radically changing the structure of British industry. For instance, of the 2,000 or so industrial firms with a quotation on some U.K. stock market in 1954, more than 400 had been taken over or had disappeared through merger by the end of 1960. Such a phenomenon deserves to be investigated in its own right.

Secondly, the period 1954–60 is more suitable for the purposes of this enquiry than the earlier postwar years, which were marked by the continuance of many wartime controls, in both the product and the capital markets. These controls were very largely relaxed by 1954 and finally disappeared well before 1960.

Thirdly, and more importantly, the Board of Trade's standardised data on quoted public companies, which constitute the main source of information for this study, have been made available to the Department of Applied Economics only for the years 1948–60.† But it is important to point out that, although more data (especially for more recent years)

---

† The date for the post-1960 period are also in theory available from the Board of Trade. We have not been able to process them as yet, because the task would require rather large computing (and human) resources. Owing to major changes in company taxation (i.e. corporation tax) in the 1960s, and some changes in the Board's methods of preparation of data, there are also considerable problems of linking the data with the earlier time periods.

are always welcome, the amount available is sufficient, and displays enough industrial and temporal variation, for meaningful conclusions to be drawn about the comparative economic and financial characteristics of taken-over companies, at least during the period studied.

1.5   PLAN OF THE BOOK

In this chapter we have discussed the central purpose of this study, its general conception, the broad issues to which it is related and the nature of the data used. Chapter 2 deals with the main features of the take-overs and mergers which occurred among quoted industrial firms in the U.K. over the period 1948–60, and especially over the period 1954–60. This chapter presents, *inter alia*, a detailed statistical profile of the 'deaths', and causes of deaths, of quoted manufacturing firms in the U.K. over the period studied.

In chapters 3 to 5 the economic and financial characteristics of taken-over firms are compared with those of the surviving firms. The analysis of chapter 3 is done on a univariate basis and that of chapters 4 and 5 on a multivariate basis, i.e. in terms of all or suitable subsets of all characteristics taken together. Multiple discriminant analysis and Mahalanobis distance analysis are employed for the latter purpose, and these chapters include *inter alia* a discussion of the appropriate statistical methodology for dealing with multivariate comparisons.

In chapter 6, the empirical conclusions of chapters 3 to 5 are discussed in relation to the main economic issues – of stock-market discipline and of the theory of the firm – raised in the present chapter. Lastly, in chapter 7, the records of the *acquiring* firms are analysed and compared in turn with those of the acquired and of the non-acquiring firms. Some further aspects of the question of stock-market efficiency are also discussed in that chapter.

Readers may like to note that in the following chapters, the main conclusions – especially the main empirical conclusions – are normally summarised at the end of each chapter. Although all the qualifications to the conclusions cannot be given in the summaries (for these the reader must refer to the text of the chapters themselves), they may be found useful for cross-reference purposes as well as giving a brief abstract of what is contained in each chapter.

Finally, although it should be clear from the account given above, it is perhaps worth stressing again the empirical character of this study. Its usefulness must be judged mainly by the value of the data presented and the way these have been analysed.

2. TAKE-OVERS AND MERGERS IN U.K. MANUFACTURING INDUSTRY, 1948–60

INTRODUCTION

Since the middle 1950s a wave of take-overs, historically unprecendented in its scope and its effects, has swept through British industry. The following simple statistics speak for themselves: of the 2,126 firms engaged in manufacturing industry (excluding steel), which were quoted on the U.K. stock exchanges in 1954, more than 400 had been acquired by 1960.† Of the 100 or so largest firms in 1954 in the five industry groups in manufacturing which are the subject of detailed analysis in the following chapters (food, clothing and footwear, drink, electrical engineering and non-electrical engineering), 10 were taken over during the next 6 years.‡ The number of unquoted manufacturing companies and other smaller concerns acquired in the same period runs into thousands.§

This take-over movement has been far larger than those which occurred at the turn of the century and in the early 1920s, the major earlier amalgamation movements to have left their mark on British industry. It is far from having run its course. In this chapter we shall study in some detail the main features of the take-over and mergers which occurred in U.K. manufacturing industry over the period 1948–60, and especially in the period 1954–60; in particular we shall analyse the time pattern of take-overs, and the industrial characteristics and size distribution of the taken-over firms. The statistics presented in the main tables of this chapter have been collected from primary sources and are not available elsewhere in published form.‖

The main characteristics of the population of quoted firms – 'births',

---

† A further 21 companies had disappeared from the list through mergers. See sections 2.1 and 2.2 below for the source of these figures and for definitions of the terms 'take-over' and 'merger'. Readers are reminded that the words 'take-over' and 'acquisition' are used interchangeably throughout this study. ‡ See section 2.4 below.
§ Cf. R. W. Moon, *Business Mergers and Take-over Bids*, 3rd ed. London, 1968, p. 15.
‖ The main primary sources are the Board of Trade files on the individual quoted companies and the historical status indicator in the standardised company accounts prepared by the Board of Trade for each company. The Board has published some valuable information on take-overs and mergers in a number of articles, e.g. 'Acquisitions and amalgamations of quoted companies 1954–61', *Economic Trends*, No. 114, April 1963; 'Acquisitions and amalgamations of quoted companies 1962–63', *Economic Trends*, No. 146, Dec. 1965. However the information given in these articles is invariably presented from the point of view of the acquiring company, rather than from that of the acquired company. To this extent, this information is complementary to that presented in the following sections.

STO

'deaths', the number of 'surviving' firms – in manufacturing industry, over the whole period 1948–60 and during the second half of the period in particular, are discussed in section 2.1. In this section the incidence of births and deaths is compared with that observed for earlier periods in the U.K. economy. An analysis of the causes of death of firms in the two periods is presented in section 2.2. In the next two sections further statistics are presented relating to take-overs, mergers, liquidations and the size distribution of taken-over companies within the selected group of industries which receive particular attention in the rest of the book. The main conclusions of this chapter are summarised in section 2.5.

2.1 BIRTHS, DEATHS AND SURVIVING FIRMS IN MANUFACTURING INDUSTRY

Information about some of the main features of the U.K. industrial firms which were in existence over the periods 1948–60 and 1954–60 and were quoted on the stock exchanges is given in summary form in table 2.1. This table contains figures for firms in all sections of manufacturing industry except steel. Steel firms have had to be excluded for obvious reasons: the industry was nationalised at the beginning of the period under review; it then went through a process of denationalisation and reorganisation which makes it, for our purposes, unsuitable for comparison with other industries.

Strictly speaking, the population of firms analysed here consists of all quoted public companies in manufacturing industry for which the Board of Trade since 1953 (and the National Institute of Economic and Social Research before that date) has prepared standardised consolidated accounts.† Thus only quoted firms engaged in trade *in the U.K.* are included; those operating wholly or mainly overseas, such as the oil companies, are excluded. A quoted company is defined here as one whose shares (ordinary, preference or both) are quoted on the U.K. stock exchanges. Companies whose loan stock only is quoted are also included in this definition. However, in addition to the quoted companies there are also a rather small number of large unquoted companies which are important because of their size and for which the

---

† The Companies Act of 1948 made it in effect necessary for all public companies to provide consolidated accounts for each company group as a whole. It also imposed certain detailed minimum requirements on the accounting information to be provided by each company. It is therefore only since 1948 that it has been possible to put on a standardised basis the accounting information for quoted public companies, so that inter-firm comparisons of their characteristics can be made. This task was first undertaken by the National Institute of Economic and Social Research, which prepared standardised accounts for quoted public companies in manufacturing and certain other industries for the period 1948–53. This work has been continued since then by the Statistics Division of the Board of Trade.

Board of Trade prepares standardised accounts. In this study, when quoted companies are mentioned they include these few unquoted firms.†

The figures given in table 2.1 are for the individual manufacturing industries, as they are defined by the Standard Industrial Classification (S.I.C.) orders, and for all the industries taken together. The definitions of the orders changed in 1958, but as most of the period with which this study is concerned falls before that year, pre-1958 S.I.C. orders are used throughout.

The reader will probably find it easier to understand the significance of the figures in table 2.1 if we run through the information given in the column for a single industry. If we examine the data for chemicals, for instance, we find that of the 121 firms quoted on the U.K. stock exchanges which started out in the industry in 1948,‡ only 89 existed continuously throughout the period 1948–60. 36 new firms were 'born', i.e. added to the population of quoted firms over the period. To dispel any misunderstanding which may arise from the use of such biological terms as 'birth' and 'death', it is perhaps worth emphasising that the occurrence of a birth does not necessarily imply that a new concern has been started. It may merely mean that a long established firm has only just found it worthwhile to obtain a quotation on the stock market.

Of the 41 firms which are recorded as having 'died' in the chemical industry over the period 1948–60, 28 disappeared through acquisition. The causes of death, i.e. the disappearance from the list, of the remaining 13 are analysed in the next section, but it is again important to note that they need not all have literally died – in the sense of ceasing to trade. A few of them may, indeed, have disappeared from the list in this particular sense (say through liquidation); others may still be trading in their usual manner as independent concerns – for example some of them may, voluntarily or involuntarily, have merely lost their quotation on the stock market. Similarly it is obvious, but it is important to bear in mind, that even a company which has been acquired may very often carry on with its normal trading activities. An acquisition only implies a change in the legal ownership of the company.

Row 6 of table 2.1 is headed 'double counting' because it shows the number of firms which both were born and died during the period under consideration; thus, of the 121 quoted firms which *started out* in the chemical industry in 1948, 32 (total deaths – 'double counting'

---

† For further details and a more comprehensive definition of the companies included in the Board of Trade list, the interested reader is referred to Singh and Whittington [1968], pp. 207–8.

‡ The figures for the year 1948 refer to companies' accounting years finishing between 6 April 1948 and 5 April 1949; other years are similarly defined.

TABLE 2.1. *Industrial firms quoted on the U.K. stock exchanges 1948–60 and 1954–60 : births, deaths and continuing firms*

Period			Ind. 01 Bricks, Pottery, Cement, etc.		Ind. 02 Chemicals		Ind. 04 Non-electrical engineering		Ind. 05 Electrical engineering	
			No.	% of row 5	No.	% of row 5	No.	% of row 5	No.	% of row 5
1948–60	1.	Companies in 1948	105	70.0	121	77.1	270	70.1	113	73.4
	2.	Cos. which continued throughout the period	80	53.3	89	56.7	212	55.1	83	53.9
	3.	Births[a]	45	30.0	36	22.9	115	29.9	41	26.7
	4.	Deaths (all causes)[b]	29	19.3	41	26.1	75	19.5	35	22.7
	4a.	Deaths through acquisition	18	12.0	28	17.8	62	16.1	24	15.6
	5.	Total number of cos. included in the record (row 1+row 3)	150	100.0	157	100.0	385	100.0	154	100.0
	6.	Double counting[c]	4		9		17		5	
	7.	No. of cos. at end of period (1960)	121	80.7	116	73.9	310	80.5	119	77.3
1954–60	1.	Cos. in 1954	123	86.0	141	91.6	324	86.6	125	82.2
	2.	Cos. which continued throughout the period	102	71.3	105	68.2	261	69.8	93	61.2
	3.	Births	20	14.0	13	8.4	50	13.4	27	17.8
	4.	Deaths (all causes)[d]	22	15.4	38	24.7	64	17.1	33	21.7
	4a.	Deaths through acquisition	16	11.2	27	17.5	54	14.4	23	15.1
	5.	Total no. of cos. included in the record (row 1+row 3)	143	100.0	154	100.0	374	100.0	152	100.0
	6.	Double counting	1		2		1		1	
	7.	No. of cos. at end of period (1960)	121	84.6	116	75.3	310	82.9	119	78.2

Period	Ind. 06 Vehicles		Ind. 07 Metal goods		Ind. 08 Cotton, etc.		Ind. 09 Woollens	
	No.	% of row 5	No.	% of row 5	No.	% of row 5	No.	% of row 5
1948–60								
1. Companies in 1948	89	77.4	159	69.7	95	69.3	66	80.5
2. Cos. which continued throughout the period	60	52.2	127	55.7	49	35.8	51	62.2
3. Births[a]	26	22.6	69	30.3	42	30.7	16	19.5
4. Deaths (all causes)[b]	32	27.8	41	18.0	65	47.4	20	24.4
4a. Deaths through acquisition	26	22.6	31	13.6	30	21.9	16	19.5
5. Total number of cos. included in the record (row 1 + row 3)	115	100.0	228	100.0	137	100.0	82	100.0
6. Double counting[c]	3		9		19		5	
7. No. of cos. at end of period (1960)	83	72.2	187	82.0	72	52.5	62	75.6
1954–60								
1. Cos. in 1954	100	93.5	195	88.2	119	97.5	76	96.2
2. Cos. which continued throughout the period	76	71.0	162	73.3	69	56.5	59	74.7
3. Births	7	6.5	26	11.8	3	2.5	3	3.8
4. Deaths (all causes)[d]	24	22.4	34	15.4	50	41.0	17	21.5
4a. Deaths through acquisition	22	20.6	27	12.2	24	19.7	14	17.7
5. Total no. of cos. included in the record (row 1 + row 3)	107	100.0	221	100.0	122	100.0	79	100.0
6. Double counting	—		1		—		—	
7. No. of cos. at end of period (1960)	83	77.6	187	84.6	72	59.0	62	78.5

TABLE 2.1 (cont.)

Period		Ind. 10 Hosiery, etc.		Ind. 11 Clothing and Footwear		Ind. 12 Food		Ind. 13 Drink	
		No.	% of row 5	No.	% of row 5	No.	% of row 5	No.	% of row 5
1948-60	1. Companies in 1948	119	68.4	92	73.0	121	74.2	180	86.5
	2. Cos. which continued throughout the period	93	53.4	69	54.7	73	44.8	102	49.0
	3. Births[a]	55	31.6	34	27.0	42	25.8	28	13.5
	4. Deaths (all causes)[b]	32	18.4	27	21.4	57	35.0	85	40.9
	4a. Deaths through acquisition	21	21.1	22	17.5	48	29.4	71	34.1
	5. Total no. of cos. included in the record (row 1+row 3)	174	100.0	126	100.0	163	100.0	208	100.0
	6. Double counting[c]	6		4		9		7	
	7. No. of cos. at end of period (1960)	142	81.6	99	78.6	106	65.0	123	59.1
1954-60	1. Companies in 1954	147	87.5	101	82.8	141	88.7	187	96.9
	2. Cos. which continued throughout the period	122	72.6	78	63.9	91	57.2	117	60.6
	3. Births	21	12.5	21	17.2	18	11.3	6	3.1
	4. Deaths (all causes)[d]	26	15.5	23	18.8	53	33.3	70	36.3
	4a. Deaths through acquisition	18	10.7	19	15.6	46	28.9	58	30.1
	5. Total no. of cos. included in the record (row 1+row 3)	168	100.0	122	100.0	159	100.0	193	100.0
	6. Double counting[c]	1		—		3		—	
	7. No. of cos. at end of period (1960)	142	84.5	99	81.1	106	66.7	123	63.7

Period		Ind. 14 Tobacco		Ind. 15 Paper, etc.		Ind. 16 Leather, etc.		Total of Industries 01–16 except Industry 03 (Steel)	
		No.	% of row 5	No.	% of row 5	No.	% of row 5	No.	% of row 5
1948–60	1. Companies in 1948	14	87.5	135	78.0	165	77.1	1844	74.3
	2. Cos. which continued throughout the period	7	43.7	105	60.7	122	57.0	1322	53.3
	3. Births[a]	2	12.5	38	22.0	49	22.9	638	25.7
	4. Deaths (all causes)[b]	7	43.7	37	21.4	45	21.0	628	25.3
	4a. Deaths through acquisition	5	31.2	32	18.5	27	12.7	461	18.6
	5. Total no. of cos. included in the record (row 1 + row 3)	16	100.0	173	100.0	214	100.0	2482	100.0
	6. Double counting[c]	—		7		2		106	
	7. No. of cos. at end of period (1960)	9	56.2	136	78.6	169	79.0	1854	74.7
1954–60	1. Companies in 1954	11	84.6	148	89.7	188	89.5	2126	89.2
	2. Cos. which continued throughout the period	7	53.8	120	72.7	147	70.0	1609	67.5
	3. Births	2	15.4	17	10.3	22	10.5	256	10.7
	4. Deaths (all causes)[d]	4	30.8	29	17.6	41	19.5	528	22.2
	4a. Deaths through acquisition	4	30.8	27	16.4	26	12.4	405	17.0
	5. Total no. of cos. included in the record (row 1 + row 3)	13	100.0	165	100.0	210	100.0	2382	100.0
	6. Double counting[c]	—		—		—		11	
	7. No. of cos. at end of period (1960)	9	69.2	136	82.4	169	80.5	1854	77.8

[a] Births: year 1949 onwards. If born in year 1948, the firm will be included among those existing in 1948. A similar convention is used in the bottom half of the table. For definition of 'birth', see text.

[b] Deaths: year 1949 onwards. For definition of 'death', see text.

[c] Double counting refers to those firms which were born and died during the period under consideration.

[d] Deaths: year 1954 onwards.

= 41 − 9),† died during the period 1948–60. The bottom part of the table gives analogous information for the sub-period 1954–60.

Before we comment on the main features of table 2.1, it is of some interest to consider the significance of quoted companies in manufacturing industry.

The significance of quoted companies in manufacturing

In manufacturing industry the firms with a quotation on the stock market are of overwhelming importance. A 1953 survey showed that there were 1,945 quoted public companies, 1,457 unquoted public companies and 11,640 active non-exempt private companies engaged in manufacturing in England and Wales.‡ However, the quoted public sector accounted for 65 % of the total net assets employed by these companies. The average size of a quoted firm in manufacturing (measured in terms of the book value of net assets) was six times that of an unquoted firm, and thirteen times that of a non-exempt private firm.

The Board of Trade and Central Statistical Office calculations confirm the disproportionate significance of quoted public companies in manufacturing. They show that in 1958 quoted public companies accounted for 81 % of the gross trading profits of *all* companies in manufacturing industry as a whole, the proportion ranging from 57 % in the clothing and footwear industry to 79 % in food, drink and tobacco and 98 % in chemicals and allied trades.§

Thus, by confining our analysis of take-overs and mergers in manufacturing industry to quoted public companies, we are isolating for consideration those firms which account for the bulk of profits and assets, and which are typically much larger than other types of firms in this sector of the economy.

† Rows of table 2.1 observe the following identities:

$$\text{row } 5 = \text{row } 1 + \text{row } 3$$
$$= \text{row } 2 + \text{row } 4 - \text{row } 6 + \text{row } 3$$

and

$$\text{row } 7 = \text{row } 5 - \text{row } 4$$
$$= \text{row } 2 + \text{row } 3 - \text{row } 6.$$

‡ Cf. Ronald Ma: 'Composition of the corporate sector: II – a comparison of public and private companies', *Accounting Research*, October 1958, pp. 302–23. The 'non-exempt' private companies are required to disclose their trading and financial position, whereas the exempt companies are not.

§ Ministry of Labour, *Statistics on Income, Prices, Employment and Production*, No. 1, April 1962, p. 47. The disproportionate importance of quoted public companies in manufacturing industry is, if anything, increasing over time. For statistics on later periods see 'Non-quoted companies and their finance', *Economic Trends*, No. 136, February 1965 and 'Patterns of company finance', *Economic Trends*, No. 169, November 1967.

The incidence of births and deaths

Returning to table 2.1, we notice that since births and deaths occurred at much the same rate over the period 1948 to 1960, the total number of quoted firms in manufacturing industry (excluding steel) was almost the same in 1960 (1854) as it was in 1948 (1844). The last column of the table shows that of the total number of firms in the record over the 13-year period, 25.7 % were born and 25.3 % died during the period.

However over the sub-period 1954–60 the situation was very different. The incidence of deaths (22.2 %) was much greater than that of births (10.7 %), so that of the 2126 firms existing in 1954 only 1854 survived until 1960. It is worth noticing also that most of the deaths and acquisitions recorded for the period 1948–60 in fact occurred in the sub-period 1954–60. For all industries together (see the last but one column of table 2.1), of the 628 deaths and 461 acquisitions in the period 1948–60, 528 deaths and 405 acquisitions occurred in the sub-period 1954–60. The figures suggest that, over the latter time period, a quoted manufacturing firm had a nearly 1 in 4 chance of disappearing from the list, and a nearly 1 in 5 chance of being acquired.

For firms quoted on the stock market this represents an incidence of disappearance unprecedented in the U.K. economy. The following broadly comparable figures, for both births and deaths, put the situation into its historical perspective:†

	Annual birth rates[a] of quoted public companies	Annual death rates[b] of quoted public companies
1885–96	7.5	2.3
1896–1907	5.9	1.8
1907–24	2.2	1.2
1924–39	2.7	1.9
1939–50	2.6	1.1
1949–53	2.6	0.8
1954–60	2.0	3.2

[a] Expressed as % of the number of companies at the beginning of the period.
[b] Expressed as % of the number of companies at the end of the period.

† The figures for the period 1885–1950 have been obtained from P. E. Hart and S. J. Prais, 'The analysis of business concentration a statistical approach', *Journal of the Royal Statistical Society*, Series A (General), vol. 119, part 2, 1956, pp. 162–9. The figures refer to quoted companies engaged in mining, manufacturing and distribution, except for the period 1939–50 for which steel companies were excluded. The figures for the period 1949–53 have been taken from Ronald Ma, 'Births and deaths in the quoted public company sector in the United Kingdom, 1949–1953', *Yorkshire Bulletin of Economic and Social Research*, November 1960, pp. 90–5. The figures refer to quoted companies in manufacturing, building, distribution and services.
The figures for 1954–60 are based on table 2.1. However, a small adjustment had to be

These figures show that, whilst the birth rate in the sub-period 1954–60 was slightly lower than that observed since 1907, the death rate was very much higher. The annual death rate during the years 1954–60 was nearly four times the rate recorded for the immediately preceding period 1949–53, and nearly one-and-a-half times that for the period around the turn of this century, during which the most important earlier amalgamation movement occurred in the U.K.†

Table 2.1 also shows important differences in death rates between industries. The death rate over the sub-period 1954–60 varies from 15.4% in the brick, pottery and cement industry and 17.1% in the non-electrical engineering industry to 33.3% in the food industry and 41.0% in the cotton industry. A detailed examination of the causes of death of firms is presented in section 2.2, but it is quite clear, even at this stage of the analysis, that acquisition is the predominant cause of death. The incidence of death through acquisition never falls below 10% (of the number of firms in the record during the period), and is as high as 30% or more in the drink and tobacco industries.

It would be interesting to attempt an explanation of (i) the relatively much higher rate of overall disappearance of firms in the period 1954–60 and (ii) the observed inter-industry differences in the acquisition or disappearance rate during this period. A proper examination of these issues, however, lies outside the scope of this book.‡ As mentioned in chapter 1, this study of take-overs is principally concerned with questions of stock-market discipline and with certain other aspects of stock-market efficiency. To the extent that the overall acquisition rate and the inter-industry differences in this rate are relevant to these questions, they will be discussed in the following chapters. The empirical analysis of these chapters – in which an inter-firm comparison of the characteristics of the acquired, the non-acquired and the acquiring firms is made – is restricted to firms in 5 industrial groups: food, drink, electrical engineering, clothing and footwear, and non-electrical engineering. The incidence of acquisitions and mergers in the period 1954–60 was well above average in the first two of these industries, and a little below average in the latter three. There were 1000 quoted firms on the record in these industries during the period; of these, 200 had been

made to the figures for 'deaths' in this table in order to make them comparable with those of the earlier periods. In table 2.1, in the very small number of cases where two firms A and B 'merge' together to form a new firm C, both A and B are deemed to have 'died'. In Hart and Prais' figures only the smaller of the two firms is recorded as having died. See further the discussion in the next section which bears on this point.

† On the amalgamation movement at the turn of the century in the U.K. and for a comparison with that experienced during roughly the same period in the U.S., see Nelson [1959], pp. 129–38.

‡ These questions are being investigated in a separate study by Mr A. Hughes of King's College, Cambridge.

acquired by the end of 1960. However, the analysis in the following chapters is confined to about 180 of these firms, which were acquired during the years 1955–60.

2.2 ANALYSIS OF THE CAUSES OF DEATH OF FIRMS

Table 2.2 gives a detailed analysis of the causes of death of quoted manufacturing firms in the period 1948–60 and the sub-period 1954–60. The distinction in this table between acquisitions (or take-overs) and mergers is a purely legal one. When company A† acquires more than 50 % of the equity of company B, B is recorded as having been taken over or acquired by A. A merger between companies A and B is deemed to occur when the two companies amalgamate to form a new legal entity, say company C. Thus the distinction between acquisition and merger in this table turns on whether or not the amalgamation involves the creation of a new legal entity in place of two or more existing ones. From an economic point of view, this distinction is quite arbitrary in one sense, since the choice by firms of a legal form by which to effect an amalgamation has little to do with broader economic considerations.‡ However, in another sense, which is especially important in the context of this study, the difference between take-over and merger in the statistics presented in table 2.2 is indeed significant. This is because in the case of a take-over of company A by company B, only one company (A) is regarded as dying; if A and B merge, both are included as dying, although clearly both cannot be regarded as having been forced out of existence by a more successful or a bigger company.

This problem is usually dealt with in the literature by regarding the smaller of the two companies involved in a merger as being essentially an acquisition of the larger.§ This procedure has much to recommend it – on both *a priori* and practical grounds – when there are large differences in the 'sizes' of the merged companies; when this is not so and especially when the companies involved in a merger are nearly equal in size, the method loses much of its *a priori* justification. In view of this difficulty, we have in this book both (i) analysed the acquired

---

† The figures for acquisitions in table 2.2 (and other tables in this chapter) refer only to the acquisition of a quoted public company by another *company*. The acquiring company need not be a quoted public company; it could be unquoted, private or foreign-owned. However if an individual (as opposed to a company) acquires more than 50 % of the shares in a quoted public company, this is not listed as an acquisition in the statistics presented here. The incidence of such take-overs is however unlikely to be of any significance as far as quoted public companies are concerned.

‡ Cf. Moon [1968], pp. 47–66; 171–209.

§ This procedure was adopted by Hart and Prais [1956]. See also M. Gort, 'An economic disturbance theory of mergers', *Quarterly Journal of Economics*, November 1969.

TABLE 2.2. *Industrial firms quoted on the U.K. stock exchanges: causes of deaths of firms, 1948–60 and 1954–60*

a. 1948–60

Cause of death[a]	Ind. 01 Bricks, Pottery, etc.		Ind. 02 Chemicals		Ind. 04 Non-electrical engineering		Ind. 05 Electrical engineering		Ind. 06 Vehicles		Ind. 07 Metal goods		Ind. 08 Cotton, etc.		Ind. 09 Woollens	
	No.	%[b]	No.	%[b]	No.	%[b]	No.	%[b]	No.	%[b]	No.	%[b]	No.	%[b]	No.	%[b]
1. Acquisition	18	62.1	28	68.3	62	82.7	24	68.6	26	81.2	31	75.6	30	46.1	16	65.6
(a) acq. by co. in same industry	9	31.0	14	34.1	25	33.3	14	40.0	16	50.0	10	24.4	15	23.1	10	50.0
(b) acq. by co. in different ind.	5	17.2	5	12.2	28	37.3	6	17.1	8	25.0	18	43.9	4	6.1	5	25.0
(c) acq. by co. not in population	4	13.8	9	21.9	9	12.0	4	11.4	2	6.2	3	7.3	11	16.9	1	5.0
2. Merger	3	10.3	—	—	1	1.3	5	14.3	2	6.2	2	4.9	5	7.7	—	—
(a) merger with co. in same ind.	3	10.3	—	—	—	—	4	11.4	2	6.2	2	4.9	4	6.1	—	—
(b) merger with co. in different ind.	—	—	—	—	1	1.3	1	2.9	—	—	—	—	1	1.5	—	—
3. *Total acquisitions and mergers*	*21*	*72.4*	*28*	*68.3*	*63*	*84.0*	*29*	*82.9*	*28*	*87.5*	*33*	*80.5*	*35*	*53.8*	*16*	*80.0*
4. Liquidation	4	13.8	2	4.9	6	8.0	3	8.6	—	—	3	7.3	20	30.8	—	—
5. Ceased to trade	1	3.4	—	—	—	—	—	—	—	—	1	2.4	2	3.1	—	—
6. Loss of quotation	—	—	1	2.4	—	—	1	2.9	—	—	—	—	1	1.5	—	—
7. Conversion to private co., property co., etc.	—	—	2	4.9	1	1.3	—	—	—	—	1	2.4	3	4.6	—	—
8. Withdrawn from population (other causes)	1	3.4	1	2.4	—	—	1	2.9	2	6.2	2	4.9	—	—	—	—
9. Rebirth/reorganisation; miscellaneous	2	6.9	7	17.1	5	6.7	1	2.9	2	6.2	1	2.4	4	6.1	4	20.0
10. *Total deaths*	*29*	*99.9c*	*41*	*100.0c*	*75*	*100.0c*	*35*	*100.2c*	*32*	*99.9c*	*41*	*99.9c*	*65*	*99.9c*	*20*	*100.0c*

Cause of death[a]	Ind. 10 Hosiery, etc.		Ind. 11 Clothing & footwear		Ind. 12 Food		Ind. 13 Drink		Ind. 14 Tobacco		Ind. 15 Paper, etc.		Ind. 16 Leather, etc.		Total of Inds. 1–16 (except Industry 3)	
	No.	%[b]	No.	%[b]	No.	%[b]	No.	%[b]	No.	%[b]	No.	%[b]	No.	%[b]	No.	%[b]
1. Acquisition	21	65.6	22	81.5	48	84.2	71	83.5	5	71.4	32	86.5	27	60.0	461	73.2
(a) acq. by co. in same industry	8	25.0	6	22.2	36	63.1	67	78.8	4	57.1	25	67.6	9	20.0	268	42.5
(b) acq. by co. in different ind.	9	28.1	13	48.1	5	8.8	2	2.3	—	—	5	13.5	10	22.2	123	19.6
(c) acq. by co. not in population	4	12.5	3	11.1	7	12.3	2	2.3	1	14.3	2	5.4	8	17.8	70	11.1
2. Merger	—	—	—	—	2	3.5	7	8.2	—	—	—	—	—	—	27	4.5
(a) merger with co. in same ind.	—	—	—	—	—	—	7	8.2	—	—	—	—	—	—	22	3.7
(b) merger with co. in different ind.	—	—	—	—	2	3.5	—	—	—	—	—	—	—	—	5	0.8
3. *Total acquisitions and mergers*	*21*	*65.6*	*22*	*81.5*	*50*	*87.7*	*78*	*91.8*	*5*	*71.4*	*32*	*86.5*	*27*	*60.0*	*488*	*77.7*
4. Liquidation	6	18.7	2	7.4	4	7.0	1	1.2	1	14.3	—	—	10	22.2	62	9.9
5. Ceased to trade	1	3.1	—	—	—	—	—	—	—	—	—	—	1	2.2	6	0.9
6. Loss of quotation	—	—	—	—	—	—	2	2.3	—	—	—	—	1	2.2	6	0.9
7. Conversion to private co., property co., etc.	1	3.1	2	7.4	1	1.7	2	2.3	—	—	—	—	2	4.4	15	2.4
8. Withdrawn from population (other causes)	—	—	—	—	1	1.7	1	1.2	1	14.3	—	—	2	4.4	12	1.9
9. Rebirth/reorganisation; miscellaneous	3	9.4	1	3.7	1	1.7	1	1.2	—	—	5	13.5	2	4.4	39	6.2
10. *Total deaths*	*32*	*99.9*[c]	*27*	*100.0*[c]	*57*	*99.8*[c]	*85*	*100.0*[c]	*7*	*100.0*[c]	*37*	*100.0*[c]	*45*	*99.8*	*628*	*99.9*[c]

TABLE 2.2 (*cont.*)

b. 1954–60

Cause of death[a]	Ind. 01 Bricks, Pottery, etc.		Ind. 02 Chemicals		Ind. 04 Non-electrical engineering		Ind. 05 Electrical engineering		Ind. 06 Vehicles		Ind. 07 Metal goods		Ind. 08 Cotton, etc.		Ind. 09 Woollens	
	No.	%[b]	No.	%[b]	No.	%[b]	No.	%[b]	No.	%[b]	No.	%[b]	No.	%[b]	No.	%[b]
1. Acquisition	16	72.7	27	71.0	54	84.4	23	69.7	22	91.7	27	79.4	24	48.0	14	82.3
(a) acq. by co. in same industry	8	36.4	14	36.8	23	35.9	13	39.4	12	50.0	6	17.6	11	2.0	9	52.9
(b) acq. by co. in different ind.	3	13.6	5	13.2	24	37.5	6	18.2	8	33.3	17	50.0	4	8.0	4	23.5
(c) acq. by co. not in population	5	22.7	8	21.0	7	10.9	4	12.1	2	8.3	4	11.8	9	18.0	1	5.9
2. Merger	3	13.6	—	—	1	1.6	5	15.1	—	—	2	5.9	1	2.0	—	—
(a) merger with co. in same ind.	3	13.6	—	—	—	—	4	12.1	—	—	2	5.9	—	—	—	—
(b) merger with co. in different ind.	—	—	—	—	1	1.6	1	3.0	—	—	—	—	1	2.0	—	—
3. *Total acquisitions and mergers*	*19*	*86.4*	*27*	*71.0*	*55*	*85.9*	*28*	*84.8*	*22*	*91.7*	*29*	*85.3*	*25*	*50.0*	*14*	*82.3*
4. Liquidation	1	4.5	2	5.3	5	7.8	3	9.1	—	—	1	2.9	18	36.0	—	—
5. Ceased to trade	1	4.5	—	—	—	—	—	—	—	—	1	2.9	2	4.0	—	—
6. Loss of quotation	—	—	1	2.6	—	—	—	—	—	—	—	—	—	—	—	—
7. Conversion to private co., property co., etc.	—	—	2	5.3	1	1.6	—	—	—	—	1	2.9	3	6.0	—	—
8. Withdrawn from population (other causes)	—	—	1	2.6	—	—	1	3.0	2	8.3	2	5.9	1	2.0	—	—
9. Rebirth/reorganisation; miscellaneous	1	4.5	5	13.2	3	4.7	1	3.0	—	—	—	—	1	2.0	3	17.6
10. *Total deaths*	*22*	*99.9*[c]	*38*	*100.0*[c]	*64*	*100.0*[c]	*33*	*99.9*[c]	*24*	*100.0*[c]	*34*	*99.9*[c]	*50*	*100.0*[c]	*17*	*99.9*[c]

Cause of death[a]	Ind. 10 Hosiery, etc.		Ind. 11 Clothing & footwear		Ind. 12 Food		Ind. 13 Drink		Ind. 14 Tobacco		Ind. 15 Paper, etc.		Ind. 16 Leather, etc.		Total of Inds. 1–16 (except Industry 3)	
	No.	%[b]	No.	%[b]	No.	%[b]	No.	%[b]	No.	%[b]	No.	%[b]	No.	%[b]	No.	%[b]
1. Acquisition	18	69.2	19	82.6	46	86.8	58	82.9	4	100.0	27	93.1	26	63.4	405	76.7
(a) acq. by co. in same industry	5	19.2	3	13.0	34	64.2	56	80.0	3	75.0	21	72.4	9	21.9	227	43.0
(b) acq. by co. in different ind.	9	34.6	13	56.5	5	9.4	2	2.9	—	—	4	13.8	10	24.3	114	21.6
(c) acq. by co. not in population	4	15.4	3	13.0	7	13.2	—	—	1	25.0	2	6.9	7	17.1	64	12.1
2. Merger	—	—	—	—	2	3.8	7	10.0	—	—	—	—	—	—	21	4.0
(a) merger with co. in same ind.	—	—	—	—	0	—	7	10.0	—	—	—	—	—	—	16	3.0
(b) merger with co. in different ind.	—	—	—	—	2	3.8	—	—	—	—	—	—	—	—	5	0.9
3. Total acquisitions and mergers	18	69.2	19	82.6	48	90.6	65	92.9	4	100.0	27	93.1	26	63.4	426	80.7
4. Liquidation	6	23.1	1	4.3	3	5.7	1	1.4	—	—	—	—	9	21.9	50	9.5
5. Ceased to trade	1	3.8	—	—	—	—	—	—	—	—	—	—	1	2.4	5	0.9
6. Loss of quotation	—	—	—	—	—	—	—	—	—	—	—	—	—	—	2	0.4
7. Conversion to private co., property co., etc.	1	3.8	2	8.7	1	1.9	2	2.9	—	—	—	—	2	4.9	15	2.8
8. Withdrawn from population (other causes)	—	—	—	—	1	1.9	1	1.4	—	—	—	—	1	2.4	10	1.9
9. Rebirth/reorganisation; miscellaneous	—	—	1	4.3	—	—	1	1.4	—	—	2	6.9	2	4.9	20	3.8
10. Total deaths	26	99.9[c]	23	99.9[c]	53	100.1[c]	70	100.0[c]	4	100.0[c]	29	100.0[c]	41	99.9[c]	528	100.0[c]

[a] See the text for explanations of the headings.

[b] The number of firms in each row is expressed as a percentage of the total number of deaths (row 10) in that industry.

[c] Rows 3 to 9 should add to 100.0. The discrepancy is due to rounding errors.

companies on their own, i.e. ignoring the merged firms, in table 2.2, and (ii) where appropriate included the smaller of the merged companies among the acquired companies. It must be noted in this context that the number of firms which disappeared through merger is very small relative to the number which were acquired – 27 as opposed to 461 in the period 1948–60 and 21 as opposed to 405 in the period 1954–60 (see the last column of both parts of table 2.2).

The figures for acquisitions (row 1 of both parts of table 2.2) have been divided into 3 categories, according to whether the amalgamation occurred with a firm in the same industry, a firm in a different industry, or a firm outside the population of quoted firms for which the Board of Trade prepares standardised consolidated accounts.† Thus, for example, part *b* of table 2.2 shows that, of the 45 companies acquired in the food industry in the sub-period 1954–60, 35 amalgamated with firms in the same industry, 5 amalgamated with firms in other industries, and 7 amalgamated with firms which were not in the population. Of these 7 firms which were not in the Board's population, investigation shows that 2 were foreign-owned companies, 2 were finance companies and 3 were private companies. The Board does not normally analyse the accounts of such companies.

Table 2.2 (part *b*) also shows that both the firms which disappeared through merger from the list of food industry firms during the period 1954–60 amalgamated with firms in other industries.‡ A minor point to note is that in none of the 15 industries in table 2.2 were there any cases of *mergers* with firms which were not in the Board of Trade population. This possible sub-category of mergers corresponding to row 1(*c*) for acquisitions is therefore omitted from the table.

The other causes of death (rows 5 to 9) shown in the table are largely self-explanatory. As noted above, a quoted public company which converts into a private company or a property or finance company (row 7) is normally deleted from the Board of Trade population. Some of the other reasons for which a firm may withdraw from this population (row 8) are (i) a change in all or a substantial portion of its normal trading activity to one which falls outside the industries covered by the Board, and (ii) a change in the location of its activity.

† In addition to quoted firms engaged in manufacturing industry in the U.K., the Board of Trade also analyses the accounts of quoted companies engaged in construction, transportation, distribution, and a few service industries. See, for instance, 'Acquisitions and amalgamations of quoted companies, 1954–61', *Economic Trends*, No. 114, April 1963, pp. 66–7.

‡ The two firms which disappeared through merger in the food industry were Aplin and Barrett and Cow and Gate. They merged in 1959 with a quoted company (South County Dairies) in retail distribution and with other unquoted companies, to form a new company, Unigate.

If a firm transfers the major portion of its business overseas, it is also deleted from the Board's population. Rebirth/reorganisation (row 9) usually implies only a temporary disappearance of the firm from the population while its capital structure is being reorganised. The important point to note, however, is that whereas the figures for acquisitions, mergers, liquidations, loss of quotation, etc., in rows 1 to 6 of table 2.2 (both parts) are mostly accurate at least in a formal sense (i.e. they meet certain definite legal and formal criteria), this cannot be said of the figures in rows 7 to 9. The latter figures depend less on formal criteria than on the judgement of the officials of the Board of Trade and are in that sense not so reliable.

The following main points emerge from table 2.2.

(i) *Major cause of death.* As was noted in the last section, acquisitions are by far the most frequent cause of death in *each* industry in both periods (1948–60 and 1954–60). Thus, whereas for all industries together, liquidations accounted for only 9.5 % of the deaths of firms during the sub-period 1954–60, acquisitions accounted for more than 75 % of them.

It has sometimes been suggested that the acquisition figures are overstated relative to the figures for liquidations, since some firms find it worthwhile to acquire loss-making companies (for tax reasons) instead of letting them go into liquidation.† An investigation of the profitability records of acquired companies showed however, that although there may be some support for this proposition in the period 1948–53, there is scarcely any in the period 1954–60, at least so far as the acquired *quoted* companies are concerned. Thus, as was pointed out in chapter 1, if we wish to understand the nature of the 'selection mechanism' at work in the case of firms which are quoted on the stock market, it is essential to study the characteristics of the acquired firms.

It is also interesting to observe that acquisitions and mergers have only *recently* emerged as the predominant cause of death of firms. Traditionally, the chief cause of death of quoted firms has been liquidation. P. E. Hart and S. J. Prais examined the causes of death of a sample of 400 U.K. quoted firms in the period 1885–1950, and found that 'some 37 per cent of deaths are due to liquidation, 34 per cent to amalgamation and 27 per cent to the loss of active quotation'.‡ These figures stand in striking contrast to those given in table 2.2.

It is possible to think of several factors which could have contributed to this change in the mode of disappearance of firms on the stock market. However, it appears to this writer that the two most important factors are probably the following. First, the decrease in the incidence of liquidation for quoted companies has to a large extent been the result

---

† Ma [1960], p. 95.   ‡ Hart and Prais [1956], p. 165.

of the much greater stability in aggregate economic activity in the post-war period than earlier. Secondly, with the tremendous growth and dispersal of share ownership – which implies both a relative weakening of family control in the typical quoted company and the existence of a much more active stock market – take-over of one firm by another through the acquisition of shares has become much more feasible than used to be the case. If these arguments are correct, it is to be expected that in future take-overs will be an even more important cause of death of firms, relative to liquidations, than over the period 1954–60.

(ii) *Industrial concentration.* Although this study is not concerned with investigating the effects of take-overs on the structure of industry and industrial concentration, the figures in table 2.2 do throw some light on this important topic. For all industries together, of the 488 acquisitions and mergers in the period 1948–60, 290 involved amalgamations within the same industry group. In the drink industry 95 % of the acquisitions and mergers involved amalgamation with quoted firms in the same industry. In food, which was already highly concentrated, more than 70 % of the mergers and acquisitions of quoted firms were with firms in the same industry. The proportion is also high for several other industries.

To the extent that we are considering rather broad industry groups, it can justifiably be argued that these figures overstate the effect of acquisitions and mergers on industrial concentration. But it must be remembered that in one important respect they probably understate it: the figures do not include acquisitions by firms 'not in the population'. Amalgamations of this kind may also contribute to increased concentration, for example, in those instances where the acquiring firm (as is often the case) is a foreign firm or a private firm engaged in the same industry as the acquired firm. Furthermore, the figures for acquisitions and mergers do not include those cases in which one firm acquires a substantial or even a controlling minority interest in another. The definition of an 'acquired firm' as one in which the acquiring firm owns more than 50 % of the shares rules out such cases, although they have important implications for industrial concentration. The example of the Whitbread 'umbrella' in the drink industry immediately springs to mind in this connection. This company bought a minority interest (seldom less than 10 %) in a number of other brewing companies through which it sold its bottled beer.† There are probably other similar cases of 'trade investments' by firms in other firms, not amounting to majority ownership, which are nevertheless significant from the point of view of concentration.

---

† See W. Mennel, *Take-over: the Growth of Monopoly in Britain, 1951–61,* London, 1962, pp. 42–7; also Moon [1968], pp. 142–3.

Thus, given the unprecedentedly high acquisition rate, and given that a very large proportion of acquisitions and mergers have involved firms in the same industry, it is more than likely that, as a result of the amalgamations which occurred in the 1950s, there has been an appreciable rise in the degree of concentration in manufacturing industry. Recent studies of industrial concentration in the U.K. in fact clearly show that concentration has been increasing since the 1950s,† and, although the subject has not yet been properly explored, most people who work in this field would probably accept the view that acquisitions and mergers have been an important source of increased concentration.‡

The fact that so many acquisitions and mergers have taken place between firms in the same industry also highlights the differences between the legal and institutional environments in which large quoted firms operate in the U.K. and the U.S. Apart from the absence in the U.K. of antitrust laws, which would have prohibited outright a good many of the horizontal amalgamations effected within manufacturing industry, there has in fact been an attitude of benevolent approval, if not positive government encouragement, of the merger movement since the middle 1950s. Mergers have been regarded by successive governments, rightly or wrongly, as important instruments in rationalising British industry, and reorganising it along more efficient lines.§

2.3   TIME PATTERN OF ACQUISITIONS, MERGERS AND TAKE-OVERS: SELECTED INDUSTRIES, 1955–60

In this section and the next some additional aspects of acquisitions and mergers in 5 industries (food, drink, electrical engineering, clothing and footwear and non-electrical engineering) over the period 1955–60 are discussed. We have already mentioned that the analysis of the following chapters is confined to firms in these industries. In the present section the time pattern of acquisitions and mergers is discussed, and in section 2.4 we examine the size distribution of merged and taken-over firms.

At the end of 1954, there were 847 firms in these industries which were quoted on the U.K. stock exchanges and which had produced annual accounts during that accounting year. Table 2.3 shows the observed probability of death by acquisition, by merger and by liquida-

† A. Armstrong and A. Silberston, 'Size of plant, size of enterprise, and concentration in British manufacturing industry, 1935–1958', *Journal of the Royal Statistical Society*, Series A (General), vol. 128, part 3, 1965; and W. G. Shepherd, 'Changes in British industrial concentration, 1951–58', *Oxford Economic Papers*, March 1966.

‡ R. E. Caves, 'Market organisation, performance and public policy' in R. E. Caves and associates, *Britain's Economic Prospects*, Washington, 1968, pp. 284–5. Mennel [1962], pp. 35–8. See also the important article, 'Behind the wave of mergers', *Financial Times*, 30 March 1961.   § Caves [1968], pp. 319–21.

TABLE 2.3. *Probability of death through acquisition, merger[a] or liquidation: selected industries, 1955–60*[b]

	Food			Drink			Clothing and footwear		
	1955–60	1955–58	1959–60	1955–60	1955–58	1959–60	1955–60	1955–58	1959–60
	No. %	No. %	No. %	No. %	No. %	No. %	No. %	No. %	No. %
No. of companies at the end of 1954	132	132	132	176	176	176	96	96	96
(a) death by acquisition	35 26.5	10 7.6	25 18.9	50 28.4	24 13.6	26 14.8	16 16.7	8 8.3	8 8.3
(b) death by merger[a]	2 1.5	1 0.8	1 0.8	3 1.7	1 0.6	2 1.1	— —	— —	— —
(c) death by liquidation	1 0.8	1 0.8	— —	1 0.6	1 0.6	— —	1 1.0	1 1.0	— —
(d) total of (a) and (b)	37 28.0	11 8.4	27 19.8	53 30.1	25 14.2	28 15.9	16 16.7	8 8.3	8 8.3

	Non-electrical engineering			Electrical engineering			All 5 industries combined		
	1955–60	1955–58	1959–60	1955–60	1955–58	1959–60	1955–60	1955–58	1959–60
	No. %	No. %	No. %	No. %	No. %	No. %	No. %	No. %	No. %
No. of companies at the end of 1954	319	319	319	124	124	124	847	847	847
(a) death by acquisition	47 14.7	25 7.8	22 6.9	22 17.7	10 8.1	12 9.7	170 20.1	77 9.1	93 11.0
(b) death by merger[a]	1 0.3	1 0.3	— —	2 1.6	— —	2 1.6	8 0.9	3 0.3	5 0.5
(c) death by liquidation	5 1.6	2 0.6	3 0.9	3 2.4	2 1.6	1 0.8	11 1.3	7 0.8	4 0.5
(d) total of (a) and (b)	48 15.0	26 8.1	22 6.9	24 19.3	10 8.1	14 11.3	178 21.0	80 9.4	98 11.5

[a] As mentioned in the text, in this table only the smaller of the amalgamating companies involved in a merger are counted as having died.

[b] Deaths by acquisition, merger and liquidation have each been expressed as a percentage of the number of firms in the list at the end of 1954.

tion for these firms, over the periods 1955–8, 1959–60 and 1955–60. Figures are given for the individual industries and for all 5 industries together.† It is important to note that in the figures for mergers given in this table, unlike in tables 2.1 and 2.2, only the *smaller* of the merged companies are counted as having died.

The table shows that, in the five industries, a typical quoted firm in 1954 had a 20.1 % chance of death through acquisition during the next six years. There was also a 1.3 % chance that the firm would be liquidated during the same period, but this probability is negligible, compared with that of take-over and merger. The table also brings out important inter-industry variations – the chance of death through acquisition or merger ranged from 14.7 % in the non-electrical engineering industry to 28.4 % in the drink industry.

This aspect of take-overs and mergers has been discussed earlier, albeit in a somewhat different way; however, the main significance of table 2.3 lies in the important information it provides about the time pattern of take-over activity over the 6-year period 1955–60. It emerges that the rate at which acquisitions occurred was much higher in the last 2 years of the period (1959–60) than over the previous 4 years (1955–8). In all industries together there were 98 take-overs and mergers in 1959–60 but only 80 in 1955–8, a period twice as long. Although there is some industrial variation, the figures for individual industries confirm the existence of a much higher rate of acquisition during the last 2 years of the period.

A similar pattern emerges from the Board of Trade's figures, which provide information on acquisitions from the point of view of the acquiring companies. The data in the accompanying table give the total capital outlays and the 'expenditure' on acquisitions of non-financial quoted firms in manufacturing, construction and distribution over the period 1954–60:‡

† The reader will notice that the figures for acquisitions given in table 2.3 do not exactly match those given in table 2.2 for the relevant industries. The discrepancy arises from three sources; the figures in table 2.3 do not include (i) firms acquired in the year 1954, (ii) firms which were acquired during the period 1955–60, but which did not exist in the list at the end of 1954, and (iii) the very small number of firms for which the Board of Trade standardised data either were not available or could not be used. All these categories of firms are included in the acquisition figures given in table 2.2.

Similarly the figures for the total number of quoted firms in the list at the *end* of 1954 (table 2.3) differ from those for the year 1954 given in the bottom half of table 2.1. This is mostly because the companies which were taken over during 1954 are included in table 2.1, but not in table 2.3.

‡ The source of these figures is H. B. Rose and G. D. Newbould, 'The 1967 take-over boom', *Moorgate and Wall Street*, Autumn 1967, p. 6. Rose and Newbould have obtained the data from the table on the 'Sources and uses of capital funds' of quoted companies in the *Annual Abstract of Statistics*, Central Statistical Office. The figures given in that table under the heading 'total uses of funds' are referred to as 'total' capital 'outlays' in the figures quoted on p. 38.

	Total capital outlays[a] £m.	Expenditure on acquiring subsidiaries[b]	
		£m.	% of total outlays
1954	1,236	193	8.3
1955	1,547	97	6.3
1956	1,574	119	7.6
1957	1,546	128	8.3
1958	1,190	121	10.2
1959	1,717	277	16.1
1960	2,541	338	13.3

[a] Purchases of fixed and current assets, plus expenditure out of provisions.

[b] 'Cash paid *plus* the value of shares (including preference shares, debentures etc.) issued by a company for a controlling interest (that is, more than half in nominal value of the equity share capital) in another company. The value of shares is that attributed to them in the accounts of the acquiring company. Payments which a company makes to acquire minority interest in existing subsidiaries which are not wholly owned are excluded.' Board of Trade.

These figures bring out clearly the sharp rise in the acquisition expenditure of quoted firms, both in absolute terms and as a percentage of their total capital outlays, during the years 1959–60.

The variation in the time pattern of take-over activity over the period 1955–60 is of some significance in the analysis of the following chapters. It has been suggested that not only was there a large increase in the number of take-overs in 1959–60 relative to the period 1955–8, but there was also probably a *qualitative* change in the kind of company taken over. This point will be discussed further in chapter 3.

2.4 PROBABILITY OF DEATH THROUGH ACQUISITION BY SIZE OF FIRM: SELECTED INDUSTRIES, 1955–60

Table 2.4 is designed to answer a question of the following kind: whether a quoted firm which was small in size at the end of 1954 was more likely to be taken over during the next four (1955–8) or six years (1955–60) than a firm which was large at that time. It should be noted that the figures for acquisitions in this table do not include firms which disappeared through mergers. Since even the smaller of the firms involved in a merger was usually larger than the average taken-over firm, it was thought best in the first instance to exclude mergers altogether for the purposes of this exercise.

The table gives figures for the five individual industries and for firms in all these industries taken together. The observed probability of death through acquisition has been computed for the periods 1955–8, 1959–60 and 1955–60. The firms' size in 1954 is measured by the book value of their 'equity assets' in that year.† The table shows, for example, that in the drink industry, of the 17 quoted firms with equity assets of less than £250,000 in 1954, 4 were taken over in the period 1955–8 and 5 in the period 1955–60. For a drink firm in the lowest size class in 1954, this gives probabilities of 23.5 % and 29.4 % respectively of being acquired over the periods considered. Similarly of the 40 firms in the drink industry the value of whose equity assets ranged from £½ million to £1 million in 1954, 16 had been taken over by 1960, giving a probability of acquisition of 40 % during the next six years for a drink firm in that size class.

Considering the figures for all five industries together (the last 7 columns), table 2.4 reveals a complex, but broadly speaking inverse, relationship between size and probability of acquisition. The figures indicate that the average 'small' firm (belonging to the 3 lowest size classes with equity assets of less than £1 million) in 1954, had a chance of a little more than 10 % of being acquired during the next four years. Over the same period, the probability of acquisition for a typical firm in the two 'medium' size classes (with equity assets between £1 million and £4 million) was very slightly lower, being nearly 9 %. On the other hand, we find that the average 'large' firm, with equity assets of greater than £4 million, had an appreciably smaller probability of acquisition – less than half that for the average medium-sized or small firm. If, instead of considering a 4-year period, the probabilities of acquisition are examined over the period 1955–60, the picture remains broadly the same, except that the relative chances of acquisition for the medium-sized firms compared to those for the small firms are about a third lower.

Another important feature of the relationship between size and the probability of acquisition is revealed by a further subdivision of the highest size class. (In order not to make the table too unwieldy, these sub-divisions are not shown in table 2.4.) Such sub-division shows that among the 'large' firms, the probability of acquisition declines sharply with an increase in firm size. Thus it is found for instance that of the

† 'Equity assets' are defined as total assets (fixed and current) net of depreciation minus current and long term liabilities, minority interest and preference capital. They represent the book value of the assets attributable to the ordinary shareholders of the firm. It can be reasonably argued that 'net assets' which exclude only current liabilities from the total assets, are *a priori* a more suitable measure of firm size in this context than equity assets. (See Singh and Whittington [1968], p. 22 and notes 1, 2 and 3.) Net assets are in fact used as a measure of size in the empirical analysis of the following chapters. However, by a clerical error, the firms in table 2.4 were ordered by their equity assets rather than their net assets (the adjoining column in the data sheets). Nevertheless, on redoing this exercise, it was dicovered, not surprisingly, that the main conclusions of this section are not changed in any way when net assets are used as an indicator of firm size. In view of this and in view of the fact that the 'error' was noticed at a late stage in the preparation of the book, it was not thought necessary to alter table 2.4.

TABLE 2.4. *Probability of death through acquisition by size of firm: selected industries, 1955–60*

Drink

Size of firm [Book value of equity assets in 1954]	No. of companies with data in 1954	Taken over during 1955–8		Taken over during 1959–60		Taken over during 1955–60	
		No.	%[a]	No.	%[a]	No.	%[a]
< £250,000	17	4	23.5	1	5.9	5	29.4
< £500,000	28	6	21.4	6	21.4	12	42.8
< £1,000,000	40	8	20.0	8	20.0	16	40.0
< £2,000,000	45	3	6.6	4	8.8	7	15.5
< £4,000,000	24	2	8.3	5	20.8	7	29.2
> £4,000,000	22	1	4.5	2	10.1	3	13.6
Total	176	24		26		50	

Electrical engineering

Size of firm [Book value of equity assets in 1954]	No. of companies with data in 1954	Taken over during 1955–8		Taken over during 1959–60		Taken over during 1955–60	
		No.	%[a]	No.	%[a]	No.	%[a]
< £250,000	22	1	4.5	—	—	1	4.5
< £500,000	22	3	13.6	2	10.1	5	22.7
< £1,000,000	19	—	—	3	15.8	3	15.8
< £2,000,000	24	2	8.3	1	4.2	3	12.4
< £4,000,000	11	1	10.1	4	36.3	5	45.4
> £4,000,000	26	3	11.5	2	7.7	5	19.2
Total	124	10		12		22	

Food

Size of firm [Book value of equity assets in 1954]	No. of companies with data in 1954	Taken over during 1955–8		Taken over during 1959–60		Taken over during 1955–60	
		No.	%[a]	No.	%[a]	No.	%[a]
< £250,000	34	4	11.8	5	14.7	9	26.5
< £500,000	36	4	11.1	10	27.8	14	38.9
< £1,000,000	17	2	11.8	5	29.4	7	41.2
< £2,000,000	20	—	—	4	20.0	4	20.0
< £4,000,000	7	—	—	0	—	—	—
> £4,000,000	18	—	—	1	5.5	1	5.5
Total	132	10		25		35	

Non-electrical engineering

Size of firm [Book value of equity assets in 1954]	No. of companies with data in 1954	Taken over during 1955–8		Taken over during 1959–60		Taken over during 1955–60	
		No.	%[a]	No.	%[a]	No.	%[a]
< £250,000	51	4	7.8	5	9.8	9	17.6
< £500,000	59	3	5.1	6	10.0	9	15.2
< £1,000,000	76	9	11.8	7	9.2	16	21.0
< £2,000,000	53	7	13.2	2	3.8	9	17.0
< £4,000,000	44	2	4.5	1	2.3	3	6.8
> £4,000,000	36	—	—	1	2.8	1	2.8
Total	319	25		22		47	

Size of firm [Book value of equity assets in 1954]	Clothing and footwear							All five industries combined						
	No. of companies with data in 1954	Taken over during 1955–8		Taken over during 1959–60		Taken over during 1955–60		No. of companies with data in 1954	Taken over during 1955–8		Taken over during 1959–60		Taken over during 1955–60	
		No.	%a	No.	%a	No.	%a		No.	%a	No.	%a	No.	%a
< £250,000	35	3	8.6	5	14.3	8	22.9	159	16	10.1	16	10.1	32	20.1
< £500,000	18	—	—	—	—	—	—	163	16	9.8	24	14.7	40	24.5
< £1,000,000	25	1	4.0	3	12.0	4	16.0	177	20	11.3	26	14.7	46	26.0
< £2,000,000	9	2	22.2	—	—	2	22.2	151	14	9.3	11	7.3	25	16.6
< £4,000,000	7	2	28.6	—	—	2	28.6	93	7	7.5	10	10.7	17	18.3
> £4,000,000	2	—	—	—	—	—	—	104	4	3.8	6	5.8	10	9.6
Total	96	8		8		16		847	77		93		170	

a As a percentage of the number of companies in the size class in 1954.

104 firms in all 5 industries which had equity assets of more than £4 million in 1954, 59 had equity assets ranging between £4 million and £8 million. Of these 59 firms, 8 were acquired over the next six years, giving a probability of acquisition of 13.5 % for the typical firm in that size range. The corresponding probability of acquisition for the 30 firms with equity assets ranging between £8 million and £16 million was 6.6 %; for the remaining 15 firms with equity assets of greater than £16 million, this probability was 0.

To sum up, we observe a distinct non-linearity in the relationship between firm size and probability of acquisition. Up to a certain level of firm size, and in particular for the small and medium-sized firms, the probability of acquisition for the typical firm remains much the same or declines relatively moderately with an increase in size. However, for the larger firms, the probability of acquisition is appreciably smaller and declines monotonically and much more sharply with an increase in firm size. Furthermore, it should be noted that although the figures for the individual industries are inevitably more hetero-geneous, since the numbers of firms involved in the various size-classes are fewer, they reveal an essentially similar pattern in most of the industries. An important exception is the electrical engineering industry, where there appears to be on the whole a positive relation-ship between size and probability of acquisition, especially for the whole period 1955–60. But even in this industry it turns out that for the *large* firms the probability of acquisition declines with size, though not as sharply as in the other industries.

The above analysis is based on an ordering of firms by their absolute size. Broadly the same kind of conclusions emerge if firms are ordered instead by their relative size (say decile or quintile rankings) *within* each industry. For instance, if in terms of relative size, we define a 'large' firm as one which is ranked among the top 20 % within its own industry group, it was discovered that the average large firm in all 5 industries in 1954 had a 14.8 % chance of being acquired over the period 1955–60. The corresponding probabilities of acquisition for firms in the first (lowest), second, third and fourth quintiles were 21.8 %, 24.9 %, 20.7 % and 18.3 % respectively. When the firms in the highest quintile are subdivided into a top 10 % and a bottom 10 %, the probability of acquisition for the former was found to be a little more than half that of the latter. Similarly the subdivision of the firms in the highest decile into the top and bottom 5 % showed the probability of acquisition for firms in the former sub-category to be less than a third of that of firms in the latter.

Finally, it is important to note that although the figures in table 2.4 refer only to acquisitions, the main conclusions given above are essentially unaltered if the smaller of each pair of merged firms is included among the taken-over firms. The only difference made to the results by the inclusion of the few (8) merged firms is that the probability of acquisition for the medium-sized firms becomes somewhat larger relative to that observed for take-overs only, thus strengthening the impression of non-linearity in the generally inverse relationship between size and probability of acquisition. The observed relationship between these two variables has certain important economic implications which will be discussed in chapter 6.

2.5 SUMMARY AND CONCLUSIONS

The decade of the 1950s was marked by an unprecedented spate of mergers and take-overs in the U.K. In this chapter we have discussed the main features of the take-overs and mergers involving firms engaged in manufacturing industry (excluding steel) and having a quotation on the U.K. stock exchanges, which occurred during the period 1948–60, and especially over the second half of the period, 1954–60. Information was provided in section 2.1 on the main characteristics of the population of quoted firms in manufacturing industry – births, deaths, surviving firms, etc. The causes of death of firms were analysed in section 2.2. In the next two sections a further analysis was undertaken of acquisitions, mergers and liquidations in a selection of industries, which are the subject of detailed study in the following chapters. The following main conclusions emerged from the analysis of sections 2.1 and 2.2:

(i) It was observed that quoted public companies were of overwhelming significance in manufacturing industry. They accounted for the bulk of assets and profits of all firms in this sector of the economy, and were on the whole much larger than the unquoted or the private companies.

(ii) The death rate of quoted firms in the period 1954–60 was much higher than had ever previously been observed. The *annual* death rate over these years was 3.2%, compared with a rate of about 2% for the years around the turn of the century – the previous period of outstanding amalgamation activity in the U.K. economy.

(iii) Take-overs were the major cause of death of quoted industrial firms over the periods 1948–60 and 1954–60. During the years 1954–60 take-overs accounted for more than 75% of deaths, whereas liquidations were responsible for less than 10%.

It was noted that take-overs have only recently become the predominant cause of death for quoted firms. In the past liquidation was the most frequent reason for their disappearance. Some reasons were given for this change in the mode of death, and it was suggested that in the future take-overs, relative to liquidations, will be an increasingly important cause of the disappearance of quoted firms.

(iv) About 60 % of the acquisitions and mergers during the periods with which we are concerned involved amalgamations with quoted firms in the same industry. In the food industry, which was already highly concentrated, amalgamations within the same industry accounted for more than 70 % of all acquisitions and mergers; the percentage was as high as 95 in the drink industry. It was noted that these amalgamations have probably brought about some increase in industrial concentration.

Finally, two main points emerged from the analysis in sections 2.3 and 2.4 of the food, drink, electrical engineering, clothing and footwear and non-electrical engineering industries over the period 1955–60. First, it was found that there was a distinct variation in the time-pattern of take-over activity over the 6 years. There were more take-overs in the last 2 years of the period than in the first 4. The data on quoted firms' expenditure on acquisitions also revealed a marked increase in take-over activity during the years 1959–60. (This is a point of some significance for the statistical analysis of the following chapters.) Secondly, the analysis in section 2.4 showed that, for the typical 'small' or 'medium-sized' firm in 1954, the probability of acquisition over the next 4 or 6 years was either more or less the same or declined relatively moderately with an increase in firm size. For the large firms, i.e. those with book value of equity assets of greater than £4 million in 1954, the corresponding probability of acquisition was appreciably smaller and it declined much more sharply with an increase in firm size.

3. COMPARISON OF THE CHARACTERISTICS OF TAKEN-OVER AND NON-TAKEN-OVER FIRMS: UNIVARIATE ANALYSIS

INTRODUCTION

In the previous chapter we have looked at, among other things, the industrial characteristics of taken-over and merged firms and the time pattern of take-over activity in U.K. manufacturing industry. We shall now proceed directly to the main themes of chapter 1, i.e. the related questions of (i) the nature of the 'selection' process on the stock market, as represented by the take-over mechanism, and (ii) the nature and degree of stock-market discipline implied by this selection process. To examine these questions, we shall in this and the following two chapters analyse the economic and financial characteristics of the taken-over firms and compare them with those of firms which are not the subject of take-over or liquidation. The analysis will be done throughout on an inter-firm cross-section basis; the results of the univariate investigation will be given in the present chapter and of the multivariate investigation in chapters 4 and 5.

The order of discussion of this chapter is as follows. The particular variables used to describe the company characteristics, and the economic motivation for the inclusion of these variables, are discussed in section 3.1. In view of the well known limitations of the basic data – chiefly the accounting data – the question of their suitability for the purposes of this study is also discussed in that section. The economic and statistical considerations involved in pooling data across industries and over time are examined in section 3.2. A summary of the results of the statistical analysis of the comparative records of the taken-over and non-taken-over (i.e surviving) firms, on a univariate basis, is given at the outset in section 3.3. The statistical methods used and the way in which these results have been derived are explained in sections 3.4 to 3.6. Finally, in section 3.7, the main points of this chapter are recapitulated and some of the economic implications of the results are discussed.

3.1 DESCRIPTION OF VARIABLES

The following variables were used to describe the economic and financial characteristics of each firm:

(1) pre-tax rate of return on net assets (X_1)
(2) post-tax rate of return on equity assets (X_2)
(3) dividend return (gross of tax) on equity assets (X_3)
(4) pre-tax 'productive' rate of return (X_4)
(5) liquidity ratio (stock measure) (X_5)
(6) gearing (stock measure) (X_6)
(7) retention ratio (X_7)
(8) size ('net assets') (X_8)
(9) growth of net assets (X_9)
(10) valuation ratio (X_{10})

Variables X_1 to X_9 are based on accounting data, whilst X_{10} uses both accounting data and the stock-market valuation of the firm. The list of standardised accounting items available for each company year, from which these variables have been derived, is given in the appendix to this chapter; the precise definitions of the variables are also given there. Most of these variables were also used in Singh and Whittington [1968], where they have been described and critically discussed (pages 21–61). It is unnecessary to repeat that account here and only a *summary* description of each variable will therefore be given below. For a detailed discussion and for our reasons for choosing particular formulations of these variables, the reader is referred to the above-mentioned book, where he will also find individual frequency distributions for most variables for the continuing quoted industrial firms in the U.K. over the period 1948–60. The reader will see from that discussion that often many different accounting definitions of the same variables (such as 'liquidity', 'growth', etc.) are possible. However, given the nature of the available data, the definitions finally selected (and the ones used here) are the most appropriate both from the economic and from the practical point of view.

Turning first to X_8, 'size' is measured here in terms of the balance sheet or book value of 'net assets' of the firm. 'Net assets' are defined as total fixed assets, plus current assets net of current liabilities; assets being valued, as is the usual practice in balance sheets, at historic cost net of depreciation. Similarly 'equity assets' (in X_2) means the assets attributable to the ordinary shareholders of the firm; they are derived from the 'net assets' by deducting debentures, minority interests and preference capital.

X_1 to X_4 are different measures of the firm's earnings record. The first two, which indicate its pre-tax profitability and post-tax profitability† respectively, are self-explanatory and need no comment, except

---

† In line with the definition of net assets given above, pre-tax profits include trading profits, investment and other income of the firm. They are net of depreciation and charges for

perhaps for a reminder of their origin in accounting data. Dividend return, X_3, however, has a different meaning and significance from the similar variable, 'dividend yield', ordinarily used in financial circles. The variable used here expresses dividends, before deducting income tax,† as a percentage of the *equity assets* of the firm (as opposed to the market value of the firm, which is used in the calculation of 'dividend yield'). The fourth variable, 'productive' rate of return, excludes (from the denominator) the government securities and the securities of other companies held by the firm‡ and (from the numerator) the return on these securities, in the calculation of the rate of return on the 'net assets' of the firm. By excluding the influence of marketable securities and what are known as 'trade investments', X_4 thus measures the return on the financial capital employed *within* the firm itself.

The next three variables are financial indicators. X_5 expresses the liquidity position of the firm, being the ratio of its net current assets (cash, marketable securities and tax reserve certificates, *less* bank overdraft and loans, dividend and interest liabilities and current tax liabilities) to its total 'net assets', as defined above. X_6 represents the choice made by the firm with respect to long-term debt; it expresses long-term liabilities, plus preference capital, as a percentage of total capital and reserves, plus long-term liabilities. The retention ratio (X_7) shows the percentage of the available disposable income (earnings after tax and after fixed interest and dividend obligations have been met) retained within the firm. It thus expresses the firm's choice with respect to dividend pay-out.

In relation to X_8, 'growth', it should be noted that this variable measures the growth of the long-term financial capital (net assets), as opposed to the fixed assets, employed in the firm.§ The last variable, the valuation ratio, has been discussed in chapter 1 (p. 11); it is defined as the ratio of the stock-market value of the ordinary shares of the firm to the balance sheet value of the assets owned by ordinary shareholders.

current liabilities (e.g. bank interest), but they are taken before the deduction of taxation, long-term interest payments and payments to minority interests in subsidiaries. The pre-tax rate of return on 'net assets' (X_1) expresses pre-tax profits as a percentage of 'net assets'. Similarly, corresponding to the definition of 'equity assets' given in the text, post-tax profits are obtained by deducting from the pre-tax profits on the net assets of the company the following: interest on long-term liabilities, share due to minority interest, preference dividend and taxes. See also appendix to this chapter.

† Company taxation and the taxation of shareholders, before the introduction of corporation tax in the middle 1960s, were on a rather different basis in the U.K. than in the U.S.

‡ The securities held in subsidiaries (i.e the companies in which a firm holds more than 50 % of the equity) are not excluded.

§ This was also the definition of growth used in Singh and Whittington [1968]. Since that study was completed we have calculated the other measure of growth (growth of fixed assets) as well and we find that it makes little difference to the results.

Having looked at the accounting definitions of the variables, it is important at this stage to see their economic meaning in the context of some of the issues raised in chapter 1. It will be recalled that one of the main questions we are concerned with is the extent, if any, to which the stock market – through the take-over mechanism – disciplines firms with a bad record of past performance. To put it simply, do firms with a bad performance record have a higher probability of being acquired than firms with better records? The 4 rates of return (X_1 to X_4) and the rate of growth (X_9), measured over suitable lengths of time, are used in this study as indicators (in their different ways) of the past performance of the firm.

In relation to the question of the nature of the selection mechanism on the stock market, we are also interested in finding other meaningful distinguishing features which set apart the taken-over firms from those which do not get taken over. For example, it can be argued that the size of the firm has an independent and systematic influence on its chance of being taken over. The large companies are not only more expensive to buy but once bought are also more difficult to absorb in the existing organisation of the acquiring company. Therefore, one expects that, of firms with the same record of past performance (or of future prospects), the larger the size of the firm, the smaller the chance that it will be acquired. Similarly with respect to X_5, the liquidity variable, it can be argued that the liquidity position of the firm may systematically influence its chance of acquisition. However, in this case one cannot say *a priori* what the direction of that influence will be. Casual observation suggests that many firms are acquired precisely because they are liquid: the size of their liquid assets attracts the raiders. On the other hand, it is possible to maintain that the firms which are particularly illiquid will find it more difficult to avert a take-over. Only a systematic empirical examination of the records of the taken-over and the non-taken-over firms can determine the extent and the direction of the *independent* influence of the liquidity position of the firm on the probability of its acquisition.

The valuation ratio, X_{10}, is a rather different kind of indicator than the four rates of return, X_1 to X_4. The relative valuation ratios of the firms represent the market's evaluation of their future earning prospects, per unit of their assets. The valuation ratio reflects the past performance of the firm only to the extent that the market judges its future prospects by its past record. As indicated in chapter 1, Marris has argued that (for firms of the same size) the higher the valuation ratio of the firm, the smaller the chance that it will be acquired. The main motivation for this hypothesis appears to be the simple notion that the numerator of the valuation ratio (i.e. the stock-market value of the firm's equity shares) represents the price that a raider would have to pay for the acquired firm. Although the actual price paid for the acquired firm is usually somewhat higher than its quoted stock-market value prior to acquisition, the latter is a reasonably good indicator of the former. Therefore, of two firms with the same book value of equity assets (i.e. with the same denominator of the valuation ratio), the one with a lower valuation ratio would on average be more likely to be acquired. Although the well known limitations of the accounting data may introduce a considerable degree of 'noise', Marris expects that on the whole this relationship between the valuation ratio and the chance of acquisition will still hold.

It is also possible to provide a somewhat different justification for the inclusion of the 'valuation ratio'. One could argue (with the neo-classicals) that on the whole the stock market works in such a way that firms with a bad performance record (as measured, say, by their achieved profitability) have a very high chance of being acquired. However, one could go further and say that of two firms with the same past profitability record, the one which in the view of the market has better future prospects (i.e. a relatively higher valuation ratio and hence 'price–earnings ratio')† is less likely to be acquired than the other. In other words, it is a tenable hypothesis that the 'selection process' on the stock market takes into account not only the past performance of the firm, but also the market's assessment of its future prospects.

With respect to X_8, the gearing variable, it can be argued that, other things being equal, the more highly geared the firm, the greater its chance of acquisition. This is for the simple reason that of two firms with the same value of net assets and other relevant attributes, it will be cheaper for an acquiring firm to gain control of the more highly geared firm, since it need not buy the debentures, etc.

Finally, the retention ratio, X_7, is included because casual observation indicates that several of the taken-over firms in the period studied had a relatively high retention ratio. In fact in many contested take-over battles the defending management would pledge to increase dividends

† If earnings per share are taken after tax, the price–earnings ratio (P/E) is linked to the valuation ratio and post-tax profitability by the indentity:

$$P/E = X_{10}/X_2.$$

In view of the accounting problems involved in asset valuation, P/E would be regarded by many people as perhaps a better measure of the market's evaluation of a firm's future prospects than the valuation ratio. However, in practice we found that the P/E did not perform any better than the valuation ratio in discriminating between the taken-over and the non-taken-over firms. In view of this and in view of the fact that Robin Marris' model of the growth of the firm and his work on take-over bids (see chapter 1) are couched explicitly in terms of the valuation ratio, we decided to use this variable rather than P/E throughout this study.

and lower the retention ratio if allowed to continue.† This is not to say that the retention ratio necessarily has an independent influence on the chance of acquisition; it is more than likely that any association which may be discovered between the two variables is due to the fact that the retention ratio is related to the valuation ratio or to the other variables.

To sum up, the variables X_1 to X_{10}, either individually or in conjunction with other variables, can affect a firm's chance of acquisition. The statistical analysis of this chapter will be concerned with determining to what extent, if any, it is possible to distinguish between the taken-over and the non-taken-over firms on the basis of each of these variables, taken by itself. Multivariate analysis, in terms of all or suitable subsets of these variables, will be attempted in the next two chapters.

However, before going on to statistical analysis, there are two further points to be noted about the variables X_1 to X_{10}.

Long-term and short-term record

In comparing the economic and financial characteristics of taken-over and non-taken-over firms, both the short-term and the long-term records of the firms have been used. For this purpose, measurements of most of the 10 basic variables, X_1 to X_{10}, were obtained for the current year and for the averages of the previous 2, 3 and 6 years. In particular, for variables X_1 to X_7 the short-term record is indicated by measurement of the variable in question over the current year and by measurement of its average value over the past 2 years. The long-term values of these variables are given by average measurements over the last 3 and 6 years. For X_{10}, valuation ratio, however, only 1-year, 2-year and 3-year measurements have been made. The short-term value of X_8, growth, is indicated by the growth of net assets over the previous 3 years, and its long-term record by growth over the previous 6 years. Size, X_9, is always measured by the current value of net assets.

Thus the analysis of this chapter involves a cross-section comparison of taken-over and non-taken-over firms in terms of 34 variables, on a univariate basis. The 34 variables represent measurements over various lengths of time of the 10 basic variables X_1 to X_{10}.

Limitations of the accounting data

In view of the fact that all the variables given above are based on accounting data, and in view of the known limitations of such data,‡ it is necessary to consider the suitability of these data for the problems considered in this study. The basic defect of accounting data derives from the fact that the accounting conventions used in the valuation of a

---

† Cf. Alex Rubner, *The ensnared Shareholder*, Harmondsworth, 1966, pp. 109 and 118.
‡ For a detailed discussion of these problems, see Singh and Whittington [1968], pp. 229–34.

firm's assets do not usually conform to economic principles and may differ between firms. However, it should be noted that, in the context of this particular study, these limitations are of much less significance than may at first appear. In the first place, this is a comparative interfirm study – the records of a group of companies are being compared either within the group itself or with another group of firms usually in the same industry. To the extent that the accounting conventions within an industry for firms quoted on the stock market are similar, this should greatly reduced the handicap imposed by the use of accounting data, although it is true that it does not necessarily eliminate it.†

Secondly, and for the purposes of this study more importantly, it must be recognised that accounting data, in spite of their defects, represent in most cases the best available indication to investors and shareholders on the stock market of the current and past record of a firm. These are the data used and discussed in the financial press and in the financial community generally, to indicate company performance.

3.2 STATISTICAL ANALYSIS: THE PROBLEM OF 'POOLING'

In making statistical comparisons of the characteristics of the taken-over and the surviving firms on a cross-section basis, the first problem which arises is that of 'pooling'. Do we compare the characteristics of the two groups of firms within each year and each industry separately, or do we pool firms across all the industries and all years? Pooling is obviously helpful from a statistical point of view in that it leads to larger samples and, therefore, to more reliable results. Its legitimacy, however, depends on certain economic and certain purely statistical considerations, which will be examined in turn below.

From an economic point of view, it is possible to maintain that pooling firms over the whole period 1955–60 – the period considered in this analysis – is not legitimate. It could lead to misleading results since there is reason to believe that there were major changes in the economic environment and in the nature of take-over activity over the years 1955–60. For instance, it was seen in the last chapter that there was a very distinct pattern in take-over activity over this period. More quoted industrial firms were taken over in the last 2 years of the period than in the previous 4 years (see chapter 2, table 2.3). Similarly, expenditure on acquistions by quoted firms was running at an appreciably higher rate in 1959–60 than in 1955–8.

Several writers have asserted that not only was there a quantitative increase in take-over activity during 1959-60 (and in the following

† See further discussion on this point in the next chapter.

years), but also a significant qualitative change in it. In part, the latter reflected important differences in the economic and institutional environment in which the companies operated during this later period. The abolition of the differential profits tax in 1958 and the enormous jump in the share price index in 1959 were important features of the changed economic environment.† In particular, as a result of the stock-market boom, the undervaluation of company shares in relation to their underlying assets or earning capacity, which had occurred throughout the early and middle 1950s, was by and large corrected by the end of that decade.‡ For these and other reasons, it has been suggested that, whereas in the period 1954–8 purely 'financial' considerations were the dominant motives for take-overs, in 1959–60 (and the following years) commerical considerations became far more important.§

It therefore appears that in comparing the records of firms which were acquired and those which were not the subject of take-over or liquidation, it would be appropriate from an economic point of view to group together, at least *in the first instance*, only the years 1955–8 and 1959–60. Similarly, it is important from the economic point of view to do the analysis first on an individual industry basis. There are basically two reasons for this. First, as mentioned earlier, it is much more likely that the accounting conventions used by firms will be similar within the same industry than among firms in different industries. Secondly, and perhaps more importantly, it is possible that the nature of take-over activity and the dominant motivations (in the sense of stimuli) for take-overs may differ between industries. For example, it can be argued that the motives and/or the opportunities for take-over, and hence the characteristics of the acquired companies, are likely to be different in, say, an industry where there have already occurred a number of take-overs than in one where there has been little take-over activity in the recent past, or in an industry populated by small firms than in one dominated by large firms, etc.||

Turning to statistical considerations about the legitimacy of pooling, the essential point is that if there are major differences in the characteristics of the firms among the samples which are being pooled, this

---

† Cf. J. F. Wright, 'The capital market and the finance of industry', in *The British Economy in the Nineteen-fifties*, G. D. N. Worswick and P. H. Ady, eds., Oxford, 1962, pp. 484–96. Moodies' index of share prices, with 1947 = 100, stood at 116.9 in 1954, at 135.9 in 1957 and at 139.1 in 1958. In the share price boom which followed, it jumped to 199.0 in 1959 and to 251.6 in 1960.

‡ See further Singh and Whittington [1968], p. 59.

§ Rose and Newbould [1967], pp. 7–8. A similar view is expressed in Wright [1962], p. 467, and in Board of Trade, 'Acquisitions and amalgamation of quoted companies, 1962–63', *Economic Trends*, No. 146, December 1965.

|| See further chapter 6 on this. See also Gort [1969].

introduces an important source of bias in the analysis. This statistical bias could exist even if the above-mentioned possible economic objections to pooling data across all industries and all years were not valid or were found to be unimportant. It is easy to construct numerical examples to show that, on account of this bias, we may conclude from statistical analysis that there are no differences in the characteristics of taken-over and non-taken-over firms when in fact they exist, and vice versa.

It is, therefore, relevant to find out how legitimate pooling over the various years and industries is from this particular point of view. For this purpose, the means and variances of the individual characteristics of *all* companies were computed within each industry for each year from 1954 to 1960. As an illustration of the results, and for their own interest, a selection from these calculations, relating to two individual characteristics of company records in two industries, is presented in table 3.1.

TABLE 3.1. *Pre-tax profitability and growth: electrical engineering (Industry 5) and drink (Industry 13), 1954–60*

Year	Industry	Current pre-tax profitability (%)			Growth ($t-3 = 100$)		
		Mean	Variance	N[a]	Mean	Variance	N[a]
1954	5	21.7	212.2	121	131.5	3527.3	117
1955	5	22.0	130.4	123	137.0	2814.9	118
1956	5	19.9	119.9	123	134.9	2354.6	114
1957	5	20.3	166.1	124	129.5	1392.4	115
1958	5	19.6	138.0	125	123.8	852.9	115
1959	5	18.9	135.6	120	122.1	664.5	110
1960	5	18.1	176.5	116	124.4	1688.6	107
1954	13	11.2	36.1	172	109.3	340.3	165
1955	13	11.6	46.2	170	109.7	352.0	165
1956	13	12.5	35.9	162	112.1	286.0	159
1957	13	13.4	39.5	157	113.2	337.8	155
1958	13	12.9	35.5	149	113.1	292.1	148
1959	13	13.1	51.3	140	114.8	488.2	138
1960	13	13.7	34.0	121	119.5	753.5	119

[a] N = number of companies.

The table shows the average value and variance of current pre-tax profitability and short-term growth of quoted firms in the electrical engineering industry and the drink industry, from 1954 to 1960.† It

† The figures for the year 1954 (say) refer to the companies' accounting years ending during the course of the 'financial year' 1954, i.e. during the period 6 April 1954 to 5 April 1955. This convention is used with respect to all the other years in table 3.1 and in the rest of the book.

should be noted, first, that the pooling of taken-over and non-taken-over firms over (say) the period 1955–8 normally involves the comparison of their records over the period 1954–7, since the last complete annual accounts of a taken-over company are usually available only for the year previous to the date of take-over. Similarly, pooling over the years 1959–60 involves comparing the record of the two groups of firms during 1958–9.

Table 3.1 shows very clearly that *within* either industry the inter-year differences in the pre-tax profitability and growth of firms tend to be very small. In particular, if we consider the years 1954–7 and 1958–9 respectively, the inter-year differences, in spite of the large number of observations, are by and large statistically insignificant (say at the 5 % level of significance). There would not, therefore, be any problem of statistical bias in pooling data over each of these two time-periods. On the other hand, it is also obvious that a straightforward pooling of firms across industries would not be legitimate from a statistical point of view. The average pre-tax profitability of firms in the electrical engineering industry, for instance, often runs at nearly twice the level observed for firms in the drink industry. In fact, in general, inter-industry differences in profitability and a number of other characteristics of firms tend to be highly significant (at the usual 5 % or 1 % levels). Pooling data across industries could, therefore, produce results which are seriously biased, unless a suitable sample design is used to overcome this problem.

To sum up, we have seen that from an economic point of view, at least in the first instance, it would be appropriate to pool taken-over (and for purposes of comparison, non-taken-over) firms only over the periods 1955–8 and 1959–60 respectively. Economic considerations also suggest that it is important to do the analysis initially on an individual industry basis since it is possible that there might be systematic inter-industry differences in the characteristics of the taken-over firms. A statistical analysis of the observed characteristics of firms showed that pooling, *within the same industry*, over the periods 1955–8 and 1959–60 would be in order from the statistical point of view. However, it was also found that pooling of firms across industries must be handled very carefully in order to avoid the possibility of a serious statistical bias. In view of these economic and statistical considerations, in the following investigation the comparative records of the taken-over and the non-taken-over firms were first analysed on an individual industry basis for each of the two time-periods, 1955–8 and 1959–60 respectively. Later, by using *appropriate* statistical methods and a proper sample design, we have also considered the results of data pooled over all the years and all the industries.

3.3 A SUMMARY OF THE RESULTS OF THE STATISTICAL ANALYSIS

Since the records of the taken-over and the non-taken-over firms are compared here in terms of a very large number of variables (34) and as there are many different sets of data analysed (pertaining to the individual industries and time-periods as well as pooled data) it is proposed first to review in a very general way the nature of the differences which exist between the two groups of firms.

Table 3.2 shows in simple, commonsense terms, without the use of any statistical tests, how some of the more important characteristics of the taken-over firms (the rates of return, growth and the valuation ratio) differ from those of the non-taken-over firms. The table provides a first glance at the relative characteristics of the two groups of firms; with respect to any particular characteristic, say profitability, it simply shows how profitable the average taken-over firm is, relative to the average non-taken-over firm. In this table, which is presented for purely illustrative purposes, the records of taken-over firms for the average of the 2 accounting years preceding the take-over are compared with the corresponding records of firms which were not taken over.† 2-year records were chosen because they give on the whole a clearer idea of the nature of differences between the two groups.

It will be recalled from chapter 2 that the statistical analysis of this and the following chapters is confined to five industries: food, non-electrical engineering, electrical engineering, clothing and footwear and drink. The reader is also reminded that the comparison of the characteristics of the two groups of firms is undertaken throughout on an inter-firm cross-section basis. Thus if we take pre-tax profitability on net assets (X_1), table 3.2 shows that over the period 1955–8, the (two-year) pre-tax profitability of the average (arithmetic mean) taken-over firm in the non-electrical engineering industry was 64.2 % of that of the mean non-taken-over firm in that industry. However, for the period 1959–60, the relative profitability of the average taken-over firm in this industry was considerably higher, being 91.3 % of that of the average non-taken-over firm. Columns 3 to 10 of the table give similar information for the other 4 industries. To save space, the numbers of taken-over and non-taken-over firms included in each set of data are not shown in this table – this information is available in tables 3.3 to 3.6 and table 4.1 (a). It should also be noted that the figures for the valuation ratio (X_{10}) are shown for only 3 of the 5 industries.‡

† Except in the case of growth (X_9). As was mentioned in section 3.1, the short-term growth of net assets is measured over three accounting years preceding the take-over.
‡ In view of the frequent and usually quite complicated capital changes which occur in company accounts, the computation of valuation ratios requires a very large amount of

TABLE 3.2. *Relative characteristics of taken-over and non-taken-over firms: a first glance*[a]

Variable[b]	Non-electrical engineering		Food		Electrical engineering		Drink		Clothing and footwear	
	1955–8	1959–60	1955–8	1959–60	1955–8	1959–60	1955–8	1959–60	1955–8	1959–60
Pre-tax profitability (X_1)	64.2	91.3	75.3	88.0	89.0	55.0	78.5	82.8	108.7	64.7
Post-tax profitability (X_2)	40.9	92.3	82.2	92.3	92.2	56.1	67.7	85.9	121.4	36.8
Dividend return (X_3)	72.3	84.1	76.1	81.2	101.6	65.2	90.7	82.8	76.2	78.9
Productive return (X_4)	82.2	97.0	77.8	82.9	87.8	47.8	75.4	81.2	88.5	62.0
Growth (X_9)	49.3	81.9	51.7	51.4	169.2	54.5	33.0	96.4	91.2	0
Valuation ratio[c] (X_{10})	88.9	108.2	77.7	68.0	99.9	71.9				

[a] For each variable, the figure for the average taken-over firm is expressed as a percentage of that for the corresponding average non-taken-over firm.

[b] X_1 to X_4 and X_9 are measured in terms of percentages. X_{10} is measured in terms of units.

[c] The figures for valuation ratios were computed only for 3 industries.

Two important points emerge from table 3.2. First we find that the rates of return, the growth rate and the valuation ratio of the average taken-over firm are almost always less than those of the average non-taken-over firm. For instance, the pre-tax or the post-tax profitability of the average taken-over firm is less than that of the corresponding non-taken-over firm in 9 out of 10 sets of data examined. Secondly, although the differences between the two groups (with respect to X_1, X_2, X_3, X_4, X_9, X_{10}) are almost always in the same direction, their magnitude varies a great deal between industries and time-periods. The variation is particularly marked in the case of X_9 (growth). The short-term growth rate of the average taken-over firm relative to that of the average non-taken-over firm is for example 0 % in the clothing and footwear industry for the period 1959–60† and nearly 170 % in the electrical engineering industry for the period 1955–8.

The question therefore arises whether it is possible to say anything in general about the *extent* of the differences between the average characteristics of the two groups of firms. In view of the fact that the numbers of taken-over and non-taken-over firms differ a great deal between the various sets of data and in view of some of the factors mentioned in the previous section, one cannot simply use the data given in table 3.2 for this purpose. It would not be correct for instance, for any particular characteristic, to obtain an overall figure of the extent of the difference between the two groups by just averaging the figures for the ten individual sets of data presented in the table. However, as mentioned earlier, it is possible to minimise, if not to completely eliminate, the bias which may arise from aggregating different sets of data, by the choice of an appropriate sample design. Such a sample design (described in section 3.6 and chapter 5 below) was in fact used to pool the various sets of data. The results for this pooled sample showed that the rates of return (variables X_1 to X_4) and the valuation ratio (X_{10}) of the average taken-over firm, in the two years preceding take-over, were on the whole about 80 to 85 % of those of the average non-taken-over firm. The short-term growth rate of the average taken-over firm was over 90 % of that of the average non-taken-over firm.

The above are rather crude impressions based on a general reading of the data, without the use of any significance tests or other more rigorous statistical methods. It must be emphasised that these first

detailed work. The valuation ratios were therefore computed for only 3 of the 5 industries. The method used is broadly the same as that described in Singh and Whittington [1968], pp. 222–5.

† In fact for this period, the average growth rate of the small number (8) of taken-over firms in the clothing and footwear industry was slightly less than 0 – about −0.3 % per annum. The average growth rate of the corresponding non-taken-over firms (150) was 3.7 % per annum.

impressions do no more than convey some general flavour of the kind of differences that exist between the two groups. In order to arrive at more reliable conclusions about the nature of these differences, it is necesssary to study the comparative group characteristics in much greater detail. In particular, it is not enough, and can in fact be quite misleading, to compare the two groups on the basis of their *average* characteristics. A proper analysis requires both a knowledge and a comparison of the within group variation of these characteristics. (In fact one reason why the relative growth rates in table 3.2 vary so much between the different sets of data is that this variable tends to have a relatively high dispersion in both groups.) In the same way, it is also necessary to study the degree of overlap between the groups with respect to the various characteristics. Such questions, apart from their intrinsic interest, are of course related to that of assessing the statistical significance of the observed differences among the average characteristics of the two groups.

The above-mentioned problems are investigated in sections 3.4 to 3.6 below. The main conclusions of this more rigorous analysis are for convenience summarised here.

(i) The taken-over firms had on the whole a somewhat worse record than the non-taken-over firms with respect to all the four measures of the rate of return, the growth rate and the valuation ratio. For all industries and time-periods together, 60 to 65 % of the taken-over firms achieved levels of profitability, growth and valuation ratio which were less than the average for their respective industries. (This compares with an expectation of 50 % if there was no difference between, say, profitability of taken-over and other firms in the industry.) The differences between the groups in relation to these variables were on the whole statistically insignificant at the individual industry level, but were highly significant when the data were *appropriately* pooled across all industries and time-periods.

(ii) The average taken-over firm was also significantly (in statistical terms) smaller in size than the average non-taken-over firm. For instance, about 60 % of the taken-over firms in all industries and time-periods were smaller in size than the median for their respective industries.

(iii) With respect to the financial policy variables (liquidity, gearing and retention ratio), the two groups were on the whole statistically indistinguishable at an acceptable level of probability in the case of the first two variables. The taken-over firms, however, retained a significantly *greater* proportion of their profits than the non-taken-over firms.

(iv) The differences between the groups were *marginally* (but not consistently) greater in the period 1959–60 than in the period 1955–8, and in relation to the firms' longer-term records (2-, 3- or 6-year) than their 1-year records.

(v) It was also discovered that individually none of the variables (the four rates of return; growth; valuation ratio; retention ratio; size) for which there existed significant differences between the two groups of firms was a *good* discriminator. The characteristics of the firms overlapped to such an extent that it would lead to a very high degree of misclassification if one attempted to classify firms into taken-over and non-taken-over groups on the basis of the observed values of *any* of these variables considered on its own. The calculated values of the univariate 'distance' between groups (see section 3.4 below) for most of the statistically significant variables indicate that if these variables were used as a basis for discrimination between taken-over and non-taken-over firms, 40 % or so of the firms would be expected to be misclassified. This compares with an expectation of 50 % on the basis of random allocation.

The evidence on which the above conclusions are based and the statistical methods used to derive them are discussed in sections 3.4 to 3.6 below. Those readers who are not interested in the details of statistical methodology and have no difficulty in accepting these conclusions may wish to go straight to section 3.7. However, even these readers are advised not to skip section 3.6, since tables 3.7 to 3.9 in this section are interesting in their own right, apart from establishing the above results. Furthermore some of the material in the section is closely linked to that in the following chapters.

3.4 FOOD INDUSTRY: UNIVARIATE ANALYSIS

Three statistical tests are used in this chapter to compare, on a univariate basis, the short-term and long-term records of the two groups of taken-over and non-taken-over firms. The tests and the conclusions which they yield are described in turn below. The results for the food industry are discussed in this section and for the remaining industries in the next section.

(a) Welch–Aspin test

Columns 1 to 7 of tables 3.3 to 3.6 show the application of this test to the comparison of the characteristics of taken-over and non-taken-over firms in the food industry. Table 3.3 compares the short-term records (usually of the last accounting year and of the average for the last 2 accounting years before the take-over) and table 3.4 the long-term records (usually the average for the 3 and 6 accounting years

TABLE 3.3. *Comparison of characteristics of taken-over and non-taken-over firms: food industry, 1955–8, short-term records*

Variable	Cos. taken over			Cos. not taken over			Difference of means	Taken-over and merged companies	Number < industry average
	Mean	Variance	N_1	Mean	Variance	N_2			
a. Records for year preceding take-over									
X_1 Pre-tax profitability (%)	12.4	151.6	12	17.3	134.1	498	−4.90	13	7
X_2 Post-tax profitability (%)	8.8	123.6	12	8.9	57.9	498	−0.10	13	6
X_3 Dividend return (%)	4.3	22.4	12	6.6	17.8	498	−2.29	13	10[a]
X_4 Productive return (%)	14.7	252.0	12	20.5	323.5	498	−5.84	13	9
X_5 Liquidity (%)	−6.7	1144.4	12	6.4	557.2	498	−13.09	13	9
X_6 Gearing (%)	25.6	447.6	12	18.8	369.4	498	6.81	13	7
X_7 Retention ratio (%)	56.1	1327.6	12	49.8	1028.3	498	6.28	13	5
X_8 Size (£'000)	403.2	94665.3	12	3445.0	60826864.0	498	−3041.79[c]	9	4
X_{10} Valuation ratio (units)									
b. Average records for 2 years preceding take-over									
X_1 Pre-tax profitability (%)	13.4	115.1	10	17.8	133.4	483	−4.40	11	8
X_2 Post-tax profitability (%)	7.4	27.5	10	9.0	48.5	483	−1.52	11	8
X_3 Dividend return (%)	5.1	27.2	10	6.7	16.7	483	−1.63	11	8
X_4 Productive return (%)	16.5	224.6	10	21.2	345.9	483	−4.70	11	8
X_5 Liquidity (%)	1.5	1069.0	10	7.1	524.6	483	−5.62	11	7
X_6 Gearing (%)	22.5	457.8	10	19.1	372.0	483	3.39	11	6
X_7 Retention ratio (%)	60.6	882.5	10	49.4	1041.8	483	11.20	11	4
X_9 Growth (last 3 years) [$t-3=100$]	109.1	134.1	10	117.6	1308.0	465	−8.53[a]	11	7
X_{10} Valuation ratio (units)								8	4

[a] Indicates significance at the 10% level.   [c] Indicates significance at the 1% level.

TABLE 3.4. *Comparison of characteristics of taken-over and non-taken-over firms: food industry, 1955–8, long-term records*

Variable	Cos. taken over Mean	Variance	N_1	Cos. not taken over Mean	Variance	N_2	Difference of means	Taken-over and merged companies	Number < industry average
a. Average records for the 3 years preceding take-over									
X_1 Pre-tax profitability (%)	14.3	152.0	10	18.0	127.4	465	−3.73	11	8
X_2 Post-tax profitability (%)	7.2	34.0	10	8.8	65.8	465	−1.57	11	8
X_3 Dividend return (%)	5.0	25.8	10	6.8	16.8	465	−1.74	11	8
X_4 Productive return (%)	19.5	391.7	10	21.4	328.0	465	−1.97	11	8
X_5 Liquidity (%)	2.8	1250.6	10	7.5	521.1	465	−4.69	11	7
X_6 Gearing (%)	22.6	457.4	10	19.6	373.5	465	3.00	11	6
X_7 Retention ratio (%)	50.5	919.8	10	49.5	1071.1	465	0.94	11	4
X_{10} Valuation ratio (units)								7	4
b. Average records for the 6 years preceding take-over									
X_1 Pre-tax profitability (%)	15.7	143.7	9	18.4	120.1	420	−2.74	10	7
X_2 Post-tax profitability (%)	7.1	32.7	9	8.3	120.4	420	−1.22	10	5
X_3 Dividend return (%)	6.5	18.0	9	7.0	20.0	420	−0.44	10	7
X_4 Productive return (%)	20.6	379.9	9	21.8	289.5	420	−1.30	10	7
X_5 Liquidity (%)	2.4	1523.2	9	8.3	545.1	420	−5.93	10	6
X_6 Gearing (%)	19.8	402.2	9	20.8	357.9	420	−1.02	10	7
X_7 Retention ratio (%)	41.5	1079.6	9	50.7	1047.6	420	−9.23	10	4
X_9 Growth (last 6 years) [$t-6 = 100$]	134.2	1601.7	9	154.9	3630.1	420	−20.70	10	6

TABLE 3.5. *Comparison of characteristics of taken-over and non-taken-over firms: food industry, 1959–60, short-term records*

Variable	Cos. taken over			Cos. not taken over			Difference of means	Taken-over and merged companies	Number < industry average
	Mean	Variance	N_1	Mean	Variance	N_2			
a. Records for year preceding take-over									
X_1 Pre-tax profitability (%)	12.4	62.2	26	14.8	98.7	213	−2.35	27	17
X_2 Post-tax profitability (%)	7.5	24.0	26	8.6	50.9	213	−1.14	27	16
X_3 Dividend return (%)	5.4	16.0	26	7.0	17.5	213	−1.61[a]	27	18
X_4 Productive return (%)	13.0	80.2	26	16.7	202.4	213	−3.72[a]	27	18
X_5 Liquidity (%)	2.3	535.6	26	3.3	615.9	213	−1.00	27	16
X_6 Gearing (%)	18.7	349.5	26	16.4	310.5	213	2.28	27	13
X_7 Retention ratio (%)	53.1	1002.3	26	46.4	975.1	213	6.72	27	8[a]
X_8 Size (£'000)	1318.7	2471385.0	26	5051.9	119953728.0	213	−3733.26[c]	27	15
X_{10} Valuation ratio (units)								24	17[a]
b. Average records for 2 years preceding take-over									
X_1 Pre-tax profitability (%)	13.2	60.2	26	15.0	79.7	206	−1.78	27	14
X_2 Post-tax profitability (%)	7.6	27.1	26	8.2	35.8	206	−0.64	27	15
X_3 Dividend return (%)	5.6	15.1	26	6.9	15.9	206	−0.13	27	17
X_4 Productive return (%)	14.1	83.3	26	17.0	191.2	206	−2.93	27	15
X_5 Liquidity (%)	3.4	434.0	26	4.1	4.1	206	−0.66	27	17
X_6 Gearing (%)	18.8	352.0	26	16.8	311.6	206	2.02	27	16
X_7 Retention ratio (%)	47.2	1515.5	26	45.4	853.6	206	1.84	27	10
X_9 Growth (last 3 years) $[t-3=100]$	109.4	110.6	26	118.3	1562.5	201	−8.92[b]	27	13
X_{10} Valuation ratio (units)								24	17[a]

[a] Indicates significance at the 10% level.   [b] Indicates significance at the 5% level.   [c] Indicates significance at the 1% level.

63

TABLE 3.6. *Comparison of characteristics of taken-over and non-taken-over firms: food industry, 1959–60, long-term records*

Variable	Cos. taken over Mean	Variance	N_1	Cos. not taken over Mean	Variance	N_2	Difference of means	Taken-over and merged companies	Number < industry average
a. Average records for 3 years preceding take-over									
X_1 Pre-tax profitability (%)	14.0	66.4	26	15.4	80.5	201	−1.35	27	12
X_2 Post-tax profitability (%)	7.6	31.9	26	8.1	34.6	201	−0.48	27	13
X_3 Dividend return (%)	5.7	14.0	26	6.8	14.4	201	−1.17	27	18
X_4 Productive return (%)	15.2	95.3	26	17.6	198.4	201	−2.41	27	16
X_5 Liquidity (%)	3.7	406.4	26	4.8	473.9	201	−1.11	27	16
X_6 Gearing (%)	18.9	348.3	26	17.1	321.2	201	1.84	27	14
X_7 Retention ratio (%)	51.3	858.6	26	44.2	992.3	201	7.13	27	9
X_{10} Valuation ratio (units)								24	14
b. Average records for 6 years preceding take-over									
X_1 Pre-tax profitability (%)	15.4	69.9	23	16.8	88.0	181	−1.39	24	14
X_2 Post-tax profitability (%)	8.0	26.9	23	8.6	36.6	181	−0.54	24	15
X_3 Dividend return (%)	5.8	13.3	23	6.9	13.3	181	−1.13	24	17
X_4 Productive return (%)	16.6	104.4	23	19.5	226.4	181	−2.93	24	15
X_5 Liquidity (%)	4.4	304.0	23	6.7	423.9	181	−2.24	24	14
X_6 Gearing (%)	19.7	333.8	23	18.3	344.1	181	1.38	24	12
X_7 Retention ratio (%)	49.7	602.9	23	48.2	967.1	181	1.48	24	11
X_9 Growth (last 6 years) [$t-6 = 100$]	138.9	2775.3	23	149.2	6271.2	181	−10.29	24	14

preceding take-over respectively) of the firms taken over during the period 1955–8, with the corresponding records of *all* the non-taken-over firms over the same period. Tables 3.5 and 3.6 give similar information for the firms taken over in 1959–60.

Although the figures in tables 3.3 to 3.6 are self-explanatory, nevertheless, since these tables contain a rather large amount of information, a brief description of one of them may be in order. Turning to table 3.3, part *a* shows for instance that, over the period 1955–8, the average pre-tax profitability of taken-over firms in the food industry in the last accounting year before take-over was 12.4%. The corresponding average pre-tax profitability of *all* firms which neither were taken over, nor died through merger or liquidation, for each of the years 1955–8 was 17.3%.† However, the difference in the average post-tax profitability on equity assets for the two groups of firms was only $\frac{1}{10}$ of 1% (= −0.10, row 2, column 7). Part *b* of table 3.3 similarly shows that, for taken-over firms, the average pre-tax profitability over the two accounting years preceding take-over was 13.4%, with a variance of 115.1%^{2}; for firms not taken over the corresponding figures were 17.8% and 133.4%^{2} respectively.

The numbers of taken-over and non-taken-over firms considered for each variable are indicated by N_1‡ and N_2 respectively. The reason why N_1 and N_2 differ between the top and bottom half of table 3.3, and between tables 3.3 and 3.4, is simply that there are some firms for which 1-year records are available, but which did not exist in the list of quoted firms long enough to have 2-, 3- or 6-year records.

The results of the Welch–Aspin test,§ which tests the hypothesis that there is no difference in the mean values of the characteristics for the two groups of firms, are given in column 7. This test is essentially similar

† Two points should be noted about the set of all non-taken-over firms referred to above. First, the group of non-taken-over firms in the following pages always exludes those which died through merger or liquidation, in addition to the ones which were acquired. Secondly, since we wished to find out to what extent, if any, the past records of firms which were taken over during a particular (accounting) year were different from the corresponding records of those which were not taken over in that year, we aggregated all the firms which were taken over and all the firms which were not taken over in each of the accounting years 1955 to 1958. (A similar procedure was followed for the comparisons of the two groups in the subperiod 1959–60.) This means that the set of all non-taken-over firms includes the firms which were later acquired. In the analysis of chapter 5 a different procedure is followed and the set of all non-taken-over firms excludes all such subsequently acquired firms. However, since the number of firms taken over in any year is very small relative to the total number of firms (about 4% on average), the results obtained are very much the same on the basis of either procedure.

‡ N_1 in tables 3.3 and 3.5 differs slightly from the corresponding figures for food given in table 2.4 in chapter 2. The reason for this is that the table 2.4 figures do not include those taken-over firms which did not exist in the list of quoted firms in 1954.

§ A. A. Aspin and B. L. Welch, 'Tables for use in comparisons whose accuracy involves two variances, separately estimated', *Biometrika*, 1949, pp. 290–6.

to the ordinary t test of difference of means, except that it does not assume equal variances for the values of the variables in the two groups. In fact tables 3.3 to 3.6 show that there is on the whole little (statistically significant) difference between the variances in the two groups for most of the variables. The outstanding exception is size, for which both the average value and variance of taken-over firms are considerably lower than those of the non-taken-over group. Thus, although for many variables the t test and Welch–Aspin test will give essentially similar results, for size and possibly for a few other variables, such as growth, the results could differ considerably.†

Considering first the period 1955–8 and the long-term records of the firms (see table 3.4), the results of the Welch–Aspin test show that, although the rates of return of the non-taken-over firms are somewhat higher, and their liquidity position somewhat better, than those of taken-over firms, the two groups of firms *do not* differ significantly (at the 10 % level) with respect to these or any of the other characteristics. One natural interpretation of these results is that, on the basis of the observed long-term characteristics, it is not possible (at the 10 % level of significance) to reject the hypothesis that the two groups of firms belong to the same population. Although the mean values of some characteristics (e.g. pre-tax profitability) are higher for non-taken-over firms than for the ones taken over, there is so much variation around the mean values in the two groups that it is not possible, at an acceptable level of probability, to discriminate usefully between them on the basis of these characteristics. This interpretation of the results will be developed further later in the section.

For the same period (i.e. 1955–8) the short-term records given in table 3.3 yield essentially similar conclusions. Size (at the 1 % level) and growth (at the 10 % level) turn out to be the only statistically significant discriminators. In relation to our first impressions about the differences between the taken-over and non-taken-over firms, discussed in section 3.3, it is interesting to observe, from the bottom half of table 3.3, that although the 2-year pre-tax profitability of the average taken-over firm is only about three-quarters (75.3 %) of that of the average non-taken-over firm (as was shown in table 3.2), it is not possible to reject the hypothesis (at the 10 % level) that there is no difference between the groups with respect to this variable.

† It may be noted that since size-distribution of firms is known to depart a great deal from normality (possessing either a Pareto-type or a log-normal distribution), even the Welch–Aspin test may not be the best for this variable except when the number of companies in both groups is large. The performance of the test would of course be much better with log size, but since a distribution-free test is presented later, it was not thought necessary to use this transformation. Furthermore, the reader will recall that the relationship between size and probability of take-over was discussed in detail in chapter 2.

For the period 1959–60, again none of the differences between the mean values of the variables is significant as far as the long-term records of firms are concerned (see table 3.6). For the short-term records in this period, table 3.5 shows that, apart from size, which is significant at the 1 % level, both the dividend return (X_3) and the productive return (X_4) for the last year before the take-over are significant at the 10 % level. Short-term growth (X_9) is significant at the 5 % level. The meaning and value of the above results will become clearer when they are summarised and compared with those of other industries (in sections 3.4 (c) and 3.5 below).

(b) The binomial probability test

Another method by which the characteristics of two groups of firms may be compared involves posing the problem in the following way. Suppose there was little difference between the profitability of taken-over firms and non-taken-over firms in an industry. In that case, assuming that the two groups constituted the entire population of firms in the industry, we should expect to find that about half the taken-over firms had a level of profitability less than the industry average, and the other half a level above average. By counting the actual number of taken-over firms with profitability (before take-over) less than the industry average, we can test whether this expectation is justified.

Such a test not only has an obvious intuitive appeal, but also possesses the advantage of being distribution free. It has been performed on each of the 34 characteristics of taken-over (and merged) firms in columns 8 and 9 of tables 3.3 to 3.6 above. Thus table 3.3 shows that of the 13 firms (column 8), which were taken over or died through merger in the food industry over the period 1955–8, 7 had a level of pre-tax profitability in the last (accounting) year before take-over less than the industry average for that year. This result is in accord with the hypothesis that the pre-tax profitability of taken-over firms is much the same as that of other firms, the same conclusion as was reached on the basis of the Welch–Aspin test.

For size, on the other hand, where 10 of the 13 taken-over firms were below the industry average,† the hypothesis of no difference between the groups is more difficult to sustain. The chance of getting this

---

† Strictly speaking, in order for the binomial probability test to be completely non-parametric, the *median* rather than the (unweighted) arithmetic mean should be used as a measure of the 'average'. But since the mean values were readily available, and calculation of the medians for such a large number of sets of data would have been a laborious task, we used the means for this exercise. However, on checking these results for a few sets of data against those obtained by the use of the medians, it was dicovered that whereas, using either method, the figures obtained for variables such as X_1, X_2 etc. were much the same (but see section 3.6, p. 74) rather different figures were obtained for size (X_8) and to some extent for growth (X_9). It was, therefore, decided to use the median as a measure of average for these two variables throughout this analysis.

number or more of taken-over firms with a smaller size than the industry average, if in fact there is no difference between the sizes of taken-over and other firms in the industry, is less than one in 20. Using a two-tailed significance test, the null hypothesis for this variable is rejected at the 10 % level, as indicated in the last column of table 3.3.†
It is also worth noting from this table that size is a much less significant discriminator on the basis of the binomial probability test than on the basis of the Welch–Aspin test. The results of a non-parametric test are, however, to be preferred in the case of size, since, as mentioned earlier, the distribution of this variable is far from being normal.

It should be noted that, in the application of this test, we have included among the taken-over firms the *smaller* of the firms which disappeared through a merger. This accounts for the difference between columns 3 and 8 of tables 3.3 to 3.6. Calculations were done for taken-over firms alone as well, but the results were very much the same as those reported for take-overs plus mergers, except in the case of size. In the latter case, even the smaller of the companies involved in a merger was usually larger in size than the average taken-over firm. Furthermore, it may be noted that the variable X_{10}, valuation ratio,‡ which was not subjected to the Welch–Aspin test, has been considered in relation to the present test. This variable performs no better in the period 1955–8 than the measures of rate of return. However, its performance in discriminating between the two groups of firms for the period 1959–60 is shown in table 3.5 (short-term) to be a shade better than that of dividend return (X_3) or productive return (X_4).

Lastly, we may note that the results of the binomial probability test on the whole confirm the conclusions of the Welch–Aspin test, except in the case of size. The former test shows this variable to be a much less significant discriminator than does the Welch–Aspin test.§

---

† The number of taken-over firms with a measurement less than the industry average is regarded as a binomial variable. Normal approximation to binomial has been used in the application of significance tests. Two-tailed tests have been used throughout since one cannot assume that for every characteristic, more than half the total number of firms would always have a value less than the industry average. This is in fact not true in the case of several characteristics; even for size, it is not true in the electrical engineering industry.

‡ The number of companies for which data were available for the computation of the valuation ratio was less than that for other variables. This explains the discrepancy in the rows of column 8 of tables 3.3 to 3.6.

§ It should be noted that size would appear to be a somewhat better discriminator on the binomial probability test if we excluded mergers. As pointed out above, even the smaller of the companies involved in a merger – the ones included here – tended to be larger in size than the average taken-over company. However in view of the fact that only a handful of companies disappeared through merger, size would still be a less significant discriminator on the binomial probability test than on the Welch–Aspin test, even if mergers were excluded.

(c) The distance between groups

So far in this section we have seen that there are some variables which can discriminate between the groups of taken-over and non-taken-over firms, in the sense that the mean values of these variables in one group are significantly different from those observed in the other group. The question now arises: what is the *extent* of discrimination achieved by these 'significant' variables? Or to put it another way, what is the degree of overlap between the groups with respect to these variables? In particular, suppose that, on the basis of the observed values of one of these variables, we tried to classify the entire population of firms in some industry into two *a priori* groups of taken-over and non-taken-over firms, using of course a suitable decision criterion which minimised the chances of misclassification.† The proportion of firms misclassified as a result of this exercise would give us some idea of the extent of discrimination between groups achieved by the variable, and could serve as an index of the degree of overlap between them.

A simple way of estimating this probability of misclassification is to calculate the Mahalanobis 'standardised distance' between the two groups. This statistic emerges as a by-product of the research in tables 3.3 to 3.6. Mahalanobis distance between two groups is defined as being equal to $|d/s|$, where d is the difference between the means of the two groups and s is an estimate of their common standard deviation. If the variable is normally distributed and has equal variance in both groups, and the two populations are of the same size, there is a simple relationship between $|d/s|$ and the probability of misclassification. Some values of this probability for given values of $|d/s|$ are shown at the top of p. 69.‡

These figures show that when $|d/s| = 0$, i.e. when the two groups are literally indistinguishable, the probability of misclassification is at its maximum of 50 %. In general, the greater the value of $|d/s|$ the lower is the probability of misclassification and *vice versa*.

† For instance, in the case of a normally distributed variable with equal variance for the two groups, and if the consequences of misallocation are the same for both groups, the decision rule which minimises the probability of misclassification is a straightforward one. If m_1 is the mean of the first group and m_2 that of the second one, and $m_1 < m_2$, the decision rule which will minimise the probability of misclassification is simply to assign a particular member of the population to group 1 if its value is less than $m_1 + m_2/2$ and to group 2 if its value is greater than $m_1 + m_2/2$. The mean of the two groups can thus serve as the boundary for classification. Cf. C. R. Rao, *Advanced Statistical Methods in Biometric Research*, New York, 1952, ch. 8; and G. W. Snedecor and W. G. Cochran, *Statistical Methods*, 6th ed., Ames, Iowa, 1967, pp. 415–18.

‡ Cf. W. G. Cochran, 'On the performance of the linear discriminant function', *Bulletin of the International Statistics Institute*, Tome 39, Book 2, reprinted in *Technometrics*, May, 1964, p. 180. Strictly speaking, the relationship between $|d/s|$ and the probability of misclassification, shown above, holds only for the population (as opposed to the sample) values of the two variables.

$|d/s|$	Probability of mis-classification (%)
0.000	50
0.251	45
0.501	40
0.771	35
1.049	30
1.349	25
1.683	20
2.073	15
2.563	10
3.290	5
4.653	1

Table 3.7 gives the value of $|d/s|$ for food industry firms for those variables which were found to be significant on *either* the Welch–Aspin test *or* the binomial probability test in tables 3.3 to 3.6. This table thus also has the virtue of conveniently summarising the information given in the latter tables.† Although strictly speaking the relationship between $|d/s|$ and the probability of misclassification holds only with the qualifications mentioned above, the statistic $|d/s|$ can nevertheless be used as a *rough* index of the degree of overlap between the groups for most of our variables.‡

Table 3.7 shows that for variables other than size, even in the small number of cases where the mean values of the taken-over companies are significantly different from those of the non-taken-over companies, there is a very considerable overlap between the groups. Almost all these variables have values of $|d/s|$ of less than 0.5, indicating a 40 % or greater probability of misclassification, as against an expectation of 50 % on random selection, if any of them were used to discriminate between the groups.§

† Note that the values of $|d/s|$ are not given for variable X_{10} (valuation ratio).

‡ If the underlying populations are not equal in size, as indeed they are not in the case of taken-over and non-taken-over firms, the appropriate decision rule which will minimise the probability of misclassification will be different from that given above in n.†, p. 68. Cf. Rao [1952], pp. 286–300. The statistic $|d/s|$ can, however, still be used as a measure of the degree of overlap between the groups, since the lower the value of $|d/s|$, the greater will be the chance of misclassification even on the basis of the modified decision rule.

§ It should be noted that a random or a naive model yields an expectation of misclassification of 50 % only on the assumption that the underlying populations are equal in size. If they are not, an appropriate naive model would yield a lower probability of misclassification. For instance if it is known that, say, only 5 % of the firms are taken over in any year, one could lower the probability of misclassification to 5 % by simply classifying each firm as a non-taken-over one. However, in this situation if the value of $|d/s|$ for some variable is greater than zero, the probability of misclassification on the basis of that variable (following the modified optimum decision rule – see n. ‡ above), will be less than 5 %. And, in general, provided the underlying assumptions stated in the text are not seriously violated,

TABLE 3.7. *Significant discriminators and distance between taken-over and non-taken-over firms: summary table for food industry*

	1955–8		1959–60	
Record	Significant discriminating variables	Distance between groups	Significant discriminating variables	Distance between groups
Long-term (6 years)			Dividend return[a]	0.31
Long-term (3 years)				
Short-term (2 years)	Growth[a]	0.24	Growth[b]	0.24
			Valuation ratio[a]	
Short-term (1 year)	Size[c]	0.39	Size[c]	0.36
	Dividend return[a]	0.54	Dividend return[a]	0.39
			Productive return[a]	0.27
			Retention ratio[a]	0.21
			Valuation ratio[a]	

[a] Significance at 10% level. [b] Significance at 5% level.
[c] Significance at 1% level.

For the size variable, which is very far from being normally distributed for at least one group of firms (i.e. the non-taken-over ones), the simple relationship between the probability of misclassification and the values of $|d/s|$ may not hold. Nevertheless, it should be noted that the high probabilities of misclassification indicated by the low values of $|d/s|$ tend to confirm the results obtained for this variable on the (distribution-free) binomial probability test.

3.5   OTHER INDUSTRIES: UNIVARIATE ANALYSIS

Corresponding to the basic tables (tables 3.3 to 3.6) for the comparison of the characteristics of the taken-over and the non-taken-over firms in the food industry, we constructed similar tables for each of the other four industries – drink, electrical engineering, clothing and footwear and non-electrical engineering. For reasons of economy and space, these tables are not reproduced here.† Instead the summary statistics

the greater the value of $|d/s|$, the lower the probability of misclassification relative to that based on the best random strategy. Cf. the discussion between John Netter and William Beaver on 'Financial ratios as predictors of failure', in *Empirical Research in Accounting: Selected Studies, 1966*, Chicago, 1967, pp. 112–19 and 123–7. See also chapter 6 below.

It is important to emphasise that in the discussion of this chapter, we are using $|d/s|$ simply as a rough index of the degree of overlap between the groups.

† The interested reader can obtain a complete set of these basic tables from the Department of Applied Economics, University of Cambridge.

for these industries, corresponding to table 3.7 for the food industry, are given in table 3.8. This table shows, as in the case of food, the variables for which the mean values of the taken-over and non-taken-over firms are significantly different on either the Welch–Aspin test, or the binomial probability test (at the 1% or 5 % level of significance).†
They also give for these variables the values of the Mahalanobis distance, $|d/s|$, between the two groups.‡

Since table 3.8 already summarises the information given in the basic industry tables, and the meaning of the statistics presented in it has been discussed in the previous section with respect to table 3.7 for the food industry, no attempt is made here to give a verbal summary of the results for individual industries. However, the general impression which emerges from this table may be summed up as follows. The number of significant discriminators varies a great deal between industries and between the two time-periods, but for the various sets of data considered there are very few variables, apart from size,§ for which there exist in general statistically significant differences between the two groups of firms on *either* of the tests. For instance, in one of the four industries (clothing and footwear), there is no significant (at the 5 % level) difference between the pre-tax or post-tax profitability of taken-over and non-taken-over firms, for either the short- or the long-term measurements of these variables. In two others (drink and non-electrical engineering), the differences for these variables are significant in only one of the two time-periods.

The most important point which emerges from table 3.8 is that, even when there *do* exist significant differences between groups for some variable for one or the other set of data, the distances between the groups tend on the whole to be rather small. In most of the sets of data examined, there is so much overlap among the characteristics of the taken-over and non-taken-over firms, that none of the 'significant' variables is even a moderately good discriminator. The figures for $|d/s|$ indicate that in industries other than electrical engineering, 40 % or more of the firms, as against a maximum of 50 % on the basis of random selection, would be expected to be misclassified if any of these variables

† The variables which were significant only at the 10% level have been omitted from this table.

‡ As was mentioned in n.‡, p. 55 above, measurements for valuation ratio (X_{10}) have not been made for firms in the drink industry and the clothing and footwear industry. Note also that the values of $|d/s|$ are not given for this variable.

§ The results for the significance of the size variable in table 3.8 need to be interpreted with care. As noted in the case of the food industry in section 3.4, for size the binomial probability test is the more appropriate one to use. By this test, size is a much less significant discriminator than it is by the Welch–Aspin test. In fact by the former test, this variable is significant at the 5 % level in only 3 of the 8 sets of data for which results are summarised in table 3.8.

TABLE 3.8. *Significant discriminators and distance between taken-over and non-taken-over firms: summary tables for 4 industries*

Record	1955–8		1959–60	
	Discriminating variables at 5% or 1% level of significance	Distance between groups	Discriminating variables at 5% or 1% level of significance	Distance between groups
	a. Drink			
Long-term (6 years)	Growth[c]	0.433	1. Pre-tax profitability[b] 2. Post-tax profitability[b] 3. Dividend return[b] 4. Productive return[c] 5. Retention ratio[c]	0.311 0.259 0.334 0.328 0.210
Long-term (3 years)			1. Pre-tax profitability[c] 2. Dividend return[b] 3. Productive return[b]	0.350 0.353 0.342
Short-term (2 years)	Growth[c]	0.418	1. Pre-tax profitability[c] 2. Post-tax profitability[b] 3. Dividend return[b] 4. Productive return[c] 5. Gearing[b]	0.378 0.304 0.145 0.357 0.413
Short-term (1 year)	1. Size[c] 2. Productive return[b]	0.277 0.247	1. Pre-tax profitability[c] 2. Post-tax profitability[b] 3. Dividend return[b] 4. Productive return[b] 5. Gearing[b] 6. Size[b]	0.322 0.288 0.350 0.329 0.364 0.187
	b. Non-electrical engineering			
Long-term (6 years)	Dividend return[c]	0.280	Growth[b]	0.320
Long-term (3 years)	Dividend return[c]	0.308		
Short-term (2 years)	1. Pre-tax profitability[b] 2. Dividend return[c] 3. Productive return[b] 4. Growth[c]	0.684 0.344 0.162 0.471		
Short-term (1 year)	1. Dividend return[c] 2. Size[c]	0.416 0.072	Size[c]	0.230

TABLE 3.8. (*cont.*)

Record	1955–8		1959–60	
	Discriminating variables at 5% or 1% level of significance	Distance between groups	Discriminating variables at 5% or 1% level of significance	Distance between groups
		c. Electrical engineering		
Long-term (6 years)	1. Pre-tax profitability[c]	0.432	1. Post-tax profitability[c]	0.308
	2. Productive return[b]	0.412	2. Productive return[c]	0.565
			3. Dividend return[b]	0.472
			4. Pre-tax profitability[b]	0.789
Long-term (3 years)	1. Productive return[c]	0.452	1. Pre-tax profitability[b]	0.780
	2. Pre-tax profitability[b]	0.477	2. Post-tax profitability[b]	0.666
			3. Productive return[b]	0.647
			4. Dividend return[b]	0.589
			5[a]. Valuation ratio[c]	—
Short-term (2 years)			1. Pre-tax profitability[c]	0.821
			2. Productive return[c]	0.717
			3. Retention ratio[c]	0.689
			4. Post-tax profitability[c]	0.747
			5. Dividend return[b]	0.621
			6[a]. Valuation ratio[b]	—
Short-term (1 year)			1. Pre-tax profitability[c]	0.989
			2. Post-tax profitability[c]	1.035
			3. Productive return[c]	0.781
			4. Dividend return[b]	0.757
			5. Retention ratio[b]	0.729
			6. Size	0.170
		d. Clothing and footwear		
Long-term (6 years)	1. Dividend return[b]	0.601		
	2. Retention ratio[b]	0.490		
Long-term (3 years)				
Short-term (2 years)				
Short-term (1 year)	Dividend return[b]	0.588	Size[b]	0.207

[a] The distance statistic has not been computed for variable X_{10}, valuation ratio.
[b] Significance at 5% level.
[c] Significance at 1% level.

was used to discriminate between the two groups of firms. In electrical engineering, the values of $|d/s|$ are somewhat higher for the short-term measurements (1-year or 2-year) of several of the variables and the corresponding percentage of misclassifications would, therefore, be expected to be somewhat lower (perhaps 30 to 35%).

3.6 ALL INDUSTRIES AND ALL SAMPLES TOGETHER: UNIVARIATE ANALYSIS

In the previous two sections we have applied three different tests to each of a number of industries and time-periods. It is important, however, to make some assessment of the collective significance of all the statistics presented. For example, we find in tables 3.7 and 3.8 that in only 3 out of 10 sets of data (there being 5 industries and 2 time-periods) are there significant (at the 5% level) differences between the average 2-year pre-tax profitability records of taken-over and non-taken-over firms. On the other hand, the basic tables for the individual industries (corresponding to tables 3.3 to 3.6 for food) show that in 9 out of the 10 sets of data, this variable has a *higher* average value for the non-taken-over than for the taken-over firms. (See also table 3.2 in this connection.) The probability of this difference between the two groups of firms being in the same direction in 9 out of 10 independent samples, if in fact the groups are indistinguishable with respect to this variable, is very small. It would therefore be wrong to conclude on the basis of the various individual sample results that the two groups of firms belong to the same population as far as pre-tax profitability is concerned.

It is quite possible that the reason we have not, in the previous two sections, found many significant differences between the two groups, is that the sample sizes tend to be small for the taken-over group of firms. The example above suggests that the observed differences may well prove to be statistically significant if the results of the various samples are considered simultaneously.

This problem can be tackled in various ways. On the face of it, the easiest would be to pool the data for all industry groups and time-periods. However, as was mentioned in section 3.2, the existence of significant inter-industry differences in the firms' records can lead to a serious statistical bias, unless the samples are carefully designed to overcome this problem. Another, and in fact simpler, way out of this difficulty is the use of the binomial probability test which, it will be recalled, is based on a comparison of the record of each taken-over firm with the average record of firms in the *same industry* for the *same* year. For this particular test, pooling does not lead to any obvious statistical bias.† The results of the test, for the data pooled across all industries and time-periods, are given in table 3.9.

This table, which refers to both the firms' short-term and long-term records, shows very clearly that there are indeed significant differences between the two groups of firms for several variables. The taken-over group has a significantly worse record (at the 1 % level), short-term as well as long-term, than the non-taken-over group on the basis of any of the 4 rates of return, and also growth, valuation ratio and size. For example, if we consider the record of the year before take-over, we find that 62.3 % of the firms taken over over the whole period 1955–60, in all 5 industries, achieved a level of pre-tax profitability less than their respective industry average for that year. Given that there were 185 taken-over firms, this result contradicts (at the 1 % level) the hypothesis of no difference in the pre-tax profitability of the taken-over and the other (i.e the non-taken-over) firms in the industry. The corresponding percentages of taken-over firms with records (in the accounting year preceding the take-over) inferior to their respective industry averages were 59.5 % for X_2, 66.0 % for X_3, 65.9 % for X_4, 60.5 % for X_8 and 61.5 % for X_{10}. All these variables are significant at the 1 % level except for X_2, which is significant at the 5 % level.

For the financial policy variables (liquidity (X_5), gearing (X_6) and retention ratio (X_7)), the hypothesis that the taken-over firms are indistinguishable from the rest is not rejected at an acceptable level of probability in the case of X_5 and X_6, for either the short-term or the long-term measurements of these variables. However, X_7 is significant at the 5 % level; the results indicate that the taken-over firms on the whole retained a *markedly greater* proportion of their profits than the non-taken-over firms. This tendency was particularly marked in the period 1959–60.

Finally, table 3.9 reveals on the whole *marginally* greater differences between the two groups of firms in the period 1959–60 than in 1955–8, and in their longer-term (2-year, 3-year and 6-year) records compared with their 1-year records. It is also interesting to observe that dividend return (X_3) and productive return (X_4) appear from these tables to be

† As for the possible economic objections to pooling data across industries and the two time-periods discussed in section 3.2, it should be noted that there is in an important sense an impressive degree of uniformity in the nature of the differences we have found between the two groups. Although there are some industries and time-periods in which the differences between the taken-over and non-taken-over firms are larger than in others, the evidence indicates that, for most of the variables, the 'distances' between the groups (i) tend on the whole to be small and (ii) are almost always in the same direction. (For a discussion of the relationship between 'distance' and the statistical significance of a variable see below, p. 77.) It will therefore not be inappropriate from an economic point of view to pool together these various sets of data.

TABLE 3.9. *Comparison of the records of taken-over (and merged) firms with average industry records: pooled data, all industries and time-periods, binomial probability test*

Variable	1955–8		1959–60		1955–60	
	No. of taken-over firms	% < industry average	No. of taken-over firms	% < industry average	No. of taken-over firms	% < industry average
a. 1-year record before take-over						
Pre-tax profitability (%)	84	58.3	101	65.3[c]	185	62.2[c]
Post-tax profitability (%)	84	56.0	101	62.4[b]	185	59.5[b]
Dividend return (%)	84	65.5[c]	101	66.3[c]	185	66.0[c]
Productive return (%)	84	66.7[c]	101	65.3[c]	185	65.9[c]
Liquidity (%)	84	53.6	101	55.4	185	54.6
Gearing (%)	84	53.6	101	47.5	185	50.3
Retention ratio (%)	84	45.2	101	39.6[b]	185	42.2[b]
Size (£'000)	84	61.9[b]	101	59.4[a]	185	60.5[c]
Valuation ratio[d]	39	59.0	57	63.2[a]	96	61.5
b. 2-year average record before take-over						
Pre-tax profitability (%)	80	65.0[b]	101	64.4[c]	181	64.6[c]
Post-tax profitability (%)	80	61.3[a]	101	63.4[c]	181	62.4[c]
Dividend return (%)	80	65.0[b]	101	68.3[c]	181	66.9[c]
Productive return (%)	80	70.0[c]	101	65.3[c]	181	67.4[c]
Liquidity (%)	80	55.0	101	52.5	181	53.6
Gearing (%)	80	53.8	101	50.5	181	51.9
Retention ratio (%)	80	45.0	101	38.6[b]	181	41.4[b]
Growth (*t*−3 = 100)	79	73.4[c]	101	55.4	180	63.3[c]
Valuation ratio[d]	36	58.3	53	69.8[c]	89	65.2[c]
c. 3-year average record before take-over						
Pre-tax profitability (%)	79	67.1[c]	101	62.4[b]	180	64.4[c]
Post-tax profitability (%)	79	65.8[c]	101	56.4	180	60.6[c]
Dividend return (%)	79	63.3[b]	101	72.3[c]	180	68.3[c]
Productive return (%)	79	70.9[c]	101	69.3[c]	180	70.0[c]
Liquidity (%)	79	51.9	101	53.5	180	52.8
Gearing (%)	79	55.7	101	47.5	180	51.1
Retention ratio (%)	79	45.6	101	38.6[b]	180	41.7[b]
Valuation ratio[d]	35	60.0	53	66.0[b]	88	63.6[b]
d. 6-year average record before take-over						
Pre-tax profitability (%)	73	68.5[c]	92	63.0[b]	165	65.4[c]
Post-tax profitability (%)	73	56.2	92	65.2[c]	165	61.2[c]
Dividend return (%)	73	63.0[b]	92	73.9[c]	165	69.0[c]
Productive return (%)	73	68.5[c]	92	70.6[c]	165	69.7[c]
Liquidity (%)	73	52.1	92	57.6	165	55.1
Gearing (%)	73	53.4	92	46.7	165	49.7
Retention ratio (%)	73	38.3[b]	92	40.2[a]	165	39.3[c]
Growth (*t*−6 = 100)	73	63.0[b]	92	59.8[a]	165	61.6[c]

[a] Significance at the 10% level.   [b] Significance at the 5% level.
[c] Significance at the 1% level.
[d] Valuation ratio data available only for 3 industries (food, electrical engineering and non-electrical engineering).

the most important discriminators. In particular X_3 or X_4 seem to perform somewhat better than X_1 or X_2, i.e pre- or post-tax profitability. We do not however attach any importance to this result, since there is reason to believe that it arises purely from the nature of the statistical procedure used. It will be recalled from n. †, p. 66 above that, apart from size (X_9) and growth (X_8), the arithmetic mean rather than the median has been used as a measure of industry average for the purposes of this exercise. Since the evidence indicates that X_3 and X_4 possess a relatively positively skewed distribution, especially as compared with X_1 and X_2, the figure for the proportion of firms below the industry average would tend to be overstated for the former variables relative to that for X_1 and X_2.†

However, it must be noted that although, for the pooled data and with a sufficient number of observations, we find it possible in the case of several variables (considered individually) to discriminate between the two groups, the conclusion arrived at in sections 3.4 and 3.5, with respect to the *extent* of discrimination achieved by these variables, may be very little affected by pooling. There are essentially three reasons for thinking that this is, in fact, the case.

First, and very simply, we have found (table 3.9) that, although 65 % or so of the taken-over firms had (say) a rate of return less than their respective industry average, nearly 35 % achieved a level of profitability greater than this average. This suggests a fair degree of overlap between the two groups.

Secondly, it should be noted that the variance of d (the difference between group means) is very sensitive to sample sizes. Therefore, even an arbitrarily small value of d, for a *given* common estimate of population variance s^2, can become statistically significant if there are enough observations in both groups. However, owing to the fact that s^2 is itself *relatively* little affected by sample sizes, the 'distance' $|d/s|$ between the two groups is also relatively unaffected. (It will be recalled from sections 3.4 and 3.5 that $|d/s|$ is an indicator of the extent of overlap between the two groups.)

Thirdly and most importantly, we did investigate directly, by means of a suitable sample design, the effect of pooling on the 'distance' between groups. This exercise was carried out for three industries: food, electrical engineering and non-electrical engineering. For each taken-over firm in these industries, we matched the non-taken-over firm nearest to it in size in the same industry at the last accounting date before take-over. By taking one matched non-taken-over firm for

---

† It will be seen for example in chapter 6 (table 6.1) that in the case of X_1, the proportion of firms less than industry average remains very much the same whether this average is indicated by the median or the mean.

TABLE 3.10. *Matched samples of taken-over and non-taken-over firms: 3 industries (food, electrical engineering and non-electrical engineering) combined, 1955–60: values of t and of 'distance' |d/s| between taken-over and non-taken-over firms for selected variables, short-term (2-year) records*

Variable	Taken-over firms			Non-taken-over firms			Difference between means (d)	t	$|d/s|$
	Mean	Standard deviation	N[a]	Mean	Standard deviation	N[a]			
X_1 Pre-tax profitability (%)	14.9	8.34	87	18.29	9.99	87	−3.40	−2.44[c]	0.37
X_{10} Valuation ratio (units)	0.83	0.47	87	1.02	0.64	87	−0.19	−2.24[b]	0.34
X_5 Liquidity (%)	1.66	29.67	87	3.72	22.08	87	−2.06	−0.52	0.08
X_6 Gearing (%)	15.36	16.36	87	14.72	12.56	87	+0.64	+0.29	0.04

[a] N is the number of firms in the group.   [b] Denotes significance at the 10% level.   [c] Denotes significance at the 5% level.

each taken-over firm in each industry, this particular sample design (described more fully in chapter 5) minimises the bias due to pooling firms across industries. For a few of the variables, the 'distances' $|d/s|$, as well as the t values for the differences between the group means, relating to this set of pooled data are shown in table 3.10 opposite.

This table shows that, although for profitability and valuation ratio there are significant differences between groups for the pooled data, the 'distance' between the groups for either variable is very small and much the same as that reported in tables 3.7 and 3.8 for the individual industry samples. The table (p. 69 above) relating 'distance' to the probability of misclassification indicates that the use of either of these variables to discriminate between the two groups of firms would lead to a very high degree of misclassification (40 to 45 % as opposed to 50 % on random allocation). The same conclusion holds *a fortiori* for the other statistically significant variables in table 3.9.

To sum up we have found that, contrary to the impressions gained from section 3.4 and 3.5, if the data are appropriately pooled across industries and time-periods, there indeed exist statistically significant differences between the taken-over and non-taken-over firms, for all variables except X_5 and X_6. Pooling does not, however, alter the main point of the results of the previous two sections with respect to the distances between the groups. The distances, including those for all the significant variables, tend to be small, indicating that none of these variables is a 'good 'discriminator on its own.

3.7   SUMMARY AND ECONOMIC IMPLICATIONS

In this chapter we have discussed the question to what extent, if any, it is possible to discriminate between the taken-over firms and the non-taken-over firms, on the basis of their short-term or long-term records. These records were indicated by 34 variables, based on 10 basic ones, and the analysis was performed on a univariate basis.

It was suggested at the outset that, in making comparisons of taken-over and non-taken-over firms, there were *a priori* economic reasons for first analysing the data within each industry and for pooling together only the years 1955–8 and 1959–60 respectively. An initial statistical analysis of the firm characteristics showed that whereas the inter-year differences between firms' records were small and tended to be in-significant, the inter-industry differences were almost always highly significant. This suggested that, although inter-year pooling of firms within the same industry would be legitimate from a statistical point of view, the pooling of firms across industries would lead to statistical bias even if the *a priori* objections to inter-industry pooling were not valid or turned out to be of negligible importance. Such bias can be avoided only by the use of a suitable sample design or the choice of appropriate statistical methods.

Three statistical tests have been used to answer the main question posed in this chapter: the Welch–Aspin test, the binomial probability test and the Mahalanobis standardised distance measure. These tests have first been applied individually within each industry and to each of the time-periods 1955–8 and 1959–60, and subsequently to data *appropriately* pooled across all industries and all years.

The main conclusions which emerged from the statistical analysis have already been systematically summarised in section 3.3 and it is not necessary to repeat the whole of that account here. The essential point is that there are several variables (the rates of return, growth, valuation ratio and size) for which the average value of non-taken-over firms is on the whole significantly higher (in statistical terms) than the average value for the taken-over firms. There is, however, a very large degree of overlap between the two groups, so that the ability of these variables to usefully discriminate between them on a univariate basis is very small. The results indicate that in the cases of most of the 'significant' discriminators, 40 % or more of the firms would be expected to be misclassified (as against 50 % on random allocation), if any of them was used for classifying firms into taken-over and non-taken-over groups.

What implications can be drawn from these empirical results about the main economic issues discussed in chapter 1 and referred to at the beginning of this chapter? There are no direct implications at this stage of the analysis for the question of stock-market discipline, since the investigation so far has been conducted on a univariate basis. Although this analysis has shown that no single index of past performance (such as pre-tax profitability) is a good discriminator, it is possible that much greater discrimination between the taken-over and the non-taken-over firms might be achieved if more than one index of performance (for example, growth and profitability) were considered simultaneously. Similarly, in relation to the nature of the selection process on the stock market, although the univariate analysis has yielded some interesting insights about the take-over mechanism, it is impossible to arrive at a correct profile of the acquired firms without a multivariate analysis. In view of the inter-correlation between the variables, it is possible in principle for a variable which is a bad discriminator on its own, to become a good one in a multivariate context, and *vice versa.*†

There is, however, one issue discussed in chapter 1 on which it is

† See further chapters 4 and 5 below on this point.

possible to offer some comment at this stage. This is the notion of the threat of take-over, expressed in terms of a constraint on the valuation ratio, in Robin Marris's model of the growth of the firm. In a strong form, the constraint has been expressed as follows: unless a firm achieves a certain minimal valuation ratio it is almost bound to be acquired, but once it has achieved this value it is more or less safe from acquisition.† However, in some versions of his model, Marris has expressed the valuation ratio constraint in a weaker form, *viz.* the higher the valuation ratio of a firm, the lower the chance of its being acquired.

The results of our investigation indicate that although the valuation ratio of the taken-over firms is significantly less than that of the non-taken-over firms, there is a very considerable degree of overlap between the two groups. In the period studied, there was a relatively large number of acquired firms with above average valuation ratios, and a similarly large proportion of non-taken-over firms whose valuation ratios were below the average for their respective industries. This evidence clearly refutes the valuation-ratio constraint in the strong form described above. It also suggests that the inverse relationship between the valuation ratio and the probability of take-over is likely to be very weak. Thus the achievement of a relatively high valuation ratio, far from guaranteeing a firm against take-over, may not even greatly reduce its chance of being acquired.

APPENDIX

This appendix gives the list of standardised items of accounting information available for each company year, and the definitions of the variables used in the text to indicate the record of the company. The list of accounting items is given in section A. For a fuller explanation and notes on the various items, the reader is referred to Singh and Whittington [1968], pp. 209–16 and 232–4; the limitations of this source of data are discussed in the same publication on pages 218–21.

The definitions of the variables used to indicate company record are given in section B. For a detailed discussion of the definitions, the reader is again referred to Singh and Whittington, pp. 21–61, where the frequency distributions of most of these variables over the period 1948–60 are also presented.

A. LIST OF STANDARDISED ITEMS OF ACCOUNTING INFORMATION
FOR EACH COMPANY YEAR

ITEM NUMBER	TITLE
	Capital and reserves
1	issued capital: ordinary
2	preference

† Cf. Marris [1964], p. 234. It should be noted, however, that strictly speaking, this assertion applies to firms of the same size. But in the course of this study we have found overwhelming evidence that there is no relationship between the size of the firm and its valuation ratio. The same conclusion was arrived at in Singh and Whittington [1968], pp. 62–70. No harm is therefore done by ignoring size in the following discussion.

3 capital and revenue reserves
4 provisions
5 future tax reserves

Memorandum

6 contracts for capital expenditure outstanding

Liabilities

7 interest of minority shareholders in subsidiaries
8 long-term liabilities
9 bank overdrafts and loans
10 trade and other creditors
11 dividends and interest liabilities
12 current taxation liabilities

Memorandum

13 total depreciation

Assets

14 fixed assets: tangible, net of depreciation
15   intangible
16   trade investments
17 stocks and work in progress
18 trade and other debtors
19 marketable securities
20 tax reserve certificates
21 cash

Summary

22 total net assets

Sources of funds

23 issue of shares: ordinary
24   preference
25 increase in liability to minority interests
26 issue of long-term loans
27 bank credit received
28 trade and other credit received
29 increase in dividend and interest liabilities
30 increase in current tax liabilities
31 increase in future tax reserves
32 balance of profit: depreciation provision
33   provision for amortisation
34 balance of profit: other provisions
35   retained in reserve
36 other receipts

Uses of funds

37 expenditure, less receipts, on fixed assets: tangible
38   intangible
39   trade investments and
                                                investments in subsidiary companies

40 increase in value of stocks and work in progress
41 increase in credit given: trade and other debtors
42 expenditure ex provisions
43 sundry expenditure

Adjustments
44 consolidation adjustment
45 conversion adjustment
46 residual adjustment

Balance
47 change in securities
48 change in tax reserve certificates
49 change in cash

Appropriation of income
50 operating profit (before depreciation)
51 dividends and interest received (gross of income tax)
52 other income
53 interest paid on long-term liabilities: gross
54 tax on current profit
55 dividend, net of income tax : ordinary
56   other
57 to minority interest in subsidiaries (net of taxation)
58 prior year adjustments: tax
59   general

Summary
60 total capital and reserves (items 1–6)
61   liabilities (items 7–12)
62   fixed assets, net of depreciation (items 14–16)
63   current assets (items 17–21)
64   sources (items 23–36)
65   uses (items 37–43)
66   profit (items 50–2)
67   balance of profit (items 32–5)

Notes: Items headed '*Memorandum*' do not have any arithmetic consistency with other items, e.g. 'total depreciation' has already been deducted from the value of 'tangible fixed assets'.

Items headed '*Summary*' are the sums of groups of other items.

The following are the basic accounting equalities underlying the data:

(1) *Balance sheet:*
capital and reserves (60) + liabilities (61) = fixed assets (6) + current assets (63)

(2) *Sources and uses of funds statement:*
total sources (64) = total uses (65) + adjustments (44–6) + balance (47–9)

(3) *Appropriation statement:*
total profit (66) = interest paid (53) + tax on current profit (54) + dividends (55–6) + minority interest (57) + prior year adjustments (58–9) + balance of profits (67)

B. DEFINITIONS OF THE VARIABLES USED TO
INDICATE THE COMPANY RECORD

Variables X_1 to X_9 below were calculated for each company for each accounting year the company existed over the period 1954–60, and for which it produced data. Variable X_{10} was calculated for all companies taken over during the period 1955–60, and for a random sample of about 30 companies, in each industry in each of the years 1954 to 1960.

Notation:

t...indicates the year. Thus t takes on the values 1954, 1955, 1956, 1957, 1958, 1959, 1960.

y = standard rate of income tax.

9/20 for year 1954
17/40 for years 1955–8
31/80 for years 1959–60

In definitions given below the number prefixed by Q refer to the number of the accounting item in the list given in section A, e.g. $Q1$ is 'issued capital: ordinary'.

Definitions:

X_1 pre-tax rate of return on net assets

$$= \frac{Q66 - Q32 - Q33 - Q34 + Q59}{Q60 + Q7 + Q8 - Q4}$$

X_2 post-tax rate of return of equity assets

$$= \frac{Q35 + Q55}{Q60 - Q4 - Q2}$$

X_3 dividend return (gross of tax) on equity assets

$$= \frac{[Q55 \div (1 - y)]}{Q60 - Q4 - Q2}$$

X_4 pre-tax productive rate of return

$$= \frac{Q50 + Q52 - Q32 - Q33 - Q34}{Q14 + Q15 + Q17 + Q18 - Q10}$$

X_5 liquidity ratio (stock measure)

$$= \frac{Q19 + Q20 + Q21 - Q9 - Q11 - Q12}{Q60 + Q7 + Q8 - Q4}$$

X_6 gearing (stock measure)

$$= \frac{Q2 + Q8}{Q60 + Q8 - Q4}$$

X_7 retention ratio

$$= \frac{Q35}{Q35 + Q55}$$

X_8 size (net assets)

$$= Q60 + Q7 + Q8 - Q4$$

X_9 growth of net assets †
  (a) Short-term (last 3 years i.e. $t-3$ to t).

$$= \frac{\left[\sum_{t-2}^{t} (Q23 + Q24 + Q31 + Q35 + Q36 - Q43) + (Q7 + Q8)_t + (Q60 - Q4)_{t-3} \right]}{(Q60 + Q7 + Q8 - Q4)_{t-3}}$$

  (b) Long-term (last 6 years i.e. $t-6$ to t)

$$= \frac{\left[\sum_{t-5}^{t} (Q23 + Q24 + Q31 + Q35 + Q36 - Q43) + (Q7 + Q8)_t + (Q60 - Q4)_{t-6} \right]}{(Q60 + Q7 + Q8 - Q4)_{t-6}}$$

X_{10} valuation ratio

$$= \frac{\text{market value of equity capital (calendar year average)}}{(Q60 - Q4 - Q2)}$$

For each company year, values of each of the variables X_1 to X_7 above were calculated (a) for year t, (b) for the average of years t and $t-1$, (c) for the average of years t, $t-1$ and $t-2$, and (d) for the average of years t, $t-1$, $t-2$, $t-3$, $t-4$ and $t-5$. This resulted in 28 variables for each company year.

X_8 was calculated only for year t and X_9 was calculated over two time-periods for each company year as shown above. The value of X_{10} was calculated (a) for year t, (b) for the average of years t and $t-1$, and (c) for the average of years t, $t-1$ and $t-2$.

Thus a total of 34 variables, representing values over various time spans of the 10 basic variables given above, were calculated to indicate the record of *each company, each year*, over the period 1954–60.

† As was pointed out in Singh and Whittington [1968], various errors are introduced if growth of net assets is measured from the opening (i.e years $t-3$ or $t-6$) and closing (i.e year t) balance sheets. First, a firm which revalues its assets during a period of inflation will show a higher rate of growth in general than a firm which does not. Secondly, a firm may change its accounting date, as a result of which its growth will not be measured over the same time span as for other firms in the population which do not introduce accounting date changes. To avoid these problems, the definition of growth of net assets used here is based only partly on comparisons of opening and closing balance sheets; it is based mainly on the 'sources and uses of funds' statement, where as far as possible these problems have been eliminated. Thus the numerator of X_9 consists of size in year t, estimated by using actual figures for year t for minority interests and long-term liabilities, and 'sources and uses' figures added to the opening (i.e. $t-3$ or $t-6$) figures for the remaining components. Cf. Singh and Whittington [1968], p. 25 n. 1, and p. 236.

After the first proofs of this book had been corrected, it was discovered that the computer program used to measure growth for each company had omitted a part (mainly retentions and new issues) of the *first* year's growth. It follows that all the growth figures given here are to that extent understated, but this applies of course to each category of companies (i.e. taken-over, non-taken-over, acquiring and non-acquiring) so that the comparisons are not likely to be much affected. Nevertheless, all the relevant calculations were redone before the final proofs were passed, and it was found that none of the conclusions in the book needed to be altered.

4. COMPARISON OF THE CHARACTERISTICS OF TAKEN-OVER AND NON-TAKEN-OVER FIRMS: MULTIVARIATE ANALYSIS 1

INTRODUCTION

We have seen in the last chapter that it is not easy to distinguish between the records of taken-over and non-taken-over firms on the basis of any single one of their economic or financial characteristics. A comparison of the records of the two groups of firms on a univariate basis showed that, although there are significant differences between the groups for several of the 10 basic variables (or the 34 variables derived from them to connote the short-term and long-term records) discussed in the previous chapter, none of these variables was a 'good' discriminator on its own.

One purpose of the multivariate analysis of this and the following chapter is to investigate to what extent, if at all, the degree of mis-classification is decreased if more than one characteristic of the firms is used simultaneously to discriminate between the two groups. In principle it is obviously possible that, even if none of the variables is a good discriminator individually, the whole set of variables taken together may achieve a high degree of discrimination. In fact, if the sets of variables were *independent* of each other, it is very easy to calculate the degree of discrimination which would be achieved by considering all variables together, on the basis of the discrimination achieved by these variables individually. In terms of the notation and the concepts of the previous chapter, the extent of discrimination (i.e. the degree of misclassification following a suitable decision rule) depends on the 'distance' between the two groups. If all variables were independent of each other, the square of the combined distance between the groups would simply equal the sum of the squares of the individual distances. Thus

$$D_k = \sqrt{\sum_{i=1}^{k} \left(\frac{d_i}{s_i}\right)^2},$$

where D_k is the combined distance between the two groups on the basis of all k variables taken together and $|d_i/s_i|$ is the distance between the groups on the basis of the ith variable alone.† However, when the

† Cf. Cochran [1964].

variables are not independent of each other (as indeed is the case with the characteristics of firms being considered in this study, such as profitability, growth, liquidity etc.), there is no such simple relationship between the combined distance and the individual distances. In these circumstances, a more complex multivariate investigation is required, which takes into account the inter-relationship between the variables.

The second and related purpose of chapters 4 and 5 is to find out in a *multivariate* context which of the ten basic variables individually, and which sub-sets of these variables taken together, are most important in discriminating between the two groups. As is well known, in multivariate problems of this kind it is in general quite possible for a variable which is individually a bad discriminator to become a good discriminator when it is considered along with other variables, and *vice versa*.† In fact, *in general*, the relative discriminating powers of the variables considered on their own have no obvious relationship at all with the relative discriminating powers of the same variables in a multivariate context. However, in view of the inter-relationship between the variables, it is only in the multivariate context that a proper assessment of the relative discriminatory powers of the individual variables can be made.

The order of discussion in chapters 4 and 5 will be as follows. In section 4.1, some questions of methodology appropriate to the analysis of multivariate problems are discussed. The reader will find that certain specific multivariate methods have been used throughout the rest of the book, and it will therefore be useful to discuss at the outset their important features and their relationship to some of the possible alternative methods. The results of the multivariate comparison of the characteristics of taken-over and non-taken-over firms are presented here in two stages. The results of stage 1 are discussed in sections 4.2 and 4.3, and those of stage 2 in chapter 5. The main points of this chapter are summarised in section 4.4.

4.1 SOME NOTES ON THE METHODOLOGY OF MULTIVARIATE ANALYSIS

There are a number of different approaches to the multivariate problems posed above. In particular we may distinguish between the following four: (i) R. A. Fisher's discriminant analysis, (ii) Mahalanobis' generalised distance analysis, (iii) Hotelling's T^2 and generalised analysis

---

† *Ibid.* See also W. G. Cochran and C. I. Bliss, 'Discriminant functions with covariance', *Annals of Mathematical Statistics*, 1948, pp. 151–76, and section 4.3 below for an actual example of this phenomenon.

of variance and (iv) the regression analysis and linear probability functions. Although these various approaches have distinct historical origins,† deriving from different ways of looking at these problems, they are closely inter-related. In this section we shall briefly review the nature of this inter-relationship and indicate our reasons for preferring the use of the first two approaches, i.e. the discriminant analysis and the generalised distance analysis, in the empirical investigation which follows.

Discriminant analysis

The essential features of Fisher's linear discriminant function for the two-group case relevant to the problems mentioned above are best described with the help of the following notation. This notation will also be useful in the subsequent analysis.

Notation. Let N_1, N_2 be the numbers of objects sampled respectively from two k-variate populations. A typical observation is then denoted by x_{lgj}, which represents the value of the lth object for the gth group, for the jth variable, where

$$l = 1, 2, ..., N_g,$$

$$g = 1, 2,$$

$$j = 1, 2, ..., k.$$

The sample means for the two groups are given by the vectors:

$$\bar{\mathbf{X}}_1 = (\bar{x}_{11}, \bar{x}_{12}...\bar{x}_{1k})' \quad \text{and} \quad \bar{\mathbf{X}}_2 = (\bar{x}_{21}, \bar{x}_{22}...\bar{x}_{2k})',$$

where
$$\bar{x}_{gj} = \frac{1}{N_g} \sum_{l=1}^{N_g} x_{lgj}. \tag{1}$$

We define the vector of differences between sample means for the two groups as

$$\mathbf{d} = \bar{\mathbf{X}}_1 - \bar{\mathbf{X}}_2 = \begin{bmatrix} \bar{x}_{11} - \bar{x}_{21} \\ \bar{x}_{12} - \bar{x}_{22} \\ \vdots \quad \vdots \\ \bar{x}_{1k} - \bar{x}_{2k} \end{bmatrix}. \tag{2}$$

The estimated within samples variance–covariance matrices for the two groups, on $(N_1 - 1)$ and $(N_2 - 1)$ degrees of freedom respectively, are denoted by

$$\frac{1}{N_1 - 1} S^{(1)} \quad \text{and} \quad \frac{1}{N_2 - 1} S^{(2)} \quad \text{respectively}, \tag{3}$$

---

† For an interesting account of the historical origins of the first three approaches in the works of the English School, the Indian School and the American School respectively, see M. G. Kendall, *A Course in Multivariate Analysis*, 4th imp., London, 1968, pp. 111–16.

where for instance the typical element $s_{pq}^{(1)}$ in $S^{(1)}$ is defined as

$$s_{pq}^{(1)} = \sum_{l=1}^{N_1} (x_{l1p} - \bar{x}_{1p})(x_{l1q} - \bar{x}_{1q}) \quad (p = 1, \ldots k; \; q = 1, \ldots, k)$$

and similarly the typical element $s_{pq}^{(2)}$ in $S^{(2)}$ is given by

$$s_{pq}^{(2)} = \sum_{l=1}^{N_2} (x_{l2p} - \bar{x}_{2p})(x_{l2q} - \bar{x}_{2q}) \quad (p = 1, \ldots, k; \; q = 1, \ldots, k).$$

Furthermore we denote the pooled variance–covariance matrix, for the two groups on $N_1 + N_2 - 2$ degrees of freedom by

$$\frac{1}{N_1 + N_2 - 2} S$$

where
$$S = S^{(1)} + S^{(2)}. \tag{4}$$

A typical element, s_{pq}, of S is thus given by

$$\sum_{g=1}^{2} \sum_{l=1}^{N_g} (x_{lgp} - \bar{x}_{gp})(x_{lgq} - \bar{x}_{gq}),$$

where $(p = 1, \ldots, k; \; q = 1, \ldots, k)$.

Fisher's discriminant function

Fisher defined the discriminant function between two populations as that linear combination of variables for which the ratio of the square of the difference of its expectation in the two populations to its variance (which is assumed to be common to both populations) is maximised.[†] Thus consider the following linear combination:

$$Z_{lg} = v_1 x_{lg1} + v_2 x_{lg2} + \ldots v_k x_{lgk}, \tag{5}$$

where $v_1 \ldots v_k$ are the discriminant coefficients to be estimated.

In vector notation, $Z_{lg} = \mathbf{v}' \mathbf{x}_{lg}$, where

$$\mathbf{v} = \begin{bmatrix} v_1 \\ \vdots \\ v_k \end{bmatrix}.$$

† Cf. R. A. Fisher: 'The use of multiple measurements in taxonomic problems', *Annals of Eugenics*, vol. VII, 1936, pp. 179–88; R. A. Fisher: 'The statistical utilisation of multiple measurements', *Annals of Eugenics*, vol. VIII, 1938, pp. 376–86. For brief standard textbook treatments, see P. G. Hoel, *Introduction to Mathematical Statistics*, 3rd ed., New York, 1966, pp. 179–84; and Snedecor and Cochran [1967], pp. 414–18. For a fuller treatment of the subject, see M. G. Kendall and A. Stuart, *The Advanced Theory of Statistics*, vol. III, London, 1966, pp. 314–41. A slightly different approach, which is the basis of some standard computer programs for computing discriminant functions and allied statistics, is to be found in J. G. Bryan: 'The generalised discriminant function: mathematical foundation and computational routine', *Harvard Educational Review*, Spring 1951, pp. 90–5.

The expected values of Z in the two groups, $\bar{Z}_1$ and $\bar{Z}_2$ respectively, are then given by

$$\bar{Z}_g = \frac{1}{N_g} \sum_{l=1}^{N_g} Z_{lg}, \quad \text{where} \quad (g = 1, 2). \tag{6}$$

The pooled within samples sum of squares of Z is similarly given by

$$\sum_{g=1}^{2} \sum_{l=1}^{N_g} (Z_{lg} - \bar{Z}_g)^2.$$

Fisher's linear discriminant function then involves determining the vector of discriminant coefficients $\mathbf{v}$ in (5) in such a way that the ratio (M) is maximised where

$$M = \frac{(\bar{Z}_1 - \bar{Z}_2)^2}{\sum\limits_{g=1}^{2} \sum\limits_{l=1}^{N_g} (Z_{lg} - \bar{Z}_g)^2}. \tag{7}$$

Substituting from (2), (3), (4), (5) and (6) in (7) and simplifying it turns out that:

$$M = \frac{\mathbf{v'd\,d'v}}{\mathbf{v'Sv}}. \tag{8}$$

Maximising M with respect to $\mathbf{v}$, it is seen that the first derivative of M with respect to $\mathbf{v}$ is given by

$$\frac{\partial M}{\partial \mathbf{v}} = \frac{2[\mathbf{v'Sv}]\,[\mathbf{dv'd}] - 2[\mathbf{v'd\,d'v}]\,[S\mathbf{v}]}{(\mathbf{v'Sv})^2}.$$

The maximisation of (8) requires that

$$2[\mathbf{v'Sv}]\,[\mathbf{dv'd}] = 2[\mathbf{v'd\,d'v}]\,[S\mathbf{v}] \tag{9}$$

or

$$\mathbf{dv'd} = MS\mathbf{v}.$$

When $\mathbf{d}$ is non-zero, at the maximum $M > 0$, and from (8) $\mathbf{v'd} \neq 0$. Thus (9) can be rewritten as

$$S\mathbf{v} = c\mathbf{d}, \tag{9a}$$

where c is the well-defined non-zero constant $\dfrac{\mathbf{v'd}}{M}$.

We note that in the system of equations (9), only the ratios of v_j can be uniquely determined. Furthermore, the coefficient c in (9a) can be given any arbitrary value for an appropriate choice of the scale of the vector $\mathbf{v}$. Therefore, for convenience, replacing c by unity, we obtain

$$\mathbf{v} = S^{-1}\,\mathbf{d}. \tag{10}$$

At this stage, the following relevant features of the linear discriminant function may be noted.

(a) *Relationship to the classification problem.* Provided both populations are multivariate normal, and provided the variance–covariance matrices are *identically* the same in both populations, the probability of misclassification in the sense discussed in chapter 3 is *minimised* by the use of the linear discriminant function at (5) above.† This indeed was Fisher's aim in the whole exercise: to determine that particular function of the k variables which, taking into account the interrelationship between them, would best discriminate between the two populations, i.e. would minimise the probability of misclassification. Heuristically speaking, the linear discriminant function achieves this aim since maximisation of (7) essentially involves spreading the means of the two groups apart while the scatter of the individual observations around their respective group means is kept constant. This helps to minimise the overlap in the distribution of Z's in the two groups.

However, if the assumptions, of multivariate normality and identical dispersion matrices, are not met, and in particular if the latter assumption is violated, a quadratic discriminant function rather than a linear one is required to minimise the probability of misclassification. But quadratic discriminant functions raise very awkward problems and have proved rather intractable in practice.‡

(b) *Tests of significance.* There are two distinct problems here: (i) to devise a test of significance for the discriminant function as a whole and (ii) to consider tests of significance for the individual discriminant coefficients. The available overall tests of significance of the discriminant functions are essentially concerned with testing the hypothesis that the vectors of group means are the same in the two populations. Some of these tests do not require the assumption of multivariate normal distribution, but they all assume identical variance–covariance or dispersion matrices in the two populations.

As for the tests of significance for the individual discriminant function coefficients, there is a conceptual difficulty. This difficulty arises from the fact that these coefficients are not unique in the sense that they are estimates of definite population parameters. The *ratio* of any

† The allocation rule, based on the linear discriminant function, which will minimise the probability of misclassification is similar to that discussed for the univariate case in n.†, p. 68 above. If $\overline{Z}_1$ is the mean of computed Z values in group 1 and $\overline{Z}_2$ is the mean in group 2, and if $\overline{Z}_1 > \overline{Z}_2$, the allocation rule which will minimise the probability of misclassification (assuming the consequences of misallocation to be the same for both groups) is simply to assign an object with Z value greater than $\frac{1}{2}(\overline{Z}_1 + \overline{Z}_2)$ to group 1 and less than $\frac{1}{2}(\overline{Z}_1 + \overline{Z}_2)$ to group 2.

‡ For an example of the use of quadratic discriminant functions, see C. A. B. Smith, 'Some examples of discrimination', *Annals of Eugenics*, 1947, pp. 272–82. See also chapter 5 below.

two of these coefficients is, however, unique and an exact test is available for assessing the significance of any particular ratio.[†]

Mahalanobis' generalised distance analysis

The test of significance for the linear discriminant function as a whole, i.e. the test of the hypothesis that the vector of differences in group means in the population, $\mathbf{d}^*$ (corresponding to $\mathbf{d}$ at (2) above which refers to sample differences in group means), is 0, can also be done in terms of the Mahalanobis distance statistic. The two approaches are closely related, as will become clear below.

The Mahalanobis generalised distance statistic D^2 is defined, in terms of the notation developed at (2) to (4) above, as follows:

$$D_k^2 = (N_1 + N_2 - 2)\,\mathbf{d}'S^{-1}\mathbf{d}. \tag{11}$$

This is in fact the multivariate analogue of the statistic $|d/s|$ discussed in chapter 3. Like its univariate counterpart, this statistic can be used to indicate the degree of overlap between the two populations on the basis of their k multiple characteristics. The relationship between distance $(\sqrt{D_k^2})$ and the probability of misclassification discussed in chapter 3 holds for this statistic as well, provided the assumptions of multivariate normal distribution and identical dispersion matrices in both populations are met. In general, the greater the D_k^2 for the two populations, the lower is the probability of misclassification.

The relationship between D_k^2 and the vector of discriminant coefficients $\mathbf{v}$ is indicated by (10) and (11) above. From (10) and (11),

$$D_k^2 = (N_1 + N_2 - 2)\,\mathbf{d}'\mathbf{v}.$$

To test the hypothesis that the differences in population means, simultaneously for all variables, are zero (i.e. $\mathbf{d}^* = 0$), an F-test based on D_k^2 is available. More importantly, tests are also available for assessing the significance of the 'distance' contributed by an additional variable or an additional sub-set of variables.[‡]

Hotelling's T^2 and generalised analysis of variance

The hypothesis that $\mathbf{d}^* = 0$ can also be tested in terms of Hotelling's generalisation of Student's t. However Hotelling's T is in fact closely related to Mahalanobis' D^2 since:[§]

$$T^2 = \frac{D^2 N_1 N_2}{(N_1 + N_2)}.$$

† Cf. C. R. Rao, *Linear Statistical Inference and its Application*, New York, 1965, pp. 482–3.
‡ *Ibid.*
§ Cf. S. S. Wilks, 'Multi-dimensional statistical scatter', in *Contributions to Probability and Statistics*, Stanford University Press, 1960, Article 40, p. 495.

A somewhat different approach to this problem is in terms of the multivariate analysis of variance. This involves the use of Wilks' Λ statistic which is defined as follows

$$\Lambda = \frac{|S|}{|T|},$$

where S is the pooled *within* samples deviation cross-products matrix defined at (4) above and T is the *total* sample deviation cross-products matrix. The significance of Λ can be tested in terms of an F test due to Rao.†

Regression analysis and the linear probability function

Another way of investigating group differences in a multivariate context is to consider the problem in terms of multiple regression analysis. This method is *formally* related to the discriminant analysis discussed above. In particular, for the two-group case, Fisher showed that, if a 'dummy' dependent variable is given an arbitrary value of $\dfrac{N_2}{N_1+N_2}$ for the objects in the first group and a value of $\dfrac{-N_1}{N_1+N_2}$ for the objects in the second, the usual multiple regression equation, in k independent variables fitted by least squares, yields regression coefficients which are constant multiples of the coefficients of the discriminant function at (10) above.‡

However, there is a variant of the above approach which is sometimes used in problems of this kind. This consists of assigning values of 0 and 1 respectively to the dependent variable in the two groups rather than the values of $\dfrac{N_2}{N_1+N_2}$ and $\dfrac{-N_1}{N_1+N_2}$ respectively. If these values are given to the dummy dependent variable, it is easy to see that the linear regression equation has a straightforward interpretation as a linear probability function. Thus we consider the regression model

$$y = \beta_0 + \beta_1 x_1 + \beta_2 x_2 + \ldots \beta_k x_k + \epsilon,$$

where $\beta_0, \beta_1, \ldots, \beta_k$ are the regression coefficients to be estimated and y is the dummy variable, taking values of 0 and 1 respectively in the two groups, and $x_1 \ldots x_k$ are the independent variables.

Then if $E(\epsilon) = 0$

$$E[y/X] = \beta_0 + \beta_1 x_1 + \beta_2 x_2 + \ldots \beta_k x_k \qquad (12)$$

where X is the matrix of observations on the regressors. In other words the value of y, calculated from the fitted linear regression equation, can be regarded as an estimate of the conditional probability of y given

† Rao [1952], pp. 258–72.   ‡ See further Fisher [1938], pp. 376–86.

the X values.† This is indeed a useful way of looking at the problem, but the approach suffers from two important drawbacks:

(*a*) The assumption of homoscedasticity which is made in the classical regression model becomes untenable when the dependent variable y is dichotomous.‡

(*b*) In principle it is quite possible for the value of y in (12) above, calculated from the linear regression equation, to be greater than 1 or less than 0. This is however incompatible both with the definition of y and with the interpretation of (12) as a linear probability function.§

To sum up, in view of these drawbacks of the linear probability function, discriminant analysis and the generalised distance analysis are used in the subsequent investigation to deal with the problems posed in the introductory section. The latter two methods not only have a clear commonsense interpretation and a direct application to the problems under consideration, they also constitute a straightforward extension of some of the univariate methods discussed in the previous chapter. With the use of a linear discriminant function and the distance statistics, which as seen above are closely related, it should be possible to find out to what extent, if at all, it is possible to discriminate between the taken-over and non-taken-over firms on the basis of all (or a sub-set) of their economic and financial characteristics taken together. Furthermore, with the help of these statistics we shall also be able to assess the individual discriminatory powers of the different variables in a multivariate context.

4.2   RESULTS OF DISCRIMINANT AND DISTANCE ANALYSES: STAGE 1 (ALL FIRMS)

The results of the discriminant analysis and generalised distance analysis are reported here in two stages. In the first stage (sections 4.2 and 4.3), these methods have been applied to all taken-over (and merged) firms‖ considered as one group and to all non-taken-over firms con-

---

† For examples of the use of the linear probability function, see among others, G. H. Orcutt, M. Greenberger, J. Korbel and A. M. Rivlin, *Microanalysis of Socioeconomic Systems: a Simulation Study*, New York, 1961; and Maw Lin Lee, 'Income, income change and durable goods demand', *Journal of the American Statistical Association*, 1964, pp. 1194–202.

‡ Cf. A. Goldberger, *Econometric Theory*, New York, 1964, pp. 248–55.

§ One way in which this particular problem can be dealt with is in terms of probit analysis. See for instance: D. J. Finney, *Probit Analysis*, 2nd ed. Cambridge, 1952; J. Cornfield and N. Mantel, 'Some new aspects of the application of maximum likelihood to the calculation of the dosage response curve', *Journal of the American Statistical Association*, 1950, pp. 181–207.

‖ The smaller of the firms involved in a merger were included among the taken-over firms. Essentially similar results are obtained if merged firms are excluded. See further chapter 5 below.

sidered as another group. Following the pattern of chapter 3, the analysis has been done separately for each industry, and for each of the two time-periods 1955–8 and 1959–60. This analysis pertains to all the basic variables except X_{10} (valuation ratio) for which we did not have data for all the firms in all industries.† In the second stage (chapter 5), instead of considering *all* the non-taken-over firms as a group, we have taken 'matched' samples of these firms, matched by the 'size' of each taken-over (or merged) firm at the last accounting date before take-over. The analysis of chapter 5 pertains to only three industries, but it takes account of all variables including the valuation ratio. More importantly, it also deals with data appropriately pooled across industries and time-periods. The effects of relaxing some of the assumptions of the discriminant and distance analysis are also considered in that chapter.

Although there are many possible combinations of the variables X_1 to X_9 which can be used to discriminate between the taken-over and non-taken-over firms, only a small number are meaningful in the context of the issues which are the subject of this study. At the simplest level, from the point of view of prediction it is obvious that one should use all the available information i.e. all 9 variables together. At the other extreme, the smallest meaningful (multivariate) subset of these variables would consist of only two variables: (i) a measure of firm's rate of return and (ii) its growth rate. As was noted in chapter 3, both these variables are indicators of a firm's past performance and they have already been considered on their own. There are, however, at least two reasons for wishing to consider them simultaneously.

First, there is a purely accounting reason. It is easy to demonstrate that two firms, which have in fact the same profitability, could in principle show different accounting rates of return if their rates of growth (of the acquisition of fixed assets, more accurately) are not the same. The one with the higher growth rate will show lower accounting profitability and *vice versa*, even if the two firms follow the same usual accounting conventions. The reason for this phenomenon is that depreciation is not accurately measured by the rules of thumb normally employed by accountants for this purpose.‡ By considering growth and profitability together, this particular shortcoming of the accounting data is very much alleviated. Secondly, even if this accounting consideration is of negligible practical importance, it could be argued that profitability on growing assets indicates superior past performance (and certainly better future prospects) than the same level of profitability on stationary or declining assets.

† See n. ‡, p. 55 above.
‡ Cf. G. C. Harcourt, 'The accountant in the golden age', *Oxford Economic Papers*, March 1965.

Another combination of the variables X_1 to X_9 which is economically meaningful would consist of (a) a measure of the firm's profitability and its growth rate as above and (b) the three financial policy variables (liquidity, gearing and retention ratio), i.e. 5 variables in all. It was seen in chapter 3 that the non-taken-over firms have a significantly lower retention ratio than the taken-over firms. It would be interesting to find out whether retention ratio and the other financial policy variables can provide any greater discrimination between the groups than is achieved on the basis of profitability and growth taken by themselves.

It would be reasonable to maintain that, since size can have a systematic influence on the chance of acquisition, it should also be included among each of the two smaller combinations (profitability and growth; profitability, growth and financial policy variables) of variables mentioned above. However, it is known† – and it is fully confirmed by the analysis of this study – that size is not related to profitability, growth or any of the other variables being considered. The contribution made by size on its own in discriminating between the taken-over and non-taken-over firms has already been discussed in some detail in chapters 2 and 3. Therefore, if one wishes to study the multivariate performance of the other variables, it is not necessary to include this one among them. (Size is, of course, included in the larger combination – the complete set of variables X_1 to X_9, which may be used for prediction.)

In order to discriminate between taken-over and non-taken-over firms, linear discriminant functions were computed on the basis of all 9 variables together and on the basis of each of the two smaller combinations of these variables mentioned above. The overall significance of the discriminant functions was tested by computing Mahalanobis D_k^2, and by testing the null hypothesis that $D_k^{*2} = 0$, where D_k^* refers to the multivariate distance between the *two populations*. If the null hypothesis is not rejected at an acceptable level of probability, it means that the hypothesis, that the groups cannot be distinguished on the basis of their multiple characteristics, cannot be ruled out at that level of probability. In that case the computed discriminant function is essentially illusory, in the sense that the degree of overlap between the two populations is so great that, if this function were used to discriminate between them, it could lead to the same degree of misclassification as would be achieved on random allocation. If, on the other hand, the null hypothesis, $D_k^{*2} = 0$, is rejected at an acceptable level of probability, it suggests that there are real differences between groups and that the computed

† See Singh and Whittington [1968], pp. 62–70.

linear discriminant function discriminates between them in an optimal way. However, as Kendall and Stuart remark, that way 'may not be very good even if it is the best available'.† In other words, even if the null hypothesis is rejected, to assess the *extent* of discrimination achieved one must go further and look at the probability of misclassification entailed by the use of the computed discriminant function.

The values of D_k^2 computed on the basis of all 9 variables (X_1 to X_9) together and the tests of the null hypotheses that $D_k^{*2} = 0$, for individual industries and time-periods,‡ are given in table 4.1. In this table, the performance of non-taken-over firms is compared with that of taken-over (and merged) firms on the basis of their average records for the 2- and 6-year periods preceding the take-over. The two groups of firms were also compared on the basis of their 1-year and 3-year records. These comparisons, showed on the whole less discrimination between the groups than was found on the basis of 2-year or 6-year records. Therefore only the latter results are reported here.§

The first two columns in table 4.1 indicate the industry and the time-period; the third column gives the value of D_k^2. The fourth gives the 'variance-ratio', based on D_k^2, which has been shown to have an F distribution with F_1 and F_2 degrees of freedom.||

The variance ratio is given by:

$$F = \frac{N_1 + N_2 - k - 1}{k} \frac{N_1 N_2}{(N_1 + N_2)(N_1 + N_2 - 2)} D_k^2, \qquad (13)$$

where

N_1 is the number of taken-over and merged firms,
N_2 is the number of non-taken-over firms,
F_1 is equal to k (number of variables),
$F_2 = N_1 + N_2 - (k + 1)$.

F_1 is given in column 5 of this table. In column 6, in order to indicate the number of taken-over (and merged) and non-taken-over firms in

† Kendall and Stuart [1966], p. 323.
‡ Except the non-electrical engineering industry, for which the analysis has been done only for the period 1959–60. The analysis for the period 1955–8 was omitted for this industry because the number of non-taken-over firms (= 1234) in this set of data was larger than the capacity of the computer programmes being used. However this has been rectified at stage 2 (chapter 5), where matched samples of the two groups of firms have been considered for this set of data as well.

Similarly in the clothing and footwear industry, because of the relatively small number of taken-over firms in each of the sub-periods 1955–8 and 1959–60, the two sub-periods were amalgamated. Trials runs on the two sub-periods separately produced results similar to those for the whole period (1955–60) given in table 4.1.
§ The 1-year and 3-year results were reported in A. Singh, *Take-overs, the Capital Market and the Theory of the Firm: An inter-firm study of industrial acquisitions and mergers in the U.K.*, unpublished Ph.D. dissertation, University of California, Berkeley, 1970.
|| Rao [1965], p. 480.

TABLE 4.1. *Distance between all taken-over (and merged) firms and all non-taken-over firms: multivariate analysis:* *Mahalanobis D² for 9 variables together* $(X_1, X_2, X_3, X_4, X_5, X_6, X_7, X_8, X_9)$ *and F test for D²*

Industry	Time period	D_k^2	F based on D_k^2	F_1	F_2	$F_{F_2}^{F_1}(0.05)$
a. Short-term records (average for the 2 years preceding take-over)[a]						
Electrical engineering	1955–8	0.879	0.94	9	10+453−10 = 453	1.90
	1959–60	0.764	1.07	9	14+210−10 = 214	1.92
Food	1955–8	1.150	1.35	9	11+467−10 = 468	1.90
	1959–60	0.460	1.17	9	27+202−10 = 219	1.92
Non-electrical engineering[b]	1959–60	0.256	0.60	9	24+575−10 = 589	1.90
Drink	1955–8	0.510	1.28	9	24+619−10 = 633	1.90
	1959–60	0.312	0.91	9	28+258−10 = 276	1.91
Clothing and footwear[b]	1955–60	0.355	0.59	9	16+346−10 = 352	1.90
b. Long-term records (average for the 6 years preceding take-over)						
Electrical engineering	1955–8	0.948	0.91	9	9+428−10 = 427	1.90
	1959–60	0.971	1.35	9	14+190−10 = 194	1.92
Food	1955–8	0.935	1.00	9	10+420−10 = 420	1.90
	1959–60	0.254	0.94	9	24+182−10 = 196	1.92
Non-electrical engineering[b]	1959–60	0.483	0.97	9	19+506−10 = 515	1.90
Drink	1955–8	1.038	2.52[c]	9	23+574−10 = 587	1.90
	1959–60	0.534	1.45	9	28+249−10 = 267	1.92
Clothing and footwear[b]	1955–60	0.505	0.78	9	15+323−10 = 328	1.90

[a] Note that X_9 (growth) is measured over the 3 years preceding take-over.
[b] See n. ‡, p. 97.   [c] Significant at the 5% level.

each set of data, N_1, N_2 and $(k+1)$ are shown separately. Thus, for instance, in part a of table 4.1, row 5, column 5, $F_2 = 589$, $N_1 = 24$, $N_2 = 575$ and $k+1 = 10$. Finally column 6 gives the critical F-value for F_1 and F_2 degrees of freedom at a 5 % level of significance.

The conclusion which emerges overwhelmingly from the two tables is that the null hypothesis is almost never rejected. In only 1 out of the 16 sets of data examined in these tables does the value of D_k^2 turn out to be significant at the 5 % level; it is nowhere near this level of significance for the other sets of data. These results strongly suggest that it is not possible, on the basis of the multiple characteristics of the firms, and taking into account the inter-relationships between the various characteristics, to reject the hypothesis that the two groups (taken-over and merged firms on the one hand and non-taken-over firms on the other) belong to the same population.

However, before such a conclusion can be accepted, there is at least one difficulty which must be considered immediately. It will be recalled from chapter 3 that the univariate analysis showed that there *were* significant differences between the mean values of the two groups of firms in several cases and for many variables. In these cases, although on a univariate basis the 'distances' between the two groups tended to be rather small (suggesting a high degree of misclassification if these variables were individually used to discriminate between the two groups of firms), they were nevertheless significant.† However, when all the multiple characteristics of the firms are considered together (table 4.1), we find that the distances between the groups are no longer significant.

This apparent inconsistency between the results of a univariate and a multivariate analysis of the same data is not a particularly uncommon occurrence; it arises from the fact that, although the multivariate distance between the groups ($\sqrt{D_k^2}$) always increases with the addition of each variable, many of these variables contribute very little additional distance. However, the inclusion of these (from the point of view of discrimination) unhelpful variables decreases the variance ratio in (13), which makes it impossible to reject the hypothesis that the two groups of firms belong to the same population. It turns out that, provided the sample size is large *in both groups*, even a small increase in distance, resulting from the inclusion of additional variables, can be helpful in the application of the F-test given above.‡ But in view of the fact that

---

† We did not in fact directly test the significance of the univariate distances in chapter 3. We used a statistic similar to the t statistic for testing the significance of differences between group means. These results, subject to the qualifications discussed on p. 65, would be essentially similar to those obtained by testing the significance of the *distances* between the groups. This is because, in the univariate case, the variance ratio based on D_k^2, given above, reduces to t^2.

‡ Cf. Rao [1952], pp. 252–7.

the number of taken-over and merged firms in table 4.1 is small in many cases, it is possible that the inclusion of the 'unhelpful' variables may have produced the strikingly negative results which emerge from these tables.

In order to deal with this problem, the analyses (discriminant and distance) were done on the basis of the two smaller combinations of variables discussed above. The first combination consisted of the following variables:

(1) X_1 (pre-tax profitability) as a measure of the firm's rate of return†
(2) X_9 (growth)
(3) X_5 (liquidity)
(4) X_6 (gearing)
(5) X_7 (retention ratio)

The results showed that the null hypothesis ($D_k^{*2} = 0$) was not rejected at the 5 % level in a single one of the 16 sets of data corresponding to those reported in table 4.1.‡ There were, however, a few sets of data (confined to the electrical engineering and drink industries) for which D_k^2 was significant at the 10 % level.

The analysis was then done on the basis of an even smaller sub-set of variables: profitability (X_1) and growth (X_9).§ The results of the distance analysis on the basis of these two variables are given in table 4.2, which corresponds in every way to table 4.1. The former table shows a slightly brighter picture than the latter. The null hypothesis is rejected at the 5 % level in 3 (electrical engineering, 1959–60, for both short-term and long-term records; drink 1959–60, for long-term records) out of 16 sets of data analysed in this table.

We must, therefore, conclude from the distance analysis that there are very few cases in which it is possible, on the basis of the multiple characteristics of the firms, to reject the hypothesis that the taken-over and the non-taken-over firms belong to the same population. The results show that in view of the inter-correlation between the variables, the inclusion of the additional variables makes on the whole little contribution to the univariate distances between the groups.

† X_2, X_3 or X_4, instead of X_1, were considered in some trial runs. The results did not on the whole show any greater discrimination between the groups.
‡ To save space, these results are not reported here; they are available in Singh [1970].
§ The analysis on the basis of the smaller combinations of variables (X_1 and X_9; X_1, X_5, X_6, X_7 and X_9) has one important *statistical* advantage over that attempted on the basis of the entire set of variables. The smaller combinations exclude size which is an awkward variable for the discriminant and distance analyses. Size, as seen in chapter 3, is far from being normally distributed and its variance differs very considerably between the two groups. See further discussion bearing on this point in chapter 5.

TABLE 4.2. *Distance between all taken-over (and merged) firms and all non-taken-over firms: multivariate analysis: Mahalanobis D^2 for 2 variables together (X_1, X_9) and F test for D^2*

Industry	Time period	D_k^2	F based on D_k^2	F_1	F_2	$F_{F_2}^{F_1}(0.05)$
a. Short-term records (average for the 2 years preceding take-over)[a]						
Electrical engineering	1955–8	0.55	2.68	2	$10+453-3 = 460$	3.02
	1959–60	0.53	3.49[c]	2	$14+210-3 = 221$	3.04
Food	1955–8	0.13	0.70	2	$11+465-3 = 473$	3.02
	1959–60	0.08	0.97	2	$27+202-3 = 226$	3.04
Non-electrical engineering[b]	1959–60	0.02	0.20	2	$24+571-3 = 592$	3.02
Drink	1955–8	0.20	2.34	2	$24+619-3 = 640$	3.02
	1959–60	0.20	2.55	2	$28+258-3 = 283$	3.03
Clothing and footwear[b]	1955–60	0.02	0.12	2	$16+346-3 = 359$	3.02
b. Long-term records (average for the 6 years preceding take-over)						
Electrical engineering	1955–8	0.22	0.97	2	$9+428-3 = 434$	3.02
	1959–60	0.55	3.60[c]	2	$14+190-3 = 201$	3.04
Food	1955–8	0.12	0.59	2	$10+419-3 = 426$	3.02
	1959–60	0.04	0.39	2	$24+182-3 = 203$	3.04
Non-electrical engineering[b]	1959–60	0.11	1.01	2	$19+508-3 = 524$	3.02
Drink	1955–8	0.16	1.78	2	$23+574-3 = 594$	3.02
	1959–60	0.38	4.82[c]	2	$28+249-3 = 274$	3.03
Clothing and footwear[b]	1955–60	0.005	0.03	2	$15+323-3 = 335$	3.03

[a] Note that X_9 (growth) is measured over the 3 years preceding take-over.
[b] See n. ‡, p. 97. [c] Significant at the 5% level.

4.3   DISCRIMINANT FUNCTIONS AND THE
PROBABILITY OF MISCLASSIFICATION

The coefficients of the computed discriminant functions and the figures for the probability of misclassification entailed by the use of these functions in discriminating between the two groups of firms, provide further information which is relevant to the main questions raised in the introduction to this chapter.

Discriminant coefficients

Linear discriminant functions were calculated for each set of data for which distance statistics are reported in section 4.2. The latter, it will be recalled, were in fact used to test the overall significance of these functions. The coefficients of the computed linear discriminant functions give an indication of the relevant discriminatory powers of the individual variables in a multivariate context. As an illustration, corresponding to part *b* of table 4.1, the linear discriminant functions for the four sets of data in the drink industry and the electrical engineering industry are given in table 4.3. This table gives the vector **v** of discriminant coefficients of the function:

$$Z_{lg} = v_1 x_{lg1} + v_2 x_{lg2} + \dots v_k x_{lgk}.$$

Corresponding to each **v**, table 4.3 also gives the corresponding 'scaled' vector, $\mathbf{v}_s$, which has been obtained from **v** by multiplying each element of the latter by the square root of the corresponding diagonal element of the pooled matrix S, defined at (4) above. This procedure standardises the discriminant coefficients and the elements of $\mathbf{v}_s$ thus reflect the relative contribution to the discriminant made by each variable.†

The following important points emerge from the information contained in table 4.3, and from a study of the computed discriminant coefficients for other industries:

(i) The relative discriminatory powers of the variables in a multivariate context are often quite different from those observed on a univariate basis. For example, the basic individual industry tables in chapter 3 showed that the most important discriminator in the drink industry for the period 1955–8, on a univariate basis, was the variable X_9 (growth). In fact for this set of data X_9 was the only significant discriminator; it was significant both at the 1 % level on the Welch–Aspin test and at the 10 % level on the binomial probability test. However, the coefficients of the linear discriminant function in table 4.3 show that, in a multivariate context, the most important discriminator

† Cf. W. W. Cooley and Paul R. Lhones, *Multivariate Procedures for the Behavioral Sciences*, New York, 1962, pp. 116–23.

is pre-tax profitability (X_1), and X_9 is relatively much less helpful. Similarly in case of the three financial policy variables (X_5, X_6, X_7), the univariate analysis showed retention ratio (X_7) to be almost always the best discriminator. This impression is not confirmed on the whole by the multivariate analysis.

TABLE 4.3. *Discriminant coefficients (v) and the scaled discriminant coefficients (v_s) for drink and electrical engineering: long-term records (average records for the 6 years preceding take-over)*

	Drink				Electrical engineering			
	1955–8		1959–60		1955–8		1959–60	
Variable	v	v_s	v	v_s	v	v_s	v	v_s
Pre-tax profitability (X_1)	0.69	88.92	0.49	45.67	0.65	129.31	0.83	100.84
Post-tax profitability (X_2)	−0.33	−28.50	0.63	34.04	0.01	8.22	0.09	21.22
Dividend return (X_3)	0.30	18.42	−0.57	−23.93	−0.69	−56.77	0.45	22.38
Productive return (X_4)	−0.56	−88.41	−0.12	−13.51	−0.24	−81.40	0.17	36.86
Liquidity ratio (X_5)	0.08	32.46	0.04	8.52	0.17	91.81	−0.15	−49.52
Gearing ratio (X_6)	0.03	11.12	−0.01	−1.33	0.00	1.49	−0.01	−3.31
Retention ratio (X_7)	0.04	26.04	−0.10	−35.76	−0.11	−47.36	0.21	74.27
Size (X_8)	0.00	6.16	0.00	15.88	0.00	18.16	0.00	70.87
Growth (X_9)	0.02	12.24	−0.07	−43.40	−0.01	−10.52	−0.05	−53.91

(ii) The computed vectors **v** and $\mathbf{v}_s$ for the various sets of data show that the relative discriminatory power of the variables differs very considerably between industries and time-periods. However, it is almost always the case that of all the variables the rates of return (particularly X_1) are the best discriminators.

The probability of misclassification

Tables 4.1 and 4.2 showed that there are a few sets of data for which D_k^2 is significantly different from 0 at the 5 % level. This means that for these sets of data there are real differences between the taken-over and the non-taken-over firms and that the computed linear discriminant functions discriminate best between them. The question, however, still remains: how good are these discriminant functions, i.e. what is the extent of discrimination achieved by them?

One simple way of answering this question is to obtain the 'theoretical' probability of misclassification from the table given on p. 69 above which relates distance ($\sqrt{D_k^2}$ in the notation of this chapter) to the probability of misclassification. However, the accuracy of this answer depends among other things on the following conditions: (i) that there is no (or negligible) sampling error in the measurement of D_k^2 and (ii) that the data possess multivariate normal distribution and identical dispersion matrices in both groups. Nevertheless, it is worth noting that the computed values of D_k^2 in tables 4.1 and 4.2, even when they are significantly different from 0, tend to be relatively small, indicating a relatively high probability of misclassification. Furthermore, it is important to note that in three of the four sets of data for which the hypothesis that $D_k^{*2} = 0$ was rejected in the above tables, it was not possible to *reject* the hypothesis (at the 5 % level) that $D_k^{*2} = D_p^{*2}$ where D_p^{*2} refers to the squared distance between the two populations on the basis of X_1 alone.† In other words, even for those sets of data where the hypothesis that the two groups emanate from the same multivariate population was rejected, the distance between groups on the basis of all or a subset of all variables together was not usually significantly greater than that based on pre-tax profitability alone.

A second and more direct way of answering the question posed at the beginning of this subsection is to compute the actual (empirical) probabilities of misclassification which the use of the computed discriminant functions would entail. This procedure is to be preferred to that of calculating the theoretical probabilities of misclassification since all the assumptions underlying the latter may not be met in practice. The empirical probabilities of misclassification were computed in each case where the linear discriminant function was found to be statistically significant at the 5 % level. The results showed that the probabilities of misclassification were on the whole not much smaller than would be expected on the basis of a random or a naive model. This point is discussed further in chapter 5, where the detailed figures for the empirical probabilities of misclassification are given.

4.4   Summary and conclusions

The purpose of the multivariate analysis of this and the following chapter is to answer two questions. First, to what extent, if at all, is it possible to distinguish between the taken-over and non-taken-over firms on the basis of all or suitable subsets of all characteristics considered simultaneously? Secondly, in view of the inter-correlation between variables, what are the relative discriminatory powers of these variables in the multivariate context?

† This hypothesis was tested by means of an F-test due to Rao [1965], where

$$F = \frac{N_1 + N_2 - k - 1}{k - 1} \frac{N_1 N_2 (D_k^2 - D_p^2)}{(N_1 + N_2)(N_1 + N_2 - 2) + N_1 N_2 D_p^2}$$

on $(k-1)$ and $N_1 + N_2 - k - 1$ degrees of freedom.

Discriminant analysis and generalised distance analysis are used here to investigate these questions. A brief account of these methods and our reasons for choosing them rather than some alternative methods (such as regression analysis and linear probability functions) was given in section 4.1. The results of the discriminant and distance analyses are reported in two stages. The results of stage 1 were given in sections 4.2 and 4.3; stage 2 results will be discussed in the next chapter.

The analysis of stage 1 attempts to discriminate between all taken-over (and merged) firms considered as one group and *all* non-taken-over firms considered as another group. It was done separately for each individual industry and for each of the two time-periods, 1955–8 and 1959–60. The results can be summarised as follows.

When taken-over and non-taken-over firms are compared on the basis of their multiple characteristics, for most sets of data it is not possible to reject the hypothesis (at the 5 % level of significance) that the two groups of firms emanate from the same population. It appears that, because of the inter-correlation between variables, the inclusion of additional variables does not in general make a significant contribution to the univariate distances between groups. But even in the very small number of cases in which the null hypothesis is rejected, there is a large degree of overlap between the characteristics of the two groups of firms, so that the extent of discrimination which can be achieved by the linear discrimination function is very small indeed, although it is greater than can be expected on the basis of a random model. Further-more, the evidence indicates that even this degree of discrimination is not usually significantly greater than that achieved on the basis of profitability alone.

These conclusions are subject to several qualifications:

(i) The analysis of this chapter did not include X_{10}, the valuation ratio, which is an important variable.

(ii) The analysis has been done separately for each industry and time-period. As was seen in the case of the univariate analysis in chapter 3, it would be incorrect to draw *general* conclusions about the nature of the differences between taken-over and non-taken-over firms on the basis of these individual sample results. It is also necessary to consider all samples simultaneously by analysing data which are *appropriately* pooled across industries and time-periods before we can properly answer the two questions posed in the introduction to this chapter and in the first paragraph of this section. This is a most serious qualification to the above results.

(iii) The sensitivity of the conclusions to the statistical assumptions which underlie discriminant and distance analyses has not been assessed. It will be recalled from section 4.1 that both methods assume that the data possess multivariate normal distribution and identical dispersion matrices in the two groups, which needless to say are rather strong assumptions. Moreover, discrimination has been considered in this chapter entirely in terms of a linear combination of variables. The possibilities of non-linear discriminations have not been discussed.

All these and some other qualifications are examined in chapter 5.

5. COMPARISON OF THE CHARACTERISTICS OF TAKEN-OVER AND NON-TAKEN-OVER FIRMS: MULTIVARIATE ANALYSIS 2

INTRODUCTION

In this chapter, we present the second stage of the results of the discriminant and distance analyses. These results pertain to 'matched' samples of taken-over and non-taken-over firms. The procedure adopted was as follows: we matched each taken-over (or merged) firm with the non-taken-over firm nearest to it in size in the same industry at the last accounting date before take-over.† Matched samples of this kind were obtained from three industries: electrical engineering, food and non-electrical engineering.

One purpose of the analysis of this chapter is to examine the effects of the valuation ratio (X_{10}) which is *a priori* an important variable and which it was not possible to consider at stage 1 because valuation ratio data are not available for all firms.‡ Secondly and more importantly, with the matched samples it is possible to analyse data pooled across industries and time-periods. By taking one matched non-taken-over firm for each taken-over firm in the corresponding industry year, this particular sample design minimises the possible bias due to aggregation. The third purpose of this chapter is to discuss whether or not the statistical assumptions of the discriminant and distance analysis are valid for the data analysed, and to the extent that the data depart from these assumptions, to determine the degree of sensitivity of the conclusions to any such departures. The results of the multivariate analysis of the matched samples are reported in sections 5.1 and 5.2 and of the sensitivity analysis in section 5.3. The main conclusions are summarised in section 5.4. The economic implications of the empirical conclusions of this chapter (as well as those of chapters 3 and 4) will be considered in chapter 6.

---

† If a matched non-taken-over firm was subsequently acquired in the period 1955–60, it was normally omitted and the non-taken-over firm nearest to it in size was chosen in its place.

‡ Valuation ratios were calculated for the matched samples of taken-over and non-taken-over firms in the three industries mentioned above. There are a small number of taken-over firms for which we could not obtain the valuation ratios, mostly because Moodies cards for these firms were not available. These firms (and their non-taken-over matches) were excluded from the analysis of this chapter. This is the reason for any discrepancy between the figures for taken-over firms in this chapter and those given in chapter 4.

It should be noted that the procedure adopted in selecting matched samples of taken-over and non-taken-over firms nets out the effects of size. This is no loss as far as the economic interpretation of the results is concerned since, as noted earlier, size is not related to any of the other variables and the nature of the discrimination achieved with the help of size alone has already been investigated in the previous chapters. But, as we shall see in section 5.3, the exclusion of size from the multivariate analysis is definitely helpful from the statistical point of view. There are also certain other incidental statistical advantages to be derived from the investigation of matched samples.

5.1 DISCRIMINANT AND DISTANCE ANALYSES: STAGE 2 (MATCHED SAMPLES)

For the matched samples, the discriminant and distance analyses were done separately for each industry, for each of the two time-periods (1955–8 and 1959–60) and for both periods together (1955–60). The analysis was also done for all three industries together. The following combinations of variables were considered:

(a) All variables (X_1 to X_{10}) except size (X_8)
(b) Pre-tax profitability (X_1), growth (X_9), valuation ratio (X_{10}), liquidity (X_5), gearing (X_6)
(c) X_1, X_9 and X_{10}
(d) X_1 and X_9.

The reasons for choosing to consider (a) and (d) have already been explained in chapter 4.† We discussed in chapter 3 the justification for including valuation ratio in (c). Briefly, it could be reasonably argued that the selection process on the stock market might take account not only of the past performance of firms, but also of the market's evaluation of their future prospects. On this argument, of two firms with the same record of past performance (say in terms of growth and profitability), the one with the worse future prospects under existing management (i.e. lower valuation ratio) is more likely to be acquired. In (b), liquidity and gearing were included in order to find out what contribution to discrimination these financial policy variables make in a multivariate context.‡ Retention ratio (X_7) was excluded from (b), since once growth, profitability and valuation ratio are included, there does not seem to be any reason for expecting the retention ratio to have an

† Size was excluded from (a) for the obvious reason that with the matched samples, one is considering the possibility of discrimination between taken-over and non-taken-over firms of the same size.
‡ See chapter 3 for a discussion of our expectation with respect to the effects of these variables, particularly gearing, in a multivariate context.

independent influence on the probability of acquisition. X_7 is, however, included in (a).

The results of the discriminant and distance analyses for the combination of variables in (a) (i.e. all variables except size) are given in table 5.1, which corresponds to table 4.1 above. A linear discriminant function is computed for each set of data and the overall significance of each computed discriminant function is judged, as before, by computing D_k^2 and testing the null hypothesis that $D_k^{*2} = 0$. Part a of table 5.1 is based on the firms' short-term records: the average value for 2 accounting years preceding the take-over for all variables except X_{10} and the average value for the last available calendar year for the variable X_{10}.† Exactly corresponding records are considered for both the taken-over and the matched non-taken-over firms. Part b of table 5.1 is similarly based on the long-term records: the average value for the 3 accounting years preceding the take-over for all variables except X_{10} and the average value for the last available 2 calendar years for X_{10}.‡

The table shows the squared multivariate distances between the taken-over and the non-taken-over firms for each of the individual industries and for the data pooled across all 3 industries. The results for the individual industries are shown only for both time-periods together, i.e. the whole period 1955–60; for pooled data the results are shown separately for each of the periods 1955–8 and 1959–60, as well as for both periods together. These results indicate that on the basis of all 9 characteristics, including the valuation ratio, considered simultaneously, it is on the whole difficult to reject the hypothesis that the taken-over and non-taken-over firms belong to the same population. The null hypothesis is (barely) rejected at the 5 % level in only one (all 3 industries together; 1955–60; short-term records) of the 12 sets of data reported in this table.§ It is however rejected at the 10 % level

† Suppose the usual accounting date of a firm is 31 March and it is taken over in August 1958. The last annual accounts in our data will cover the period 31 March 1957 to 31 March 1958. We take the averages of the values at these two dates for the variables X_1, X_2 etc. For X_{10} the value taken is for the average of the *calendar* year 1957. The average market valuation of a firm for the calendar year is obtained by multiplying the number of issued shares by the mid-range of the highest and lowest prices during that year. For justification of this procedure see R. L. Marris and A. Singh 'A measure of a firm's average share price', *Journal of the Royal Statistical Society*, Series A (General), vol. 129, part 1, 1966; see also Singh and Whittington [1968], pp. 222–5. Finally it should be noted that, for the matched non-taken-over firms, exactly corresponding values for all variables are taken.

‡ Valuation ratio data were not available for enough firms over 6 consecutive years. Long-term values of most of the variables are, therefore, measured over the past 3 years rather than the past 6 years as was done in table 4.1.

§ In fact on the basis of all 9 variables, it is rejected in only one out of 24 sets of data. The results for each of the two time-periods for the individual industries have not been given in table 5.1. These results however show a similarly dismal picture and in none of the 12 cases pertaining to the separate time-periods for individual industries does D_k^2 come

TABLE 5.1 *Multivariate analysis of matched samples of taken-over (and merged) and non-taken-over firms: Mahalanobis D^2 for 9 variables together $(X_1, X_2, X_3, X_4, X_5, X_6, X_7, X_9, X_{10})$ and F-test for D^2*

Industry	Time period	D_k^2	F based on D_k^2	F_1	F_2	$F_{F_2}^{F_1}(0.05)$
a. Short-term records (average for the 2 years preceding take-over)[a]						
Electrical engineering	1955–60	1.374	1.358	9	22+22−10 = 34	2.17
Food	1955–60	0.709	1.074	9	31+31−10 = 53	2.07
Non-electrical engineering	1955–60	1.120	1.864	9	34+34−10 = 58	2.04
All 3 industries together	1955–8	0.711	1.338	9	38+38−10 = 66	2.02
	1959–60	0.627	1.564	9	49+49−10 = 88	1.98
	1955–60	0.442	2.034[b]	9	87+87−10 = 164	1.94
b. Long-term records (average for the 3 years preceding take-over)[c]						
Electrical engineering	1955–60	1.111	1.110	9	22+22−10 = 34	2.17
Food	1955–60	0.939	1.296	9	29+29−10 = 48	2.08
Non-electrical engineering	1955–60	1.683	2.088	9	26+27[d]−10 = 43	2.10
All 3 industries together	1955–8	0.791	1.286	9	33+34[c]−10 = 57	2.05
	1959–60	0.508	1.130	9	44+44−10 = 78	1.99
	1955–60	0.419	1.708	9	77+78[c]−10 = 145	1.94

[a] Note that X_9 (growth) is measured over the 3 years preceding take-over. See also p. 109.
[b] Indicates significance at the 5% level.
[c] The long-term value of X_9 is measured over the 6 years preceding take-over, See also p. 109.
[d] 1 company included by mistake.

in the non-electrical engineering industry for both short-term and long-term records, as well as for data pooled across all industries and time-periods for firms' long-term records.

It is necessary at this stage to examine the argument considered in chapter 4 that if a smaller number of variables was used D_k^2 might well be significant, particularly in view of the fact that when some of these variables were considered individually there were found to be significant differences between the mean values of taken-over and non-taken-over firms. This possibility was investigated by performing the discriminant and distance analyses on the bases of smaller subsets of variables, i.e. combinations (b), (c) and (d) listed above.

It is not necessary to give the table corresponding to table 5.1 for each of these combinations of variables, since the results are easily summarised. For combinations (b) and (c) the null hypothesis was not rejected at the 5 % level for a single set of data out of the 24 considered. It was rejected at that level of significance in one case (all industries and time-periods combined, short-term records) for combination (d). As far as the individual industries are concerned, the best results were obtained for the electrical engineering industry, 1955–60. For this industry the null hypothesis was rejected at the 10 % level, for both short-term and long-term records of firms, on the basis of combination (c) as well as (d). It will be recalled from chapter 4 that D_k^2 was found to be significant at the 5 % level for this industry, for the period 1959–60, when profitability and growth were considered together.

Overall, the best results on the basis of combinations (b), (c) and (d) were obtained for firms' short-term records for data pooled across all industries and time-periods. These results are given in the table below.

All 3 industries together (years 1955–60); short-term records: D_k^2 and tests of null hypothesis ($D_k^{*2} = 0$)

Variables considered	No. of firms in each group	D_k^2	F	F_1	F_2	$F_{F_2}^{F_1}(0.05)$
(b) $X_1, X_5, X_6, X_9, X_{10}$	87	0.19	1.64	5	168	2.27
(c) X_1, X_9, X_{10}	87	0.18	2.56	3	170	2.66
(d) X_1, X_{10}	87	0.14	3.17	2	171	3.05

close to being significant at the 5 % level. Furthermore, in relation to the *a priori* economic objections to pooling data across industries, which were discussed in chapter 3, it should be noted that the observed values of D_k^2 are broadly similar for the individual industry groups.

We must, therefore, conclude that as far as the tests of the null hypothesis (that the true multivariate distance between the taken-over and non-taken-over firms is 0) are concerned, the inclusion of the additional variable (valuation ratio) does not lead to any better results for the individual industries than those observed in chapter 4. D_k^2 is never significant at the 5 % level for any of the individual industries or time-periods. However, it is important to note that for data pooled across all industries and time-periods, D_k^2 is significant (though barely so) at that level of probability for a few combinations of variables for firms' short-term records, but not for their long-term records. It should also be noted that there are a few cases, confined to the two engineering industries and to pooled data (all three industries together; 1955–60) for firms' *long-term* records, where the null hypothesis is rejected at the 10 % level.

5.2   THE DISCRIMINANT FUNCTIONS AND THE EMPIRICAL PROBABILITIES OF MISCLASSIFICATION

In order to obtain a measure of the *extent* of discrimination achieved in the few cases in which the null hypothesis is rejected, we calculated the empirical probabilities of misclassification. The procedure used was as follows. In each set of data for which D_k^2 was found to be significant at either the 5 % or the 10 % level, the firms were classified into taken-over and non-taken-over groups on the basis of their respective discriminant scores (Z values in the notation of chapter 4). The latter (i.e. the Z values) were calculated for each firm by using the relevant (computed) discriminant function. The decision rule used (see p. 91 above) for allocating firms to the two groups was intended to minimise the probability of misclassification. The results of these calculations for pooled data, for both short-term and long-term records, are given below. The linear discriminant function employed in both cases was that based on all 9 variables together (see table 5.2 below, p. 114). As seen in section 5.1, the function for short-term records was significant at the 5 % level and that for long-term records at the 10 % level.

All 3 industries together (years 1955–60)

	Short-term records			Long-term records		
	Total	Correct	Incorrect	Total	Correct	Incorrect
Taken-over firms	87	59	28	77	50	27
Non-taken-over firms	87	53	34	78	48	30
Total	174	112	62	155	98	57
% misclassified	35.6			36.8		

Assuming that the errors of misclassification are equally important for firms in both groups, these figures show that about 35 % of the firms will be misclassified whether the firms are classified by means of all their short-term or long-term characteristics.[†] Although this figure represents definite inprovement over the error of misclassification expected on random allocation (50 %), it does indicate a rather large degree of overlap between the characteristics of taken-over and non-taken-over firms. Furthermore, it should be noted that the errors for misclassification given above are in fact an under-estimate in an important sense. This is because they are based in each case on the application of the linear discrimination function to the very set of data from which it was estimated. If these functions were used to classify other sets of data (e.g. of a different time-period), the errors of misclassification would tend to be even higher.[‡]

Another important point to note about these errors of misclassification is that they are on the whole not much greater than would be expected if the firms were classified on the basis of profitability (particularly X_1) alone. For example, the errors on the basis of some of the individual variables for pooled data (all 3 industries together; 1955–60) for firms' short-term records are as follows:

	% misclassified
Pre-tax profitability (X_1)	39.1
Growth (X_9)	44.8
Valuation ratio (X_{10})	44.8
Liquidity (X_5)	49.4
Gearing (X_6)	49.4

Thus we find that a little more than 39 % of the firms are misclassified if we use pre-tax profitability on net assests (X_1) alone for classifying firms into taken-over and non-taken-over groups for this set of data. As seen above, the probability of misclassification for the same data on the basis of the linear discriminant function using all 9 variables is only slightly lower, being 35.6 %. Moreover, the results showed that even this small improvement is mainly due to the inclusion of the other

† Similar errors of misclassification were found in the individual industries where D_k^2 was significant at the 10% level. There was of course not a single individual industry where D_k^2 was significant at the 5% level.

‡ On the downward bias in the computed figures for misclassification, which arises from this procedure of applying the linear discriminant function to the very data from which it has been computed, see R. E. Frank, W. F. Massy and G. D. Morrison, 'Bias in multiple discriminant analysis', *Journal of Marketing Research*, August 1965. See also M. Hills, 'Allocation rules and their error rates', *Journal of Royal Statistical Society*, Series B (Methodological) vol. 28, no. 1, 1966.

rates of return (X_2, X_3, and X_4) in the discriminant function. The empirical probability of misclassification on the basis of the combinations of variables (b), (c) and (d) above (all of which exclude X_2, X_3 and X_4) is in fact in each case almost exactly the same as that based on X_1 alone, i.e. about 39 %.

Similar calculations for pooled data (all 3 industries together; 1955–60) for firms' long-term records, and for the small number of other sets of data in the individual industries where the discriminant function was found to be significant at the 10 % level, lead to the same conclusion as above. This conclusion is in fact also supported by some indirect evidence. The hypothesis (first discussed in chapter 4) that $D_k^{*2} = D_p^{*2}$, where $\sqrt{D_k^{*2}}$ is the distance between the two populations on the basis of all k variables together and $\sqrt{D_p^{*2}}$ is the corresponding distance on the basis of X_1 alone, is not rejected at the 10 % level for *any* of the above sets of data.

Discriminant coefficients

In order to assess the relative discriminatory powers of the variables in the multivariate context, table 5.2 gives the vectors and the scaled vectors of discriminant coefficients for pooled data (all 3 industries together, 1955–60) for both the short-term and long-term records of firms.

TABLE 5.2. *Matched samples of taken-over (and merged) and non-taken- ove firms: discriminant coefficients* ($\mathbf{v}$)[a] *and standardised discriminant coefficients* ($\mathbf{v}_s$)[a] *for pooled data (3 industries combined, 1955–60)*

	Short-term records		Long-term records	
	$\mathbf{v}$	$\mathbf{v}_s$	$\mathbf{v}$	$\mathbf{v}_s$
Pre-tax profitability (X_1)	0.42	51.2	0.63	74.5
Post-tax profitability (X_2)	−0.51	−37.6	−0.57	−38.5
Dividend return (X_3)	0.03	1.1	0.04	1.8
Productive return (X_4)	−0.06	−12.4	−0.17	−38.7
Liquidity (X_5)	0.01	3.7	0.05	15.4
Gearing (X_6)	0.03	6.1	0.03	5.3
Retention ratio (X_7)	−0.01	−2.9	−0.04	−12.4
Growth (X_9)	0.00	2.7	0.00	4.9
Valuation ratio (X_{10})	0.74	5.5	0.49	3.8

[a] For explanation, see pp. 102–3 above.

The scaled vectors show again, as they did in chapter 4, that the rates of return (particularly X_1) are the best discriminators when all variables are considered simultaneously. Figures in table 5.2 as well as those for the individual industries (not given here) show that X_1 is usually more important than the other rates of return and far more important than valuation ratio, growth or the other variables. As far as the relative discriminatory powers of other variables are concerned, it was found that there was no consistent pattern and that they varied between industries and between different time-periods. It was notable, however, that in the multivariate context the financial variables (e.g. liquidity) were often more important than valuation ratio or growth, although the univariate analysis of chapter 3 showed the latter variables to be better discriminators individually.

Summing-up

It will probably be useful to summarise the main results up to this point of the discriminant and distance analyses of the matched samples of taken-over and non-taken-over firms. We have found that for firms of the same size, on the basis of a knowledge of their multiple characteristics, it is on the whole difficult to reject the hypothesis that the taken-over and the non-taken-over firms belong to the same population. In the few cases where the null hypothesis is rejected either at the 5 % or the 10 % level, the degree of discrimination achieved with the help of these various characteristics is not very high (about 65 % in the most favourable case) although it is higher than what can be expected on random allocation (50 %). In fact in view of the inter-correlation between variables, it is only slightly (but not significantly) greater than what is possible on the basis of profitability (in particular X_1) considered on its own. Lastly, the coefficients of the computed discriminant functions show the rates of return in general, and X_1 in particular, to be by far the most important discriminators in the multivariate context.

There are however three important points to bear in mind in relation to these conclusions. First, if the aim of the exercise is predictive accuracy, it should be possible to do somewhat better than is suggested above. The results for pooled data (all 3 industries together; 1955–60) may be interpreted in the following terms: if there was a list with an equal number of taken-over and non-taken-over firms, with each pair of firms being the *same size*, it would be possible *at best* to correctly classify about 65 % of the firms to their respective groups on the basis of a knowledge of all their short-term characteristics (using the discriminant function in table 5.2). However, since it is known (i) that the size of the firm is not related to its other characteristics and (ii) that non-taken-over firms are 'significantly' larger than the taken-over firms (chapter 3), it is reasonable to expect that the accuracy of prediction can be enhanced by using size as an additional predictor.

The question then arises what degree of predictive accuracy can be expected if size, along with all the other variables, is in fact used to classify firms into the taken-over and non-taken-over groups. One way of answering this question is to follow the method adopted so far, i.e. compute a discriminant function on the basis of all 10 variables and calculate the probability of misclassification entailed by the use of this discriminant function. This would, unfortunately, be a useless exercise for the matched samples, since in this particular sample design each taken-over firm is matched against a non-taken-over firm of the same size. (There are sound statistical reasons for the choice of this sample design as the discussion of the next section will show.) However, as size is on the whole unrelated to other variables, and the error of misclassification on the basis of size alone is easily estimated, it is possible to combine this error with that observed on the basis of all 9 variables together. For the 3 industries considered in the matched samples, it was found that about 45 % of the firms would be expected to be misclassified if size (more accurately log size) was used on its own to classify firms into the two groups.† Since the discriminant function on the basis of all 9 variables together gives a probability of misclassification of about 35 %, it can be shown that if the assumptions underlying the discriminant analysis are met, the probability of misclassification on the basis of all 10 variables would be expected to be reduced to 32 %.

This figure, it must be stressed, represents a lower bound on the probability of misclassification (see p. 113). Furthermore, it will be shown in chapter 6 that the predictive accuracy implied by it is even more modest if instead of assuming equal numbers in the two groups, the question of prediction is considered in the more realistic context where it is known that only a small proportion of firms (about 4 %) are likely to be acquired in any particular year.

The second point to note about the conclusions summarised above is that they are not affected in any way if the small number of merged firms (5) is excluded from the analysis. Thirdly, and more importantly, it must be remembered that all these results are based on certain important statistical assumptions common to the discriminant and distance analyses. Therefore, before they can be accepted, it is necessary to examine the validity of these assumptions for the data analysed here, and to assess the sensitivity of the results to any observed departures from them.

† The average univariate distance between the taken-over and non-taken-over firms for the three industry groups, on the basis of log X_8, was found to be 0.26, which indicates a probability of misclassification of about 45 %. It was decided to use log X_8 rather than X_8 for this exercise because the former is likely more nearly to meet the assumptions of normality and equal variance in the two groups. See also n. †, p. 157 below.

5.3   SENSITIVITY ANALYSIS

We saw in chapter 4 that there are two important assumptions which underlie both the discriminant and the distance analysis, namely multivariate normal distribution and identical variance–covariance matrices in both populations. The latter assumption implies not only that the variances of the k variables are the same in the two populations, but also that the same relationship (covariance) holds between any two variables, such as profitability and growth, in both populations. Furthermore, it should be noted that in the empirical analysis of the last two sections the problem of discrimination between the two groups of firms has been considered entirely in terms of a *linear* discriminant function. It is in principle possible that a non-linear function may be able to achieve discrimination where a linear one cannot.

The last two problems, it will be recalled from chapter 4, are interrelated. We noted in that chapter that when the assumption of identical dispersion matrices is not met, a non-linear function discriminates between the two populations better than a linear one. The question how far the data analysed here (both at stage 1 in chapter 4 and at stage 2 in this chapter) in fact conform with this assumption will be discussed first and that of multivariate-normality will be discussed next.

The homogeneity of variance–covariance matrices in the two groups

The similarity of the variance–covariance matrices was tested in two stages: first the significance of the differences in the variances of the individual variables was tested by means of the usual univariate F-test. At the second stage, the Bartlett–Box multivariate analogue of this test was applied to *each* set of data considered at stages 1 and 2 (chapters 4 and 5), to test the hypothesis that there are no differences in the group dispersion matrices.† It must be borne in mind however that both these tests (the univariate and the multivariate) require the assumption of normal (or multivariate normal) distribution and are extremely sensitive to any departures from normality.‡ The rejection of the null hypothesis in terms of these tests does not necessarily imply that the variance–covariance matrices are in fact different: it could mean merely that the variables are not normally distributed. The results of these tests must, therefore, be treated with caution.

As far as the variances of the individual variables are concerned, the

---

† Cf. G. E. P. Box, 'A general distribution theory for a class of likelihood criteria', *Biometrika*, December 1949, pp. 317–46. See also Cooley and Lhones [1962], pp. 60–70; T. W. Anderson, *An Introduction to Multivariate Statistical Analysis*, New York, 1958, p. 374.

‡ See for instance, G. E. P. Box, 'Non-normality and tests on variances', *Biometrika*, December 1953, pp. 318–35; H. Levene, 'Robust tests for equality of variances', *Contributions to Probability and Statistics*, Palo Alto, 1960, pp. 278–92; Anderson [1958].

data for the individual industries discussed in chapter 3 showed that they were on the whole similar in the two groups of firms. The null hypothesis, on the basis of the univariate F-test, was rejected at the 5 % level of significance in only a relatively small number of cases, for most variables except size. For size the variance of the non-taken-over group of firms was almost always significantly higher than that of the taken-over group of firms.

However, the Bartlett–Box multivariate test produced more diverse results. In the application of this test to 16 sets of data pertaining to the groups of all taken-over (and merged) firms and *all* non-taken-over firms which were considered in table 4.1 in chapter 4, the null hypothesis was nearly always rejected at the 5 % level. But this almost uniform rejection was mainly due to size, which was included in the multivariate analyses reported in this table. When size was excluded, in nearly half the sets of data analysed for various combinations of variables the null hypothesis could not be rejected at the 5 % level. In particular, the homogeneity hypothesis could not on the whole be rejected for the non-electrical engineering and the clothing and footwear industries, especially for the long-term records of firms. In two other industries (electrical engineering and food), there were found to be significant but moderate departures from the homogeneity hypothesis and in the fifth industry (drink), there were found to be significant, and on the whole rather pronounced, differences in the variance–covariance matrices of the two groups of firms.

The hypothesis that there is no difference between the variance–covariance matrices was then tested in relation to the sets of data pertaining to matched samples (stage 2). Since size was not included among the combinations of variables considered for the matched samples, the test results showed that in the majority of cases the null hypothesis could not be rejected at the 5 % level. In the remaining cases, there were significant but on the whole moderate departures from homogeneity. It should, however, be noted that in the latter cases there did not appear to be any particular pattern to the differences between the dispersion matrices in the two groups, so that the transformation of the variables could not be relied upon to bring about homogeneity.

A notable property of the Mahalanobis distance statistic, D_k^2, used throughout the analyses of chapter 4 and of the present chapter, is that it is known to be insensitive to moderate departures from the homogeneity of dispersion matrices, provided the numbers of observations in the two groups are equal.[†] More importantly, it has been demon-

† Cf. R. Reyment, 'Observations on homogeneity of covariance matrices in paleontologic biometry', *Biometrics*, March 1962, pp. 1–11.

strated in the two-group case that if the sample sizes, N_1 and N_2, are equal and N_i is large, the inequality of dispersion matrices has no effect either on the level of significance or on the power of the statistical test used in these chapters to assess the overall significance of the computed discriminant functions.† This was in fact the main motivation for the choice of the particular sample design used in the present chapter. The matched samples have an equal number of firms in the two groups; since they are 'normalised' for size, they do not on the whole display more than moderate departures from homogeneity of dispersion matrices for the various combinations of variables considered. Therefore, although it is possible that some of the results of chapter 4, particularly those pertaining to the combinations of variables which included size, may not be so reliable because of the dissimilarity of the dispersion matrices, those of the present chapter are unlikely to be affected by this factor.

Non-linear discriminant functions and other allocation rules

As suggested above, it is possible to argue that, even if a linear discriminant function is unable to satisfactorily distinguish between groups, a non-linear function may be able to do so. This would of course be a particularly valid argument where there are substantial differences between the dispersion matrices. In fact one can take it further and argue that it is not in any case sensible to discuss the problem of discrimination by looking for a *single* function of variables. It may well be that in some circumstances what is required is a classification rule or a set of rules which may or may not make use of a linear function or even a single function of the variables.‡

In the context of the empirical problem being considered in this study, such an objection must be carefully examined. For example, it is possible to argue that the firms which are taken over do in fact differ from the ones which are not taken over, but in a way which cannot be detected by multivariate discriminant analysis. In particular, it may be argued§ that the taken-over firms tend to be the ones which perform either very well or very badly. To put it crudely, in the former case the main attraction for an acquiring firm may be the management resources of the acquired firm and in the latter case it may be its

---

† K. Ito and W. J. Schull, 'On the robustness of the T_0^2 test in multivariate analysis of variance when variance covariance matrices are not equal', *Biometrika*, June 1964, pp. 71–82. It should be noted that the variance-ratio test based on D_k^2 (see p. 97 above) which has been used here to test the overall significance of a computed discriminant function is exactly the same as the one based on T^2 for testing the equality of mean vectors in the two populations. See for instance, D. F. Morrison, *Multivariate Statistical Methods*, New York, 1967, p. 125.
‡ Cf. Kendall and Stuart [1966], p. 339.
§ I am grateful to my colleague Mr G. Whittington for this suggestion.

physical assets.† If this were true, we should expect to find the situation in fig. 1 if we compared (say) the profitability–growth records of the taken-over firms with those of the ones not taken over. The crosses represent the taken-over firms and the dots the non-taken-over firms. It is clear that in these circumstances discrimination between the groups is possible, but that any single linear or even a simple non-linear function would produce an unnecessarily high degree of misclassification.

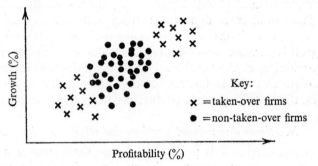

Fig. 1   Growth–profitability relationship between taken-over and non-taken-over firms (data hypothetical).

Unfortunately there does not appear to exist any neat mathematical way of dealing with this problem and one must perforce turn to simple scatter diagrams. Appendix 5.1 (charts 1 to 3) contains 2-variable scatter diagrams for the pooled matched samples (all 3 industries together; 1955–60). They compare the *short-term* records of the two groups of firms in terms of the combinations of 3 basic variables: pre-tax profitability, growth and valuation ratio. The basic data for the pooled samples, arranged for convenience in an ordered form for each of the three variables, are given in appendix 5.2. It will be recalled that for this set of pooled data, the distance analysis had shown that the null hypothesis that $D_k^{*2} = 0$ is rejected at the 10 % level if all three variables are considered simultaneously, and at the 5 % level if only profitability and growth are considered together.

A study of charts 1–3 in appendix 5.1 and the other scatter diagrams‡ does not reveal any other simple and reasonably consistent allocation rule or set of rules which would do better (in the sense of minimising the probability of misclassification) than the linear discriminant function used in the analysis of chapters 4 and 5. The same conclusion emerges from a consideration of the ordered data in appendix 5.2.

† For a more detailed discussion of this point see chapter 6.
‡ A set of scatter diagrams for the individual industries corresponding to charts 1 to 3 of appendix 5.1 are available from the author. Scatter diagrams were also prepared for various combinations of variables other than the three (pre-tax profitability, growth and valuation ratio) discussed in the text.

Multivariate normal distribution

The question of the extent to which the observed results of the discriminant and distance analyses are sensitive to possible departures from multivariate normal distribution is answered at one level by the scatter diagrams in appendix 5.1. However, following an interesting paper by M. G. Kendall,† we also tried a relatively more rigorous non-parametric method of multivariate discrimination and classification. This method is based on order statistics and its application to the various sets of data fully confirms the general conclusions of the analysis of chapters 4 and 5. In fact, as far as the possibility of discrimination is concerned, the discriminant and distance analyses of these chapters yielded better results than the non-parametric method.

5.4 SUMMARY AND CONCLUSIONS

In this chapter, the second stage of the results of the multivariate comparison of taken-over and non-taken-over firms has been presented. These results pertain to the 'matched' samples of two groups of firms, in which each taken-over firm was paired with the matched non-taken-over firm nearest to it in size in the same industry year. With the matched samples, it was possible to include valuation ratio (X_{10}) [which could not be considered in chapter 4] in the analysis. More importantly, this sample design permitted us to study the results for pooled data; it was also seen to possess certain other important statistical advantages.

The results for the matched samples may be summarised as follows:

(i) For firms of the *same* size, it is not on the whole easy to discriminate between taken-over and non-taken-over firms on the basis of their multiple characteristics. The null hypothesis that there is no difference between the groups is not rejected at the 5 % level in any of the individual industries on the basis of all, or suitable subsets of all, 9 characteristics taken together, although it is rejected at the 10 % level for a few sets of data confined to the electrical and the non-electrical engineering industries. However, it is important to note that for data appropriately pooled across industries and time-periods, the null hypothesis is rejected at the 5 % level for firms' short-term records and at the 10 % level for their long-term records.

(ii) In those sets of data where the null hypothesis *is* rejected at the 5 % or the 10 % level, the extent of discrimination achieved on the basis of the firms' multiple characteristics is not much greater than can be expected on random allocation (at best about 65 % as opposed to

† M. G. Kendall, 'Discrimination and classification', in P. R. Krishnaiah (ed.), *Multivariate Analysis*, New York, 1966.

50 %). Furthermore, it is usually about the same order of magnitude as is achieved on the basis of pre-tax profitability (X_1) alone. However, slightly greater discrimination between the groups can be achieved if size is included as an additional discriminator.

(iii) In the multivariate context, the rates of return, and particularly the pre-tax profitability on net assets (X_1), are by far the most important discriminators.

The sensitivity of the above conclusions, as well as those of chapter 4, to possible departures of the data from the main assumptions of the distance and discriminant analyses was also assessed. It was found that, although the observed departures could have affected some of the results of chapter 4, they did not affect the main conclusions of the present chapter. It was also noted that the use of a non-linear function or even a set of allocation rules, instead of a single linear discriminant function, to distinguish between the two groups of firms was unlikely to achieve a higher degree of discrimination and would probably achieve less.

APPENDIX 5.1

In order to investigate the possibility of discrimination in terms other than that of a single linear function of variates (see section 5.3), a set of two-variable scatter diagrams is presented in this appendix. These scatter diagrams pertain to matched samples of taken-over (and merged) and non-taken-over firms, described and analysed in section 5.1; they are based on combinations of 3 variables: pre-tax profitability, growth and valuation ratio.

Charts 1 to 3 refer to short-term records of firms for pooled data for all 3 industries together for the years 1955–60. The corresponding charts for the individual industries (electrical engineering, non-electrical engineering and food) are not given here, but can be obtained on application to the Department of Applied Economics, University of Cambridge.

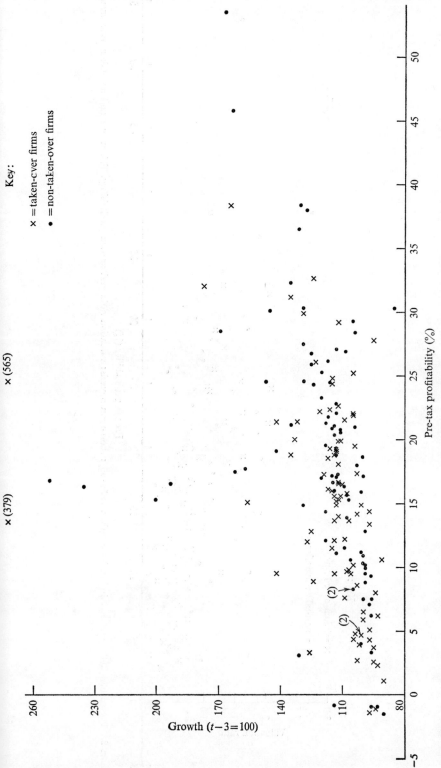

Chart 1 Pooled matched samples (3 industries together, 1955–60): short-term records: growth and pre-tax profitability. Taken-over and non-taken-over firms.

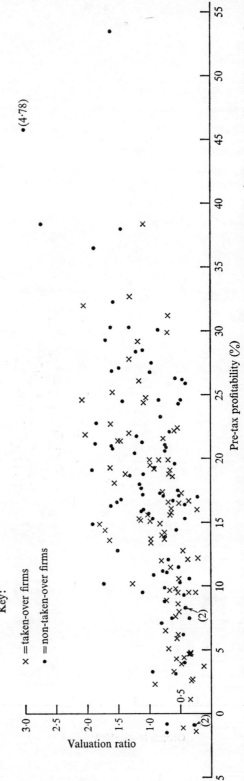

Chart 2 Pooled matched samples (3 industries together, 1955–60): short-term records: valuation ratio and pre-tax profitability. Taken-over and non-taken-over firms.

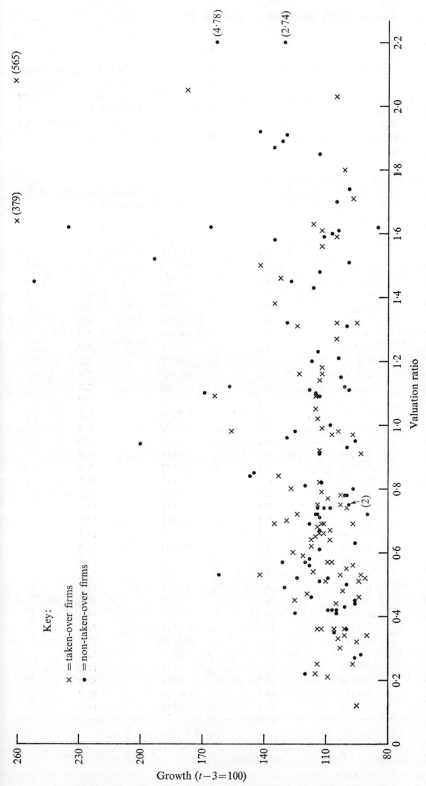

Chart 3 Pooled matched samples (3 industries together, 1955–60): short-term records: growth and valuation ratio. Taken-over and non-taken-over firms.

Key:

× = taken-over firms

● = non-taken-over firms

Growth (t−3=100)

Valuation ratio

APPENDIX 5.2

The discussion of whether or not allocation rules other than those based on a single function may be able to achieve better discrimination is made a great deal easier when the data are presented in an ordered form. The ordered data are also necessary for Kendall's method of non-parametric discrimination (see section 5.3).

The data on which the scatter diagrams for the pooled matched samples (charts 1 to 3 in appendix 5.1) are based, are given below in an ordered form for each of the variables.

Variable (X_1) pre-tax profitability (%)

Taken-over (and merged) firms		Non-taken-over firms	
Identification[a]	X_1 (%)	Identification[a]	X_1 (%)
204506	−1.4	217311	−1.5
211011	−1.1	210310	−0.9
423508	1.1	205910	−0.9
501811	2.3	429809	−0.8
208511	2.6	504310	3.1
201910	2.7	203606	3.3
208011	3.3	202909	4.0
511311	3.7	402208	6.2
503010	3.9	200811	7.1
506511	4.3	426110	7.5
202910	4.4	415908	7.5
204709	4.7	409308	8.3
207909	4.7	202510	8.3
404710	4.8	205608	8.8
413706	5.1	203510	9.3
504110	5.9	503811	9.5
206910	6.2	210511	9.9
506106	6.5	510111	10.2
426210	7.6	210510	10.3
508710	8.0	217111	10.6
509008	8.6	428411	10.9
506410	8.9	435707	11.1
416509	9.5	428706	11.2
415009	9.5	419509	11.5
419510	9.5	416611	12.1
504610	9.7	503311	12.8
203108	9.8	211407	13.9
202411	10.2	510207	14.4
511007	10.6	208311	14.9
207311	11.5	506310	15.3
415106	12.0	426309	15.3
203410	12.1	202311	15.7
401009	12.2	210011	15.9
204111	12.8	510410	16.0
217211	13.4	505511	16.3

Taken-over (and merged) firms		Non-taken-over firms	
Identification[a]	X_1 (%)	Identification[a]	X_1 (%)
409208	13.6	426310	16.4
505707	13.7	502008	16.6
200210	13.7	509706	16.7
418809	14.0	507607	16.8
411410	14.2	501011	17.0
504707	14.4	414108	17.1
504410	14.9	502511	17.1
205811	14.9	202310	17.2
501711	15.1	217711	17.3
204211	15.2	501307	17.5
423607	15.3	510409	17.7
510309	15.6	423811	18.0
204007	15.6	420411	18.7
429910	15.8	204611	18.8
401106	16.0	208310	19.1
430509	16.1	410806	19.3
405411	16.5	425109	19.6
213110	16.6	412810	20.4
213210	16.7	501910	20.6
415208	17.3	507410	20.8
202811	17.4	210210	20.9
210911	18.1	208210	21.0
203910	18.6	402310	21.1
506211	18.8	200411	21.2
513108	18.8	502708	21.3
408208	19.1	435409	21.8
422106	19.2	438510	22.1
511911	19.3	502207	22.8
402311	19.5	210209	23.3
429308	19.9	420608	24.3
424111	19.9	502210	24.5
209810	19.9	429709	24.6
429410	21.4	209809	24.6
415711	21.4	419908	25.9
430008	21.6	408410	26.2
404811	21.9	405610	26.3
206210	22.0	405210	26.8
419109	22.2	217410	26.9
412309	22.4	207711	27.1
506009	22.7	502910	27.5
412210	24.4	419208	28.4
507807	24.6	423809	28.5
411709	24.8	435511	29.3
208211	25.2	402506	30.1
202608	26.1	417009	30.3
205307	27.8	407408	30.3
418507	29.2	508409	32.3

Taken-over (and merged) firms		Non-taken-over firms	
Identification[a]	X_1 (%)	Identification[a]	X_1 (%)
208109	29.9	416207	36.5
431408	31.2	423306	38.0
509510	32.0	207110	38.4
213410	32.7	207111	45.8
438910	38.4	207407	53.5

Variable (X_{10}) valuation ratio (units)

Taken-over (and merged) firms		Non-taken-over firms	
Identification[a]	X_{10} (units)	Identification[a]	X_{10} (units)
511311	0.1	501011	0.2
401009	0.2	426110	0.3
401106	0.2	205910	0.3
423508	0.3	210310	0.3
204506	0.3	217111	0.3
204709	0.3	409308	0.4
419510	0.3	419908	0.4
404710	0.3	402208	0.4
201910	0.3	426309	0.4
208511	0.3	202909	0.4
415009	0.4	426310	0.4
207909	0.4	203510	0.4
202910	0.4	202510	0.4
203410	0.4	420608	0.5
213210	0.4	429703	0.5
204111	0.4	419509	0.5
415208	0.5	501307	0.5
412309	0.5	408410	0.5
416509	0.5	502511	0.5
511007	0.5	210510	0.5
509008	0.5	415908	0.6
405411	0.5	425109	0.6
508710	0.5	509706	0.6
503010	0.5	510207	0.6
504110	0.5	405610	0.6
206910	0.5	504310	0.6
211011	0.5	435707	0.7
419109	0.6	429809	0.7
430509	0.6	211407	0.7
203108	0.6	205608	0.7
429910	0.6	438510	0.7
426210	0.6	402310	0.7
506511	0.6	416611	0.7

Taken-over (and merged) firms		Non-taken-over firms	
Identification[a]	X_{10} (units)	Identification[a]	X_{10} (units)
203910	0.6	501910	0.7
207311	0.6	210210	0.7
208011	0.6	217311	0.7
413706	0.7	210511	0.7
408208	0.7	402506	0.8
431408	0.7	428706	0.8
506106	0.7	114108	0.8
510309	0.7	210209	0.8
208109	0.7	209809	0.8
411410	0.7	217711	0.8
424111	0.7	200811	0.8
506410	0.7	410806	0.9
504610	0.7	203606	0.9
506211	0.7	428411	0.9
200210	0.7	506310	0.9
213110	0.7	405210	1.0
415106	0.8	502910	1.0
430008	0.8	202311	1.0
418809	0.8	423809	1.1
504410	0.8	502708	1.1
209810	0.8	510409	1.1
202811	0.8	423811	1.1
501811	0.9	510410	1.1
422106	0.9	503811	1.1
429308	1.0	204611	1.1
411709	1.0	210011	1.1
505707	1.0	202310	1.1
204007	1.0	419208	1.2
402311	1.0	435409	1.2
501711	1.0	412810	1.2
217211	1.0	417009	1.3
438910	1.1	420411	1.3
412210	1.1	423306	1.4
204211	1.1	507607	1.4
418507	1.2	502210	1.4
423607	1.2	502008	1.5
202608	1.2	503311	1.5
205307	1.3	207711	1.5
206210	1.3	508409	1.6
213410	1.3	207407	1.6
202411	1.3	207408	1.6
513108	1.4	505511	1.6
429410	1.5	217410	1.6
415711	1.5	208210	1.6
409208	1.6	507410	1.6
506009	1.6	510111	1.7
511911	1.6	435511	1.7

Taken-over (and merged) firms		Non-taken-over firms	
Indentification[a]	X_{10} (units)	Identification[a]	X_{10} (units)
208211	1.6	502207	1.8
210911	1.6	416207	1.9
504707	1.7	208311	1.9
205811	1.8	200411	1.9
509510	2.0	208310	1.9
404811	2.0	207110	2.7
507807	2.1	207111	4.8

Variable (X_9) growth $[t-3 = 100]$

Taken-over (and merged) firms		Non-taken-over firms	
Identification[a]	X_9	Identification[a]	X_9
423508	90	207408	85
511007	91	217311	90
501811	93	205910	93
206910	93	415908	96
508710	94	402208	96
211011	94	203606	96
511311	95	203510	96
205307	95	210310	96
208511	95	200811	97
413706	97	510111	99
504707	97	503811	99
204506	97	503311	99
217211	97	205608	99
506511	97	210511	99
506106	100	414108	100
504110	100	426110	100
204709	101	428411	100
207909	101	420411	100
205811	101	210510	100
503010	102	428706	101
411410	103	202909	101
509008	103	210011	101
201910	103	423811	103
202811	103	419208	104
404710	104	208210	104
402311	104	409308	105
404811	105	435511	105
202910	105	202510	105
206210	105	217111	106
202411	105	426309	107
208211	105	217410	107
415009	106	211407	108

Taken-over (and merged) firms		Non-taken-over firms	
Identification[a]	X_9	Identification[a]	X_9
505707	107	202311	108
203108	107	419509	109
429910	108	426310	109
504610	108	507410	111
430008	109	501910	111
401009	109	217711	112
426210	109	410806	113
405411	110	435707	113
424111	111	438510	113
510309	111	509706	113
418507	112	502207	113
423607	112	502511	113
429308	112	204611	113
418809	112	207711	113
506009	112	429808	114
213110	112	402310	114
213210	112	412810	114
210911	112	510410	114
422106	113	202310	115
408208	113	210210	115
504410	113	502210	116
204211	113	435409	117
419510	114	408410	117
506211	114	425109	118
204007	114	416611	118
200210	114	510207	118
203410	114	502708	118
401106	115	405610	120
411709	115	210209	120
412210	115	420608	124
412309	116	419908	125
511911	116	405210	125
430509	117	423306	127
203910	117	417009	129
415208	119	502910	129
419109	121	208311	129
202608	123	429709	130
506410	124	207110	130
213410	124	416207	131
204111	125	504310	131
208011	126	508409	135
415106	127	200411	135
208109	129	208310	142
415711	132	402506	145
209810	133	209809	147
431408	135	510409	157
513108	135	501307	162

Taken-over (and merged) firms		Non-taken-over firms	
Identification[a]	X_9	Identification[a]	X_9
416509	142	207111	163
429410	142	207407	166
501711	156	423809	169
438910	164	502008	193
509510	177	506310	200
409208	379	505511	235
507807	565[b]	507607	252

[a] The first digit identifies the industry, the next 3 give the company number and last 2 the accounting year. The accounting years 1954–9 are denoted by the numbers 6 to 11 respectively. The industry coding is as follows:

$$4 \rightarrow \text{non-electrical engineering}$$
$$5 \rightarrow \text{electrical engineering}$$
$$2 \rightarrow \text{food.}$$

The reader is reminded that the last complete annual accounts available for a taken-over company are usually those for the year before that in which the take-over took place. Thus the last complete accounts available for a firm which was taken over in 1960 were nearly always for the accounting year 1959. The same was true for firms taken over in the other years. (Cf. section 3.2.)

[b] This is a genuine observation. This firm had acquired a number of unquoted firms over the previous 3 years before it was itself a victim of acquisition. However, none of the conclusions reported in the text (either for pooled data or for electrical engineering on its own) are upset if the distance and discriminant analysis are repeated by constraining this observation to a smaller value.

6. STOCK-MARKET DISCIPLINE AND THE THEORY OF THE FIRM

INTRODUCTION

In the last three chapters, the economic and financial characteristics of taken-over firms have been analysed and compared with those of non-taken-over firms, on both a univariate and a multivariate basis. The purpose of this chapter is to assess the significance of the observed differences between the two groups of firms for the central economic issue discussed in chapter 1 – that of stock-market discipline. It will be recalled that the nature and degree of the discipline exercised by the stock market through the take-over mechanism has an important bearing not only on the question of stock-market efficiency but also on the current controversy over the theory of the firm.

The present chapter is divided into four sections. In section 6.1 the main empirical conclusions of the previous three chapters are summarised, and extended in certain directions. In particular, the relationship between profitability and probability of acquisition is studied in greater depth. The implications of these conclusions for stock-market discipline and the theory of the firm are discussed in sections 6.2 and 6.3. The main points of the chapter are summarised in section 6.4.

6.1 PROFITABILITY AND PROBABILITY OF ACQUISITION

It will be useful to recall the main results of chapters 3 to 5, which are easily summarised. The comparison of the records of non-taken-over and taken-over firms on a univariate basis in chapter 3 showed that the former have on the whole a 'significantly' better performance record than the latter. For example, if we consider average performance over the two years before the date of take-over, we find that 60 to 65 % of the taken-over firms have profitability, growth and valuation ratio below the average for the industry in question. However, the results obtained in chapter 3 also showed that although for some variables (the 4 measures of rate of return; retention ratio; growth; valuation ratio; size) the average value for taken-over firms is significantly different from the average value for non-taken-over firms, the extent of overlap between the two groups of firms is so large that none of the variables is a 'good' discriminator on its own. Thus any attempt to classify firms into taken-over and non-taken-over groups on the basis of the observed values of any one of these variables considered by itself would lead to a high degree of misclassification, although less than on random allocation.

The essential overall conclusion which emerges from the multivariate analysis of chapters 4 and 5 is that, on the whole, in view of the inter-correlation between the variables, the degree of misclassification would not be much reduced if all or suitable sub-sets of all variables were considered simultaneously in an attempt to discriminate between the two groups of firms. In particular, it appears that if we compare taken-over firms with surviving firms of the *same size* generally speaking very little greater discrimination (i.e. correct classification) is achieved on the basis of all variables together than on the basis of profitability (in particular X_1) alone.

This conclusion clearly suggests that a closer look should be taken at the degree and nature of discrimination obtained by using size and past profitability records of firms. The use of size has already been systematically investigated in chapter 2; a detailed analysis of the relationship between profitability and probability of acquisition is given in table 6.1 below. This table classifies each firm which merged or was taken-over during 1955–60 according to the profitability decile in which it fell in the last accounting year before take-over, on the basis of its record over the 2 years (part *a*) or the 6 years (part *b*) preceding take-over. It also shows the observed empirical probability of take-over within a year associated with each decile range.† The pre-tax rate of return on net assets (X_1) is employed as the measure of profit-ability.‡ The use of decile rankings is intended to ensure that the observed inter-year and inter-industry differences in the profitability of firms (see chapter 3) do not distort the results.

The figures in this table speak for themselves. Thus part *a* shows that over the period 1955–60 the average pre-tax profitability record for the 2 years before take-over would rank 19.3 % of all taken-over§ firms in the 5 industries among the lowest 10 % of *all firms* in their respective industries. However, classified by the same variable, only

† These probabilities are obtained by taking an appropriate weighted average of the take-over probabilities for each of the 6 years.

‡ It will be recalled from chapters 3 to 5 that X_1 was as good a discriminator as any of the other rates of return (X_2, X_3 or X_4) in the univariate context, and much the better one in the multivariate context. Furthermore, a limited investigation of the type given above, on the basis of X_2, X_3 and X_4, produced results essentially similar to those for X_1. It was also found that 2-year average profitability was a slightly better discriminator than 1-year profitability and 6-year average profitability was similarly a somewhat better discriminator than 3-year average profitability, especially with respect to X_1.

§ The reader is reminded that throughout this chapter, as in the previous two, the taken-over firms include the small number of firms which disappeared through merger. However, as before, only the smaller of the firms involved in a merger is included.

4.4 % of the taken-over firms would be placed among the top 10 % of all firms. If pre-tax profitability is averaged over the 6 years preceding the date of take-over, then the corresponding percentages of taken-over firms in the first and tenth decile ranges are 14.5 and 5.5 respectively (table 6.1 *b*). More importantly, with respect to the probability of being taken over, the last column of table 6.1 *a* shows, for instance, that over the period 1955–60 a firm whose 2-year pre-tax profitability record put it among the lowest 10 % of all firms had on average a 7.4 % probability of being taken over within a year. The corresponding probability of take-over for a firm ranked among the top 10 % of all firms was 1.7 %.

The following main points relevant for the discussion of stock-market discipline emerge from table 6.1.

First, although the *average* profitability of taken-over firms is relatively low, nevertheless a notable feature of these results is the large number of acquired firms which have profitability above the average for *all* firms, or even a record of profitability which would place them among the top 10 % or 20% of all firms. This phenomenon will be discussed in the next section.

Secondly, table 6.1 *a* shows that within each industry and for all 5 industries together, the firms most likely to be taken over are those with a record of very low relative (short-term) profitability. However, the figures also show that although the chances of survival increase as the relative profitability of firms rises, this increase is not monotonic, and indeed follows a peculiar non-linear pattern.† For instance, we find that firms in the lowest decile range are more than four times as likely to be taken over as firms in the highest decile range (see the 'all industries' figures in table 6.1 *a*). However, the data also indicate that once a firm has achieved a 'satisfactory' level of profits in the sense that it has a level of profitability higher than the second decile, its chances of survival increase very little with an increase in profitability until the ninth or the tenth decile range is reached. There are, of course, variations on this pattern in the individual industries (the electrical engineering industry being a striking exception to the rule, as it has been in most of the previous chapters), but this is the general picture which emerges from part *a* of table 6.1. It therefore seems that as far as the firms' short-term records are concerned, there is indeed selection (for survival) on the bais of profitability, particularly against firms with very low profitability, but that the mechanism cannot be counted upon to distinguish among

† It should be noted that similar results are obtained if instead of averaging the probabilities of acquisition over the whole period 1955–60, these probabilities are averaged separately over the sub-periods 1955–58 and 1959–60 respectively. The changes in economic environment between the two shorter periods (see chapter 3) do not seem to have any effect on this and the other main results reported in this section.

TABLE 6.1. *Decile ranking of taken-over firms on the basis of profitability and the average probability of a firm being taken over within each decile range (1955–60)*

a. Average pre-tax profitability for the 2 years preceding take-over

Decile	Food — Number of taken-over firms	Food — % of taken-over firms	Food — Probability of a firm being taken over	Electrical engineering — Number of taken-over firms	Electrical engineering — % of taken-over firms	Electrical engineering — Probability of a firm being taken over	Non-electrical engineering — Number of taken-over firms	Non-electrical engineering — % of taken-over firms	Non-electrical engineering — Probability of a firm being taken over
d1	5	13.1	6.8	8	32.0	11.3	8	16.0	4.4
d2	6	15.8	8.2	2	8.0	2.8	8	16.0	4.4
d3	3	7.9	4.1	2	8.0	2.8	5	10.0	2.8
d4	5	13.1	6.8	3	12.0	4.2	3	6.0	1.7
d5	4	10.5	5.5	2	8.0	2.8	6	12.0	3.3
d6	3	7.9	4.1	5	20.0	6.8	2	4.0	1.1
d7	5	13.1	6.8	1	4.0	1.4	6	12.0	3.3
d8	2	5.3	2.7	0	0.0	0.0	7	14.0	3.9
d9	2	5.3	2.7	1	4.0	1.4	4	8.0	2.2
d10	3	7.9	4.1	1	4.0	1.4	1	2.0	0.6
Total	38	99.9[a]	5.2	25	100.0	3.5	50	100.0	2.8

Decile	Drink — Number of taken-over firms	Drink — % of taken-over firms	Drink — Probability of a firm being taken over	Clothing and footwear — Number of taken-over firms	Clothing and footwear — % of taken-over firms	Clothing and footwear — Probability of a firm being taken over	All industries — Number of taken-over firms	All industries — % of taken-over firms	All industries — Probability of a firm being taken over
d1	10	19.2	9.4	4	25.0	7.4	35	19.3	7.4
d2	7	13.5	7.4	2	12.5	3.7	25	13.8	5.3
d3	4	7.7	4.2	0	0.0	0.0	14	7.7	2.9
d4	8	15.4	8.5	2	12.5	3.7	21	11.6	4.4
d5	5	9.6	5.3	2	12.5	3.7	19	10.5	4.0
d6	5	9.6	5.3	1	6.3	1.8	16	8.8	3.4
d7	2	3.8	2.1	2	12.5	3.7	16	8.8	3.4
d8	4	7.7	4.2	0	0.0	0.0	13	7.2	2.7
d9	5	9.6	5.3	2	12.5	3.7	14	7.7	2.9
d10	2	3.8	2.1	1	6.3	1.8	8	4.4	1.7
Total	52	99.9[a]	5.5	16	100.1[a]	3.0	181	99.8[a]	3.8

the large number of firms whose profitability is neither extremely high nor extremely low.

When pre-tax profitability records are averaged over the 6 years preceding the date of take-over (part *b* of table 6.1), we find that there is a less marked decrease in the risk of being taken over as profitability increases. For all 5 industries together, the final column shows that a

TABLE 6.1 (*cont.*)

b. Average pre-tax profitability for the 6 years preceding take-over

	Food			Electrical engineering			Non-electrical engineering		
Decile	Number of taken-over firms	% of taken-over firms	Prob-ability of a firm being taken over	Number of taken-over firms	% of taken-over firms	Prob-ability of a firm being taken over	Number of taken-over firms	% of taken over firms	Prob-ability of a firm being taken over
d1	4	11.8	6.2	5	21.7	7.8	7	16.7	4.4
d2	5	14.7	7.8	4	17.4	6.2	6	14.3	3.8
d3	7	20.6	10.9	2	8.7	3.1	3	7.1	1.9
d4	3	8.8	4.7	3	13.0	4.7	2	4.8	1.3
d5	2	5.9	3.1	4	17.4	6.2	8	19.0	5.1
d6	1	2.9	1.6	3	13.0	4.7	4	9.5	2.5
d7	2	5.9	3.1	1	4.3	1.6	2	4.8	1.3
d8	5	14.7	7.8	0	0.0	0.0	4	9.5	2.5
d9	3	8.8	4.7	0	0.0	0.0	2	4.8	1.3
d10	2	5.9	3.1	1	4.3	1.6	4	9.5	2.5
Total	34	100.0	5.3	23	99.8[a]	3.6	42	100.0	2.7

	Drink			Clothing and footwear			All industries		
d1	7	13.7	7.9	1	6.7	2.0	24	14.5	5.7
d2	5	9.8	5.7	3	20.0	5.9	23	13.9	5.4
d3	6	11.8	6.9	1	6.7	2.0	19	11.5	4.5
d4	7	13.7	7.9	3	20.0	5.9	18	10.9	4.2
d5	10	19.6	11.4	1	6.7	2.0	25	15.1	5.9
d6	1	2.0	1.1	3	20.0	5.9	12	7.3	2.8
d7	4	7.8	4.5	1	6.7	2.0	10	6.1	2.4
d8	3	5.9	3.4	1	6.7	2.0	13	7.9	3.1
d9	7	13.7	7.9	0	0.0	0.0	12	7.3	2.8
d10	1	2.0	1.1	1	6.7	2.0	9	5.4	2.1
Total	51	100.0	5.8	15	100.2[a]	2.7	165	99.9[a]	3.9

[a] The total does not add to 100 because of rounding errors.

firm which was placed in the lowest decile group on the basis of long-term profitability had on average a 5.7 % chance of being acquired within a year. The probability of acquisition remains much the same from the first to the fifth decile group; it declines sharply in the sixth and then remains more or less constant till the ninth decile is reached. There is a further, relatively small, decrease in the probability of acquisition in the highest decile range; an average firm in that decile range had a 2.1 % chance of being acquired within a year.

Thirdly, one can deduce from table 6.1 how difficult it is to predict, on the basis of past profitability, which specific firms will be acquired. Here we shall consider this subject in a more realistic context than in the previous chapter where we discussed the analogous question of the probability of misclassification on the assumption that there were an equal number of taken-over and non-taken-over firms in the population. Briefly, from the practical point of view, the data of the prediction problem may be summed up as follows: it is known that (i) roughly 4 % of the firms are acquired within a year; (ii) taken-over firms have on average lower profitability than non-taken-over firms; (iii) profitability is approximately normally distributed with almost equal variances in the two groups. In these circumstances and in view of the information given in table 6.1, it is intuitively obvious that if one wished to pick out the firms most likely to be acquired, the best strategy would be to choose the firms with the lowest achieved profitability within an industry.

The results of part *b* of table 6.1 (under 'all industries') indicate that if (say) 50 firms are chosen at random from the entire list of firms for which long-term (6-year) profitability records are available, nearly 2 (half of 3.9 %, which is the average probability) of these firms can be expected to be acquired within a year. Moreover, if it is assumed that firms which have low (or high) 6-year average profitability in a particular year will probably have a similar record of relative long-term profitability over (say) the next 3 years, then approximately 6 of these 50 randomly selected firms may be expected to be acquired over a 3-year period. On the other hand, if instead of choosing firms at random the 50 firms most likely to be acquired, i.e. those with lowest profitability, were selected, we could expect more than 8 (8.55 in fact) of them to be acquired over the 3-year period (since the probability now depends on the figures for the lowest decile shown in the last column of part *b* of table 6.1 instead of the average). Thus, even if there did exist a very high degree of persistency in the long-term profitability records of firms, knowledge of these data would from a practical point of view be of only small help in choosing the most likely candidates for acquisition over the next few years.

An experiment was actually carried out to test this proposition. Of the nearly 700 firms in the 5 industries for which 6-year profitability records were available, the 50 firms with the lowest profitability rankings at the end of 1956† in their respective industries were selected.

† Since the incidence of take-overs is not uniformly distributed over the 6-year period, we took the end of 1956, rather than 1954, as our starting point.

The number chosen from each industry was proportional to the incidence of take-overs experienced by the various industries in the past.† Over the period 1957–9 only 7 of these 50 firms were acquired, as against an expectation of more than 8. In fact, the results over these years were only a little better than what would be expected from random selection of 50 out of the whole 700. This simple example illustrates the difficulty of predicting future victims for acquisition on the basis of the firms' past records.‡

6.2 STOCK-MARKET DISCIPLINE AND THE THEORY OF THE FIRM

We have seen above that within certain fairly wide ranges of profitability the probability of acquisition does not decline as profitability increases. It has also been observed that there are a number of firms with excellent profitability records (relative to their industry) which are acquired. At one level, it must be stressed, this is not a particularly surprising phenomenon. As was noted in chapter 1,§ an acquirer can have any of several motives for taking over a firm and there is no reason at all why *some* firms with above average or excellent profitability records should not be taken over. For example, in certain circumstances a large firm may take over a smaller one precisely because the latter is a profitable concern and has an efficient management, even though high profitability means that a relatively high price will normally have to be paid in relation to the value of its assets. But the efficient management can then be given more scope and an amalgamation may lead to increased profits on the combined assets of the two firms. In the case of the U.K., where there was an unprecedented wave of take-overs in the period considered in this study, another important contributory factor may also have been at work. In oligopolistic industries, the occurrence of a few take-overs by large firms leads to a situation of 'disequilibrium', where other leading firms in the industry have to indulge in defensive take-overs in order to maintain their share of the market. These defensive take-overs can obviously involve firms both profitable and unprofitable, though usually of smaller size, and it appears that in some industries, such as food, take-overs of this kind have been particularly important.

† The numbers from the various industries were also chosen in proportion to the total numbers of firms in these industries, but not surprisingly this method produced somewhat poorer results than those given in the text. Another method used was to pick out the 50 firms with the lowest profitability rankings in all 5 industries, but this also produced poorer results.

‡ As should be clear from the discussion in chapter 5, one can expect to predict only very slightly better if variables other than the firms' past profitability records are considered simultaneously. The most helpful additional variable would be size, which is not related to profitability. See p. 116 above.

§ Pp. 10–11 above.

However, although it is not out of the question for a firm with an excellent profitability record to be acquired, it would nevertheless be reasonable to expect that, in general, provided the capital market, and particularly the market for take-overs, worked reasonably well, relatively less profitable firms would be rather more likely to be taken over than more profitable ones. The main basis for this expectation is that if the firms are valued by the stock market on the basis of their achieved profits, i.e. their performance under existing managements, it will be in the interest of an acquiring firm to purchase, *ceteris paribus*, a less profitable rather than a more profitable firm within an industry. There are two reasons for this: (i) the less profitable firm will be relatively cheaper to acquire in relation to its assets and (ii) there will on the whole be more opportunity and greater certainty of increasing the profits of firms with lower profitability relative to their respective industries.

Thus if the stock market worked reasonably perfectly, then although there would be some scatter around the (inverse) relationship between profitability and the probability of acquisition, one would expect the two variables to be fairly closely related. And if in fact a close inverse relationship did exist between them, and if the probability of acquisition increased reasonably steeply with a decrease in relative profitability, the threat of take-over would provide firms with a strong inducement to constantly improve their profitability records. In that case the stock market, through its take-over mechanism, could truly be regarded as the 'guardian of efficiency'† of the operations of the individual firm. Then even firms which were effectively under managerial control or which did not go to the stock market for their financing needs (relying entirely on self-finance) would be subject to the discipline of the market. All this is familiar, being the basis of the arguments with respect to stock-market discipline and economic natural selection which were discussed in chapter 1.

The results of this study show that as far as the firms' short-term profitability records are concerned, the stock market is a very poor disciplinarian in this sense. For example, if 2-year pre-tax profitability on net assets is considered, we have found that there is a wide range of profitability (from the second decile to almost the ninth decile) within which the probability of acquisition is much the same.‡ A firm at the lower end of this range of profitability, if it is not otherwise interested in increasing its rate of profit, is clearly not *objectively* forced by the stock

---

† The reader is reminded that private profitability is taken as an indicator of efficiency in this study. Cf. chapter 1.

‡ The χ^2 test in fact showed that the hypothesis that there is no difference in the probability of acquisition for firms from the third decile to the tenth decile range, could not be rejected at the 5% level either for most of the individual industries or for all industries together. See table 6.1 (part *a*).

market to improve its performance in order to reduce the danger of take-over. These results seem to lend support to the new (managerial) theories of the firm which postulate that once the firms have achieved a certain 'satisfactory' level of profitability, they are able to pursue whatever other goals they please without greatly affecting the risk of take-over.

On the other hand, the implications of the observed relationship between *long-term profitability* and probability of acquisition – which in this context is the more crucial relationship – for assessing the efficacy of the take-over discipline are more complex. It will be recalled from table 6.1 (part *b*) that the cut-off point with respect to long-term profitability is around the median (fifth decile), both in the individual industries and in all five industries together. When all industries are considered together, the probability of acquisition is more or less the same (a little over 5 % a year) for firms with below median profitability; for firms with above median profitability, the probability of acquisition is again almost constant, except that it is half (about 2.6 % a year) what it is for firms with below average profits. This suggests that, while firms which already make above average profits are not on the whole forced to raise their profitability still further to increase their chances of survival, firms with below average profits have a reasonably strong inducement to increase profits. This is because, although for such firms the probability of acquisition within a year is only slightly over 5 %, the risk of take-over becomes quite high if their relatively poor profits performance continues over any length of time. A reduction of this risk by 50 % would obviously be regarded as worthwhile by the managements of these firms. The evidence on this issue, on the face of it, therefore indicates that the take-over mechanism provides a measure of discipline for firms with a below average record of long-term profitability.

However, before accepting this conclusion, the evidence must be considered alongside the results given in chapter 2 with respect to the relationship between *size* and probability of acquisition. Those results (see table 2.4 and section 2.4), it will be recalled, revealed a markedly non-linear pattern in the generally inverse relationship between size and the probability of acquisition. For instance it was found that up to a certain level of firm size, and in particular for the small and medium-sized firms in 1954, the probability of acquisition over the next 6 years (1955–60) declined only moderately with an increase in size. However, for the large firms, defined as those whose book value of equity assets was greater than £4 million in 1954, the probability of acquisition over the same period (i) was much lower (9.4 % for the 6-year period or 1.6 % a year, as compared with over 3 % a year for the typical medium-sized firm and over 4 % a year for the typical small firm), and (ii) fell fairly sharply and monotonically with an increase in firm size.†

Remembering that on the whole there is little relationship between size and profitability of firms, the above results in conjunction with those of table 6.1 (part *b*) lead to the following general conclusions about the best strategies for survival for firms of various sizes. For most small firms with a poor record of long-term profitability, there appears to be little effective choice if they wish to *appreciably* reduce the danger of take-over, except to attempt to improve their profits performance to a level above the average for the industry. The alternative course of increasing size is unlikely to be of much use to such firms, since they would have to become several times larger before they could attain any significant reduction in the chances of acquisition. This is not to deny that an attempt to increase profitability to a level above the industry average would not also require a very great effort: for instance, if the firm's initial profitability was about the level of the second decile, it would probably mean doubling or trebling its rate of profit if the danger of take-over was to be significantly reduced. Furthermore, it is necessary for this improvement to be a continuous one, i.e. in terms of long-term profits, since a temporary improvement brought about for instance by neglecting research, advertising etc. for a year or two, would only make the firm more vulnerable in the future.

On the other hand, the results of this investigation suggest that the best strategy for survival for a large firm or a largish medium-sized firm (e.g. one with a book value of equity assets of between £2 million and £4 million) with a poor record of long-term profitability might be to increase its size. As in the case of small firms, these firms would require a very large proportional increase in their rate of profit to appreciably reduce the danger of take-over. But unlike the small firms, since the probability of acquisition for these firms is known to fall fairly sharply and continuously with an increase in firm size, they might find it relatively much easier to increase their chances of survival by becoming bigger.‡ The evidence clearly indicates that it is in general

† It may be noted that table 2.4 is on a somewhat different basis than table 6.1 (part *b*). The former gives the probability of acquisition by size class, during the periods 1955–8 and 1955–60, for the list of firms which existed at the end of 1954. As seen in section 6.1, table 6.1 (part *b*) gives a weighted average of the probabilities of acquisition by profitability deciles for each of the years 1955–60; it thus considers not only the firms which existed in 1954, but also those which were born during the period 1955–60. It was found, however, that these differences do not affect the main points of the results given above; in fact, if the figures relating size and probability of acquisition are put in a form parallel to that of table 6.1 (part *b*), they only strengthen the argument discussed below.

‡ The information given in chapter 2 showed that for the large and the largish medium-sized firms in the five industry groups, the probabilities of acquisition *within a year* (averaged over the period 1955–60) were as follows:

possible for large firms to decrease their chances of acquisition, while maintaining the rate of profit they are earning or even lowering it, provided that they can achieve a sufficient increase in size.

But would a large firm with a poor record of long-term profitability (say less than the second or third decile) be in a position to achieve the required increase in size? Although low profitability would undoubtedly imply difficulties in raising finance for expansion, there are still a number of ways in which it could become bigger.† First, if profitability is not *very* low and the firm has little in the way of debentures already outstanding, it might be able to expand through issuing debentures. Secondly, there is a possibility of a merger on a friendly basis with another firm of similar size and in a similar position of low profitability. Thirdly and more importantly, a management-controlled large firm in this situation may increase its size by acquiring smaller firms through share exchange. In fact, given the imperfections of the stock market in the real world, it could in principle make its take-overs so as not only to experience no stock-market disapproval, but also to be able to maintain its rate of profit. For instance, it could acquire firms with the same or even relatively higher profitability, but with price-earnings ratios lower than its own. There are in practice many firms whose shares are undervalued in relation to their profits – i.e. their P/E ratios are relatively low, perhaps because they are small and unknown.‡ Through take-overs of this type or of suitable small unquoted firms, the large relatively unprofitable firm can become bigger and yet maintain its relative valuation on the stock market.§

Size	No. of firms	Probability of acquisition
> £2 million	92	3.0
> £4 million	59	2.2
> £8 million	30	1.1
> £16 million	15	0

† There is a growing literature on the relationship between growth and profitability of firms which is also relevant to the above issue. For U.K. quoted companies, the studies show that long-term profitability explains no more than 50% of the long-term growth rates of firms on a cross-section basis. For a detailed discussion, see Singh and Whittington [1968], pp. 148–90; see also Marris [1967].

‡ The financial press often reports acquisitions of this kind. Our own analysis of the records of the acquired and the *acquiring* firms (see further next chapter) is also of some relevance here. We found that in every one of the nearly 100 acquisitions examined, in which both the acquiring and the acquired firms belonged to the same industry, the acquiring firm was larger than the acquired. However, in more than 30% of the cases, the acquiring firm had lower profitability than the acquired firm.

§ If the managers are not concerned about the existing shareholders or the market price of the firm's shares, their opportunities for increasing size by this method are even greater. The managers cannot however be entirely unconcerned about the share price, since a

To sum up, the take-over mechanism on the stock market, although it provides a measure of discipline for small firms with below average profitability, does not seem to meet the motivational requirements of the orthodox theory of the firm as far as the large firms are concerned. The evidence indicates that these firms are not compelled to maximise or to vigorously pursue profits in order to reduce the danger of take-over, since they can in principle achieve this objective by becoming bigger without increasing the rate of profit. In fact, to the extent that the selection process implied by the take-over mechanism works much more stringently against the relatively smaller of these large firms with the same rate of profit, it furnishes positive support for the behavioural postulates of the new managerial theories of the firm. Many of these theories share the assumption that the managers of such firms, for various reasons (salaries, power, prestige etc.), are more interested in increasing the size of the organisation they work for than in raising its profitability. The results of this study suggest that the fear of take-over, rather than being a constraint on managerial discretion, may also encourage them in the same direction.

It is perhaps worth pointing out that although the above conclusion is not compatible with the notion of a perfect capital market and a perfect take-over mechanism in the sense discussed at the beginning of this section and in chapter 1, it is easily explained in terms of a more realistic view of the workings of the capital market. The essential point is simply that there is a basic asymmetry in the take-over process in the real world. With given rates of profit, it is much easier for a large firm to acquire a small one than the other way round. It is true that sometimes small firms do take over larger ones, but it is a rather rare occurrence particularly in relation to the 'large' firms. (See the evidence on this point in chapter 7.) As a large firm becomes bigger, the number of firms which can acquire it – the potential raiders – becomes small thus making it progressively more immune to take-over. Without this basic asymmetry in the take-over process, the large management-controlled firms would indeed be far more subject to the normal discipline of the stock market as posited in orthodox theory.

It is important at this stage to consider some reservations which might be considered to apply to the above conclusions.

First, the observed results, as they stand, would lend powerful support to the neoclassical argument that stock-market discipline forces firms, even large firms, to maximise their profitability, if further exploration

large reduction in it would make the firm vulnerable to take-over. But it is important to note in this connection that our discussion of the valuation ratio in chapter 3 showed that this is empirically a relatively weak constraint and the managers could in fact have considerable room for manoeuvre.

showed that, among the acquired firms, the profitable ones were of a *type* different from the unprofitable ones. It may well be that the managements of profitable firms are normally retained after take-over, whereas those of unprofitable firms are usually replaced. If this were the case, then, as far as the managers were concerned, a vigorous pursuit of profits would be necessary to avoid collective dismissal; a preliminary investigation of this point is attempted below (section 6.3).

Secondly, a related objection which could be raised is that the data used in this study make no distinction between 'voluntary' and 'involuntary' take-overs. There are many firms which, for various reasons might themselves wish to sell (see next section). It could reasonably be maintained that if such firms had been excluded from the analysis of this study and only 'involuntary' take-overs had been considered, the take-over mechanism might have turned out to be a much better disciplining device.

Thirdly, it is important to bear in mind that the above conclusions are based on 'objective' *ex post* probabilities of acquisition, experienced by firms of various sizes and with various achieved rates of profits. The actual behaviour of firms of course depends on their own subjective *ex ante* assessment of what these probabilities are, which need not be the same as the ones observed *ex post*. It would be interesting to find out through interviews, questionnaires etc. what subjective views the managements of firms entertain with respect to the danger of take-over and how they react to this danger, e.g. whether by attempting to increase profitability or to become bigger, etc. Such an enquiry, however, lies outside the scope of this study, which is entirely based on historic data on firm records.

Fourth, it goes without saying that the conclusions of this analysis, even disregarding the above qualifications, do not necessarily invalidate the neoclassical theory of the firm. Large firms may still be vigorously pursuing profits for all kinds of sociological and other reasons.† All that is being suggested here is that the selection argument and stock-market discipline cannot by themselves be invoked to validate profit maximisation. Neither do these results have any bearing on the actual nature of the differences between the predictions of the new theories of the firm on the one hand and of the neoclassical theory on the other. If it had been found that stock-market discipline was binding, then of course the new theories would have been invalidated *ipso facto*. However, the fact that this discipline is imperfect does not mean that the neoclassical theory is necessarily invalid or that its predictions are less useful than those of the new theories. This is a separate issue which has not been discussed here.

† Cf. Baumol [1959], p. 67; C. Wright Mills, *The Power Elite*, New York, 1959.

Fifth, it may be objected that if taken-over and surviving firms are compared, not only on the basis of their average profitability records, but also on the basis of the time-trend in these records, the differences between the two groups of firms may well be greater than those we have observed. However, the fact that the degree of discrimination achieved on the basis of 1-year profitability records is no greater (and usually less) than that achieved on the basis of the 2-year, 3-year or 6-year average records, suggests that this argument is unlikely to be valid. The limited attempts we have made to compare the time-profiles of the records of taken-over and surviving firms also point in the same direction.

Another apparent objection which could be put forward concerns the time-period considered in this study. It could be argued that in periods of 'normal' take-over activity the take-over mechanism is a good disciplining device and that the results of this study are what they are entirely because of the exceptional time-period considered.

There are two points which are relevant to this objection. First, it is indeed true that in the U.K. the years 1955–60 were marked by an extraordinarily high incidence of take-overs and mergers. However, it should be noted that this take-over movement has continued throughout the 1960s; towards the end of the decade take-over activity was probably running at a higher level than at the end of 1950s. The small amount of available evidence suggests that the relationship between profitability and probability of acquisition in the latter period is unlikely to be different from what was observed in 1955–60.† Secondly it is of course possible that outside the periods of exceptional take-over activity the take-over mechanism does work according to the requirements of orthodox theory. We are not, however, aware of any evidence on this point one way or the other. In any case, even if it did work in this manner, a selection mechanism which selects the 'wrong' kind of firms in periods of exceptional death rates which may last for several years and which cannot be predicted in advance, is unlikely to be able to impose any consistent criteria for survival on the population.

Still another qualification concerns the measures of rates of return used in this study. It is reasonable to suggest that an appropriate measure of 'efficiency' of the firm, as far as its shareholders are concerned, is the growth of earnings per share. It could be argued that if this particular measure of a firm's performance is considered, the differences between the taken-over and the surviving firms would be much greater than those we have found. The data available to us precluded us from using growth of earnings per share as a possible discriminating variable. However, in view of the pattern of results obtained in this study, it is very unlikely that this variable would lead to any better discrimination

† Cf. Rose and Newbould [1967].

between the two groups of firms than what has been observed on the basis of four different measures of rates of return, growth of 'net assets', and valuation ratio, considered individually and simultaneously.† Nevertheless, it is a question on which only concrete empirical evidence can carry conviction and it is proposed to do some research on it in the future to see whether this supposition is confirmed or not.

6.3   AN ASSESSMENT OF THE MAIN QUALIFICATIONS

We return now to a consideration of the two main reservations with respect to the conclusions of the last section. The most important of these concerns the consequences of take-over for the managers of the taken-over firms. As was pointed out above, if it were the case that these consequences were markedly more unpleasant (e.g. demotions or dismissals) for the managers of the unprofitable acquired firms than for the managers of the profitable acquired firms, the results of the previous section would have a totally different economic meaning.

A priori, it is possible to argue on either side of this issue. On the one hand, one could say that large companies take over small profitable concerns mainly with a view to acquiring their superior managerial talents. It could be equally plausibly maintained on the other hand that often large companies acquire smaller successful companies either for defensive reasons (i.e. to maintain their share of the existing market) or for the purpose of gaining an entry into a new market. In these circumstances, the consequences of take-over for the managers of the acquired firm depend less on how 'profitable' it was, and much more on the available resources and the requirements of the managerial organisation of the acquiring company. One could easily point to casual evidence in support of either of these positions, but unfortunately there does not exist any rigorous empirical evidence on this issue, which is so obviously important for the whole question of the nature of market constraints on the managers of firms. A proper examination of the subject lies outside the scope of this work, since it would be a major undertaking in its own right. However, in view of its crucial relevance to the theory of firm and the problems discussed in this study, we conducted a limited investigation. The results of this investigation are offered here as tentative evidence on the subject.

The procedure adopted was as follows. From the 'matched samples' list of 87 taken-over firms in chapter 5, we selected the 15 most profitable firms, the 15 firms in the middle profitability range and the 15 firms with lowest profitability. The names of the directors of each of these

† It will be recalled that the price/earnings ratio was also considered and that it did not produce any better results than the other variables. See n. †, p. 49.

firms before take-over were obtained from the *Stock Exchange Yearbooks*. Information was then obtained from the *Directory of Directors* as to how many of these directors were still on the board of directors of either the acquired company (if it continued its existence as a subsidiary company) or the acquiring company two years after take-over. Two years was thought to be a sufficient period of time for an acquiring firm to be able to make up its mind about what it would like to do with the former directors of the acquired company.

The accompanying table summarises the results of the investigation:

| | % of directors dismissed | | |
Profitability	Mean	Standard deviation	No. of companies
Highest profitability	45.6	29.1	15
Medium profitability	35.9	27.7	15
Lowest profitability	56.3	18.8	15

It shows that among the 15 most profitable acquired firms (with pre-tax profitability on net assets before take-over ranging from 20 % to 34 %), on an average 45.6 % of the board of directors were dismissed during the 2 years after take-over. The corresponding percentages of directors dismissed among the acquired firms with 'medium profitability' (with profits ranging from 11 % to 18 %) was 35.9, and among the least profitable (firms with profits ranging from − 7 % to 9 %) it was 56.3. The differences between these percentages for the most profitable and the least profitable firms are statistically insignificant at the 5 % level, but it appears that on the whole the consequences of take-over for the directors of the firms with the lowest profitability records were slightly worse than for those of the more profitable ones. It is also notable that in this sample the managers of the most profitable acquired firms fared somewhat worse than those of firms with medium profitability.

The relationship between the incidence of directorial dismissal (Y) and profitability of acquired firms (X_1) was also investigated by means of simple regression analysis, which yielded the following results:

$$Y = \quad 51.4 \quad - \quad 0.39X_1$$
$$(\pm 9.8) \quad (\pm 0.39)$$

No. of firms $= 45$; $R^2 = 0.0003$

The equation shows little relationship between the two variables; the regression coefficient relating Y to X_1 is negative, but is statistically insignificant at both the 5 % and 10 % levels.

It was thought that the size (X_8) of the firm might have a systematic effect on the incidence of dismissal. This possibility, however, was decisively rejected by the data. The results of the regression equation, with size as an additional explanatory variable, are given below:

$$Y = 52.14 \quad - \quad 0.39X_1 - 0.0003X_8$$
$$(\pm 9.77) \quad (\pm 0.40) \quad (\pm 0.002)$$

No. of firms $= 45$; $R^2 = 0.02$

Apart from observing that there was negligible inter-correlation between X_1 and X_8, this equation can be left to speak for itself.

The above results pertain to the entire board of directors, a number of whom tend to be part-time directors. The *Stock Exchange Yearbooks*, in their lists of directors, identify the managing directors and the secretaries of the boards. Conclusions very similar to those given above emerge when the incidence of dismissal is considered only among these identified full-time officers.

To sum up, this rather tentative investigation of the consequences of take-over for the managers of the acquired firms has shown that there is very little difference in this respect between the relatively profitable acquired firms and the relatively unprofitable ones. On average about half of the directors of the acquired firms are removed from their boards within 2 years of take-over, but the incidence of dismissal seems on the whole to have little relationship either to the size or to the profitability of the acquired firm. In spite of all its obvious shortcomings, the results of this modest research must at least be regarded as suggestive.

The second main reservation with regard to our conclusions about take-over discipline and the theory of the firm concerns the possible distinction between 'voluntary' and 'involuntary' take-overs. As the data used in this study are based on a formal definition of 'take-over' (see chapter 2), our lists of taken-over firms make no distinction between these two possible types. However, as was noted in section 6.2, such a distinction could be very important for the results of this study. It could be plausibly argued that the characteristics of the taken-over companies which themselves wish to be acquired are likely to be rather different from those of involuntary victims, and therefore that, if the former were excluded from the analysis, take-over discipline might turn out to be much more effective than it did on the results obtained here.

The most important point to note in connection with this argument is that, with the available data, it is very difficult to make a clear-cut distinction between 'voluntary' and 'involuntary' take-overs. The apparently easy way of distinguishing between the two is to regard only those acquisitions as 'involuntary' where the board of directors of the acquired company did not recommend to the share holders the bid of the acquiring company and there was a 'contest'. This procedure has two serious drawbacks. First, only a very small proportion of the taken-over companies, on this definition, would be regarded as involuntarily acquired. Rose and Newbould found that 90 % of the acquisitions in their 1967 sample of taken-over companies were 'agreed deals' and only a small number among the remainder involved a 'contest' by the directors of the acquired company.† If the disciplining mechanism on the stock market is supposed to operate only through the latter category of acquisitions, the overall importance of this mechanism, even if it were in itself efficient, would be very small, since it would be so rarely in use. Secondly, the distinction between 'voluntary' and 'involuntary' take-overs on this basis would not be unambiguous, since a formal 'agreement' to the bid does not necessarily mean that it was 'voluntary', particularly for the salaried managers.

It is, however, possible to approach this problem in a somewhat different way. One could ask what category of firms are most likely to wish to be voluntarily acquired? There is a fair degree of agreement in the literature that the incidence of firms which themselves wish to sell is likely to be much greater among small firms than among large ones.‡ There are two reasons for this. First, in very small firms, many of which are virtually owner-controlled, the owner may often wish to sell when he reaches retirement age. Secondly, a number of small companies find at some point that they have reached a certain stage in their development where future growth is only possible if they amalgamate with bigger organisations.§

The question therefore arises whether the results obtained in this study with respect to the differences between the taken-over and surviving firms would be changed if small quoted companies were excluded from the analysis. The answer to this question is implicit in the analysis of the last two chapters. Since size is not related to profitability or to any of the other variables, we should not expect to be able to achieve any greater discrimination between the two groups of firms of the *same* size, if small companies were excluded. It was, however, thought worthwhile to check this point directly by excluding from the 'matched samples' of taken-over and non-taken-over firms in chapter 5 (i) firms with book value of net assets of less than £$\frac{1}{2}$ million and (ii) firms with book value of net assets of less than £1 million. The results of the

† Cf. Rose and Newbould [1967], p. 10.

‡ Cf. J. A. Bushnell, *Australian Company Mergers, 1916–1959*, Melbourne, 1961; A. Hunter, 'Mergers and industry concentration in Britain', *Banco Nazionale del Lavoro Quarterly Review*, Dec. 1969, pp. 377–83.

§ Cf. E. Penrose, *The Theory of the Growth of the Firm*, Oxford, 1959.

discriminant and distance analysis on these restricted samples were, as expected, very much the same as those reported in the last chapter.† As for the influence of size itself on the probability of acquisition, it would tend to become more nearly linear if small companies were excluded. The probability of acquisition would tend to decline fairly steadily with an increase in firm size, which is in keeping with the conclusions of the previous analysis.

6.4 SUMMARY

The results of the empirical analysis of the comparative characteristics of taken-over and non-taken-over firms have been examined in this chapter in relation to the central economic issues raised in chapter 1 – those of stock-market discipline and the theory of the firm. These results were summarised in section 6.1 and extended in some directions. It was recalled that there was so much overlap between the characteristics of the taken-over and the surviving firms that it would lead to a high degree of misclassification if these characteristics were used, either singly or simultaneously, to discriminate between them, although the degree of misclassification would be less than on random allocation. It was also observed that very little greater discrimination between taken-over and non-taken-over firms of the same size is achieved by using all or suitable subsets of all characteristics together than on the basis of profitability alone. The ability of this variable to discriminate between the taken-over and surviving firms was, therefore, studied more closely. Table 6.1 provides figures on probabilities of acquisition for firms at different levels of profitability. Both short-term (2-year) and long-term (6-year) profitability records have been considered.

The implications of the relationship between (i) profitability and probability of acquisition and (ii) size and probability of acquisition were examined with respect to stock-market discipline and the theory of the firm. The following broad conclusions were reached.

The stock market, through its take-over mechanism, is a rather imperfect disciplinarian, particularly with respect to the large firms. It does provide a measure of discipline for small firms; for example the data suggest that small firms with below-average long-term profitability records are able to appreciably decrease their chances of acquisition only by raising the rate of profit to above the average for the industry. However, small firms which already make above average profits are not forced or encouraged by the take-over mechanism to increase their profits still further.

† These results are not given here. The interested reader can obtain them from the Department of Applied Economics, University of Cambridge.

As far as the medium-sized and large firms with low profitability are concerned, the results suggest that the best way for these firms to appreciably reduce their probability of being taken over might well be to increase their size rather than their rate of profit. In general it appears possible for the medium-sized and large firms to maintain their rate of profit, or even to lower it, and yet increase their chances of survival, provided they can achieve a sufficient increase in size. These conclusions go against the motivational requirements of the orthodox theory of the firm, and in fact provide positive support for the behavioural postulates of the new (managerial) theories of the firm. Many of these theories suggest that managers for various reasons prefer to increase the size of the organisation for which they work than to increase its rate of profit. The results of this study indicate that the take-over mechanism, rather than being a constraint or managerial discretion, may in fact also encourage them in the same direction.

In sections 6.2 and 6.3, various reservations/qualifications to the above conclusions were examined. It was found that there were two serious and extremely important reservations which required careful consideration. First, it is possible that the consequences of take-over are much more unpleasant for the managers of relatively unprofitable firms than for the managers of relatively profitable ones. If this were so, the economic meaning of the results of this study would be totally reversed. In that case, since the stock market would demonstrably possess strong sanctions which could be used against the managers of the relatively unprofitable firms, the results of this study, even as they stand, would be more in accord with the requirements of the neoclassical than of the new theories of the firm. However, a limited investigation showed that the incidence of directorial dismissal in the acquired firms within 2 years of take-over was about 45 % and that it was on the whole not related either to the size of the firm or to its profitability before take-over.

The second important objection to the main conclusions of this chapter concerned the distinction between 'voluntary' and 'involuntary' take-overs. If such a distinction were made, which it would be legitimate to do on *a priori* grounds, it could, in principle, greatly alter the results of this study. However a careful examination of this argument showed that it was unlikely to do so.

7. AN ANALYSIS OF THE ACQUIRING FIRMS

INTRODUCTION

So far we have analysed the economic and financial characteristics of the taken-over firms and compared them with those of the surviving firms. In this chapter, we present a brief analysis of the acquiring firms; for this purpose, the characteristics of the acquiring firms will be compared with those of (i) the acquired firms (section 7.1) and (ii) the non-acquiring firms (section 7.2). This analysis is not intended to be as comprehensive as that presented previously for the comparison of taken-over and surviving firms, which is the main focus of this book. A *limited* study of the characteristics of the acquiring firms is offered here for its own interest and to round out the picture of the acquired firms given so far. It does, however, also have some bearing on the following important question which forms the subject of section 7.3.

It was seen in chapter 1 that one important function which the stock market may reasonably be expected to perform is to ensure efficient utilisation of the existing assets of firms. It was also observed that the take-over mechanism is an important disciplinary device, which may be used by the market for this purpose. However, although the results of the previous chapters have shown the stock market to be an imperfect disciplinarian in this sense, this does not mean that the market is incapable of performing the task in some other way. If we assume private profitability to be an indicator of efficiency in the normal calculus of a capitalist economy, then it is reasonable to hypothesise that in another sense, through the process of take-over itself, the stock market may yet be bringing about more efficient utilisation of the existing assets of the firms. For instance, it is quite possible that through the process of acquisition and merger, the economic resources of firms are periodically reshuffled in such a way as to lead to higher relative profitability on the total assets of firms which amalgamate. In other words, although it may not always be the least 'efficient' firms which are taken over, it is possible that the firms which are involved in take-overs become as a result relatively more profitable in relation to their combined assets.

This hypothesis will be examined here (section 7.3) by comparing the relative profitability of the firms involved in take-overs, before and (with a suitable time-lag) after take-over. The main results of this chapter will be summarised in section 7.4.

7.1 The acquired and the acquiring firms

Is there any difference between the observed characteristics of the acquired and the acquiring firms? If so, which characteristics, either on their own or in combination with others, are best able to distinguish between the two groups? As in the previous chapters Mahalanobis distance analysis and multiple discriminant analysis have been used to answer these questions. The two groups of firms were compared on the basis of their records over the 2 years and 6 years preceding the date of take-over. The following characteristics were considered: a measure of the rate of return, pre-tax profitability (X_1); liquidity (X_5); gearing (X_6); retention ratio (X_7) and growth (X_9).

Since size (X_8) violates the statistical assumptions of the discriminant and distance analyses, it was not included. This is no great loss, as size is not related to any of the other variables, and the main interest of this analysis is in identifying discriminating characteristics other than the size of the firm. One's expectation that the acquiring firms are on the whole likely to be very much larger than the acquired ones is confirmed by a glance at the data. In every case, the acquiring firm is bigger than the acquired one.

The results for all 5 industries together, on both a univariate and a multivariate basis, for 2-year and 6-year periods, are summarised in table 7.1.† It should be noted that, because there are large inter-industry differences in the firms' records, only acquisitions made by firms within their own industry are considered. Thus if a firm in one industry acquired a firm in another industry, neither firm is included. Furthermore, if a firm acquired more than one firm in the same year, the acquiring firm is included twice. Thus we have an equal number of acquiring and acquired firms in the two groups.

Since table 7.1 contains a rather large amount of information, it may be of some help to describe the various entries. Columns 1 to 3 give the mean, the standard deviation and the number of firms for each of the 5 characteristics (rows 1 to 5) of the taken-over firms; columns 4 to 6 give corresponding information for the acquiring firms. The results of the univariate analysis – the t test of difference of means – are given in column 7. Column 8 (first 5 rows) gives the proportion of firms which would be misclassified if we tried to allocate them to the acquired and the acquiring groups on the basis of the observed values of each of the

---

† The analysis was also done for some of the individual industries. Since the results were essentially similar to those given above, only the aggregate results for all 5 industries together are given here. The reader is also reminded that throughout this chapter only acquisitions by quoted companies of other quoted companies are considered.

TABLE 7.1. *Differences between the acquired and the acquiring firms: univariate and multivariate analyses*

Variable	Acquired firms			Acquiring firms			t	% of firms mis-classified	v	v_s
	Mean	Standard deviation	N_1	Mean	Standard deviation	N_2				
a. All 5 industries together, 1955–60: 2-year average records before take-over										
X_1 Pre-tax profitability (%)	12.65	8.64	100	16.04	7.68	100	-2.93^b	42.0	0.91	104.2
X_5 Liquidity (%)	1.58	20.00	100	-1.27	13.61	100	1.18	50.0	-0.27	-66.1
X_6 Gearing (%)	22.11	16.09	100	24.07	17.24	100	-1.96^a	48.0	0.18	42.0
X_7 Retention ratio (%)	50.21	32.15	100	58.95	16.01	100	-2.43^a	43.5	-0.05	18.1
X_9 Growth [$t-3=100$]	110.97	13.87	100	133.88	44.60	100	-4.91^b	35.0	0.26	122.7
Z	46.8	10.4	100	57.5	15.0	100		34.0		

The computed discriminant function, $Z = 0.91X_1 - 0.27X_5 + 0.18X_6 - 0.05X_7 + 0.26X_9$, is significant at the 1% level. The relevant statistics are given below.

$D_k^2 = 0.6759$

$F = 6.6^b$; $F_1 = 5$; $F_2 = 194$; $F_{F_2}^{F_1}(0.05) = 2.26$.

Variable	Acquired firms			Acquiring firms			t	% of firms mis-classified	v	v_s
b. All 5 industries together, 1955–60: 6-year average records before take-over										
X_1 Pre-tax profitability (%)	13.90	8.35	92	16.36	8.68	91^c	-1.96^a	44.3	0.07	7.6
X_5 Liquidity (%)	3.49	21.10	92	-0.05	11.45	91^c	1.41	43.1	-0.68	-156.4
X_6 Gearing (%)	22.03	16.24	92	24.09	16.50	91^c	-0.85	44.8	0.43	94.3
X_7 Retention ratio (%)	47.72	34.69	92	59.83	16.95	91^c	-2.99^b	42.1	0.47	171.9
X_9 Growth [$t-6=100$]	139.70	43.97	92	175.55	68.62	91^c	-4.21^b	33.2	0.35	274.8
Z	79.8	26.5	92	101.7	31.1	91		37.5		

The computed discriminant function. $Z = 0.07X_1 - 0.68X_5 + 0.43X_6 + 0.47X_7 + 0.35X_9$, is significant at the 1% level. The relevant statistics are given below.

$D_k^2 = 0.56$

$F = 5.0^b$; $F_1 = 5$; $F_2 = 177$; $F_{F_2}^{F_1}(0.05) = 2.26$.

[a] Indicates significance at the 5% level. [b] Indicates significance at the 1% level. [c] 1 firm excluded by mistake.

individual characteristics.† The results of the multiple discriminant analysis are given in column 9 (vector of discriminant coefficients, $\mathbf{v}$), column 10 (scaled vector of discriminant coefficients, $\mathbf{v}_s$) and in row 6 (Z values). It will be recalled from chapter 4 that column 9 gives the weights used to combine all five characteristics into a single discriminating index Z. The Z values, i.e. the discriminant scores, are calculated for each firm by using the computed discriminant function; the results obtained by classifying firms into the acquired and the acquiring groups on the basis of their respective Z values are given in row 6. The results of the distance analysis are given at the foot of each part of the table.

This table shows that there are highly significant differences between the two groups of firms, both on the basis of many of the individual characteristics and also when all 5 characteristics are considered together. Taking the short-term records (2-year) first, part a of table 7.1 shows that the acquiring firms have significantly better profitability and growth records (at the 1 % level) than the acquired ones; they are also on average somewhat less liquid, more highly geared and tend to retain a significantly greater proportion of their profits (at the 5 % level) than the firms in the other group. The results of the Mahalanobis distance analysis show that when all 5 variables are considered together, the hypothesis that the two groups are indistinguishable on the basis of their multiple characteristics is decisively rejected (at the 1 % level). Column 10 shows growth and profitability to be the most important discriminators in the multivariate context.

Nevertheless, it should be noted that although D_k^2 is highly significant, the degree of discrimination achieved by the computed discriminant function is not very high. The empirical probability of misclassification, on the basis of Z scores, is 34 % (see column 8) as against 50 % on random allocation. In fact, in view of the inter-correlation between the variables, this degree of misclassification is only slightly lower than what is achieved on the basis of growth alone.

Table 7.1 (part b) shows an essentially similar pattern of results for firms' long-term (6-year) records. The only notable difference is that profitability (X_1) is not so important either individually or in a multivariate context as it is when short-term records are considered. In the multivariate context, growth, retention ratio and liquidity are the most important discriminators.

There are two further points to note about the differences between the acquiring and the acquired firms. First, the degree of misclassification on the basis of Z scores in table 7.1 would be greatly reduced if size

† For the decision rule used for allocation, so as to minimise the chances of misclassification, see n. †, p. 68 above.

were to be included as an additional discriminating variable. The acquiring firms, as noted above, are on the whole very much bigger than the acquired ones and size is not related to any of the other variables. The multivariate distance on the basis of the 6 variables $(X_1, X_5, X_6, X_7, X_9$ and $X_8)$ would, therefore, be equal to the computed distance on the basis of the 5 variables given in table 7.1, plus the distance between the groups on the basis of size alone. The results of this calculation for the combined distance suggest that if we were given a list of equal numbers of acquiring and acquired firms, we would be able to allocate them to their respective groups with a fairly high degree of accuracy using these 6 characteristics: more than 80 % of the firms would be expected to be correctly classified as opposed to 50 % on random allocation.†

Secondly, since we did not have data on valuation ratios for all five industries, this variable was not considered in the analysis of table 7.1. However, an examination of the restricted sample for which valuation ratio data were available showed that the acquiring firms have higher, but not significantly (at the 5 % level) higher, valuation ratios than the acquired ones. Multivariate analysis revealed that the inclusion of this variable does not lead to significantly greater discrimination between the groups than what is achieved on the basis of the 5 variables in table 7.1.

To sum up, the most important features distinguishing the acquiring from the acquired firms appear to be their much higher rate of growth and very much larger size.‡ The acquiring firms are, however, also significantly more profitable on average than the firms they acquire, although in more than 30 % of cases it was found that the acquired firm had higher profitability than the acquiring one.§ It is, therefore,

---

† Taking short-term records, table 7.1 a shows D_k^2 on the basis of X_1, X_5, X_6, X_7, X_9 together to be equal to 0.68. The squared distance between the groups on the basis of log size for the two groups is 2.25. Therefore D_k^2 on the basis of X_1, X_5, X_6, X_7, X_9 and log X_8 would be 2.93 which gives an expected probability of misclassification of about 18 %. (Cf. chapters 3 and 4.)

  The reason we have used log X_8 rather than X_8 in the above calculation is that the assumptions of normality and of equal variances in the two groups are more nearly met in the former case than in the latter. As for the possible inter-correlation between variables, log size is known to be uncorrelated at least to growth and profitability and there is evidence that it is most probably unrelated to the other variables as well. (Cf. Singh and Whittington [1968], chapters 4 and 6 and appendix F.)

‡ Readers may like to note that it is not tautological to conclude, as we have done above, that the acquiring firms have on an average a much higher rate of growth of net assets than the firms they acquire. The comparisons of acquired and acquiring firms in table 7.1, it must be remembered, are based on the records of the two groups of firms *before* acquisition; but of course the high growth rates of acquiring firms may be partly due to *previous* acquisitions.

§ It is important to note that since the acquiring firms have an appreciably higher growth rate, it is possible that their accounting rates of profit may be understated relative to those of the acquired firms. (See the discussion of section 5.1 above.)

generally the case that at least as far as the quoted firms are concerned, firms with better performance records acquire quoted firms with relatively worse records. This leads to the presumption that the changes in control over the assets of the acquired firms lead on the whole to a more profitable utilisation of these assets. Whether or not this presumption is in fact borne out will be discussed in section 7.3.

7.2 THE ACQUIRING AND THE NON-ACQUIRING FIRMS

We have seen in the previous chapters that there are some differences between the characteristics of taken-over and non-taken-over firms, but that these differences are on the whole small. The results of the last section show that there undoubtedly exist larger differences between the taken-over and the acquiring firms. This suggests that although we may not be very successful in choosing the potential take-over victims on the basis of the firms' past records, it might be possible to predict with a much higher degree of accuracy which will be the acquiring firms.

In order to examine this possibility, the economic and financial characteristics of the acquiring and non-acquiring firms were analysed by means of discriminant and distance analysis. The procedure adopted was as follows. For all the acquiring firms in the 5 industries which made acquisitions within their own industries, the records *before* acquisition were considered. For each acquiring firm, a non-acquiring firm was selected at random in the same industry-year. Any such firm which made an acquisition in some other year during the period under consideration was excluded and replaced by another non-acquiring firm selected at random. For obvious reasons (unlike in section 7.1) an acquiring firm which made two acquisitions in the same year was included only once.

The results of this comparison are summarised in table 7.2. In the first instance, the two groups of firms were compared on the basis of the same variables as were considered in table 7.1, to which table 7.2 corresponds in every way. The results show that on a univariate basis, growth and retention ratio are the only statistically significant discriminators between the two groups. As in the case of the comparison with the acquired firms, the acquiring firms are more profitable, less liquid and more highly geared than the non-acquiring firms. However, whereas the acquiring firms were 'significantly' more profitable than the acquired firms, their advantage over the non-acquiring firms does not pass the significance test at the 5 % level. It will be recalled in this connection that the non-acquired firms (which set, in view of the relatively small number of firms which are acquired in any year, would not be very different from that of non-acquiring firms) were also significantly more profitable than the acquired ones.

TABLE 7.2. *Differences between the acquiring and the non-acquiring firms: univariate and multivariate analysis*

Variable	Acquiring firms			Non-acquiring firms			t	% of firms misclassified	v	v_s
	Mean	Standard deviation	N_1	Mean	Standard deviation	N_2				
a. All 5 industries together, 1955–60: 2-year average records before take-over										
X_1 Pre-tax profitability (%)	15.9	7.7	93	15.2	8.1	93	0.66	45.7	−0.46	−49.59
X_5 Liquidity (%)	−0.9	13.7	93	1.8	20.7	93	−1.07	49.5	0.51	121.99
X_6 Gearing (%)	24.3	17.3	93	23.2	17.7	93	0.42	47.8	−0.15	−35.05
X_7 Retention ratio (%)	58.8	16.2	93	52.0	26.3	93	2.12[a]	43.1	−0.64	−190.52
X_9 Growth [$t-3 = 100$]	134.0	45.5	93	119.9	38.5	93	2.28[a]	38.2	−0.30	−169.33
Z										

The computed discriminant function, $Z = -0.46X_1 + 0.51X_5 - 0.15X_6 - 0.64X_7 - 0.30X_9$, is not significant at the 5% level. The relevant statistics are given below.

$D_k^2 = 0.209$

$F = 1.90$; $F_1 = 5$; $F_2 = 180$; $F_{F_2}^{F_1}(0.05) = 2.26$.

Variable	Acquiring firms			Non-acquiring firms			t	% of firms misclassified	v	v_s
b. All 5 industries together, 1955–60: 6-year average records before take-over										
X_1 Pre-tax profitability (%)	16.3	8.9	81	15.7	9.1	82[c]	0.43	49.1	−0.91	−103.44
X_5 Liquidity (%)	0.1	11.8	81	2.6	19.4	82[c]	−1.00	49.7	−0.12	−23.62
X_6 Gearing (%)	24.3	16.7	81	24.2	18.2	82[c]	0.04	47.9	−0.11	−23.90
X_7 Retention ratio (%)	59.7	17.4	81	52.7	23.1	82[c]	2.19[a]	44.8	0.33	86.09
X_9 Growth [$t-6 = 100$]	175.5	69.6	81	143.8	53.0	82[c]	3.27[b]	39.9	0.21	165.99
Z	39.5	14.7	81	30.7	13.5	82		36.8		

The computed discriminant function, $Z = -0.91X_1 - 0.12X_5 - 0.11X_6 + 0.33X_7 + 0.21X_9$, is significant at the 5% level. The relevant statistics are given below.

$D_k^2 = 0.380$

$F = 3.02$[a]; $F_1 = 5$; $F_2 = 157$; $F_{F_2}^{F_1}(0.05) = 2.27$.

[a] Indicates significance at the 5% level.　　[b] Indicates significance at the 1% level.　　[c] 1 firm included by mistake.

The results of the multivariate distance analysis show that D_k^2 is not significant at the 5 % level for the firms' short-term records, but that it is significant when the long-term (part b of table 7.2) records are considered. However, in the latter case, although the hypothesis that there is no 'distance' between the groups on the basis of their multiple characteristics is rejected, the degree of discrimination achieved is small. The empirical probability of misclassification is about 37 %, as against the expectation of 50 % on random allocation, and about 40 % on the basis of growth alone. The scaled vector of discriminant coefficients shows growth to be the most important discriminator in the multivariate context as well.

A higher degree of discrimination between the two groups of firms was achieved when size (X_8) and other rates of return $(X_2, X_3$ and $X_4)$ were added to the discriminant. For all nine variables together, the discriminant function was significant at the 1 % level for both the short-term and the long-term records of firms. The empirical probability of misclassification on the basis of the computed discriminant function was found to be 25 % for the firms' short-term records and 27 % for their longer-term records.† These figures and the observed values of D_k^2 suggest that if one had a list containing equal numbers of acquiring and non-acquiring firms, one would be able to allocate 75 % of the firms correctly to their respective groups on the basis of their past records. However, as has been noted earlier, from the practical point of view, the predictive accuracy implied by these figures is much more modest in the more realistic context where, instead of assuming equal numbers in the two groups, it is known that only a small percentage of firms (about 4 %) are likely to make acquisitions in any year and one is trying to predict which those firms are.

Nevertheless, it is worth noting that the past records of firms lead to better discrimination between the acquiring and non-acquiring firms, than between the acquired and non-acquired firms. It will be recalled (chapter 5) that when taken-over and non-taken-over firms of the same size were compared on the basis of all their characteristics taken together,‡ the linear discriminant function was found to be insignificant (at the 5 % level) for the firms' long-term records, and significant for their short-term records. In the latter case, the empirical probability of misclassification on the basis of the computed discriminant function was found to be about 35 %. When the influence of size was also taken

† Essentially similar results are obtained if we use log X_8 instead of X_8 and follow the procedure of the previous section in calculating the expected probability of misclassification.

‡ It should be noted that since valuation ratio data were not available for firms in all industries, the results for the acquiring and non-acquiring firms given in the text are based on all variables excluding valuation ratio. The empirical probability of misclassification is likely to be slightly lower if this variable is also included.

into account, the probability of misclassification was still at its least about 32 %.

There is another notable difference between the results for the acquiring and non-acquiring firms on the one hand and the acquired and non-acquired on the other. Growth is the most important discriminator in the former case whereas it will be recalled that profitability was found to be the most important variable in the latter, on both univariate and multivariate analyses.

To sum up this evidence, we find that the acquiring firms are larger and more dynamic than either the acquired or the non-acquiring. Apart from a higher rate of growth, they have all the other attributes one associates with 'growth-minded' firms – higher retention ratio, higher gearing ratio and less liquidity. The data also show that it is relatively easier to distinguish this particular group of firms from the rest than it is to separate the taken-over and non-taken-over firms.

7.3   PROFITABILITY OF ACQUIRING FIRMS AFTER TAKE-OVER

Another aspect of acquiring firms studied in this chapter is their record after acquisition. It was seen in section 7.1 that on the whole it is firms with better performance records which acquire firms with relatively worse records. Both for assessing the 'efficiency' of the take-over mechanism and for practical policy purposes, the important question is whether acquisitions lead to greater relative profits on the combined assets of the amalgamated firms. If they do, then, although the take-over mechanism may not be a good 'disciplinarian' in the sense discussed in the last chapter, it could still be regarded as fulfilling its task of bringing about more 'efficient' utilisation of the existing assets of the firms.

In order to investigate this question, the profitability of each acquiring firm after acquisition was compared with the combined profitability of both the acquiring and the acquired firm before amalgamation. A firm's profitability at any point of time is of course greatly influenced by the industry it belongs to and the overall state of the economy. Therefore the figures compared were those for firm profitability in relation to the average profitability of firms in the same industry-year. In particular, the relative profitability of an acquiring firm in the year of acquisition and for 1 and 2 years after acquisition were compared with the combined (weighted average) relative profitability of both the acquiring and the acquired firm before acquisition.†

---

† The reader is reminded that, as in the previous two sections, this investigation was confined to acquiring firms which made acquisitions within their own industry.

The results of this investigation for pre-tax profitability on net assets are summarised in table 7.3. The table shows for instance that for 9 of the 16 acquiring firms in the non-electrical engineering industry, the relative profitability in the year of take-over was less than the combined relative profitability of the amalgamating firms before take-over. Only 7 of the 16 firms had either equalled or improved upon the combined profitability records of the amalgamating firms. If the profitability of the acquiring firms one year after take-over is considered, we find that of the 14 acquiring firms in non-electrical engineering for which data were available,† 10 had suffered a relative decline. To put these figures in perspective, it should be borne in mind that if one compared the current relative profitability of a random sample of firms with their relative profitability for a few years before, one would expect the performance of about half of them to have worsened.

Table 7.3 shows very clearly that both for the individual industries and for all industries together, there was in a majority of cases a decline in the relative profitability of the acquiring firms, whether one considers profitability in the year of take-over or 1 and 2 years after take-over. It is important to note that about 2 years is probably the optimal length of time for this exercise since one is then effectively comparing the combined profitability of amalgamating firms before take-over with the profitability of the acquiring firm 3 (accounting) years later. If the period considered were shorter than this, it could be argued that not sufficient time had elapsed for the reorganisation of the amalgamating firms to have taken place and for the benefits of the merger to be reflected in improved profitability. A longer period would also be inappropriate since there might be further acquisitions by the acquiring firm, as well as other external factors which could affect its profitability. The actual results we obtained when we considered a period longer than 2 years after acquisition confirmed this impression.‡

Results very similar to those given above were obtained when post-tax profitability on equity assets was used as a measure of profitability. In this case, however, instead of comparing the relative profitability

† Data were available to us only for the period 1954–60. For an acquisition which took place in 1960, the last available accounts for the acquiring and the acquired firm before take-over are usually for the year 1959. The acquiring firm in this case would be included in column 1, but not in column 4 of table 7.3, since data for the acquiring firm one year after acquisition would not be available to us. This explains the discrepancy in the numbers in columns 1, 4 and 7 of table 7.3. The discrepancy between the total number of acquiring firms in column 1 of table 7.3 and the number given in table 7.1 (part *a*) arises in part from the fact that firms which made two or more acquisitions in the same year, or in years very close to each other, are included only once in table 7.3. Also firms which made acquisitions in a number of successive years were excluded from the latter table.

‡ For instance, for 3 years after acquisition, 77% showed a relative decline in profitability, compared with the figure of 57.1% for 2 years after acquisition shown in table 7.3.

TABLE 7.3. *The post-acquisition profitability records of acquiring firms: pre-tax profitability on net assets; 1955–60; individual industries*

Industry	Year of take-over			1 year after take-over			2 years after take-over		
	Number of firms	Number with worse records[a]	% with worse records[a]	Number of firms	Number with worse records[a]	% with worse records[a]	Number of firms	Number with worse records[a]	% with worse records[a]
Non-electrical engineering	16	9	56.2	14	10	71.4	11	6	54.5
Electrical engineering	8	6	75.0	5	5	100.0	2	2	100.0
Food	16	12	75.0	10	6	60.0	5	2	40.0
Drink	35	22	62.8	25	14	56.0	15	8	53.3
Clothing and footwear	2	2	100.0	2	2	100.0	2	2	100.0
Total	77	51	66.2	56	37	66.0	35	20	57.1

[a] These are the firms whose relative profitability declined compared with the combined relative profitability of the amalgamating firms before take-over.

of an acquiring firm after take-over with the combined profitability of the amalgamating firms before take-over, we compared it with its own post-tax profitability before take-over. The percentages of acquiring firms which showed a decline in their post-tax profitability records in the year of take-over and 1 and 2 years after take-over were on the whole slightly higher than the corresponding figures given in table 7.3.

Two important possible reservations to the above results need to be considered. First, it would be legitimate to argue that the figures for acquiring firms which showed a decline in their relative profitability records after take-over, especially in table 7.3, are likely to be biased upwards for accounting reasons. There may be a fall in the accounting profitability of the acquiring firm in the year of take-over compared with the combined profitability of the amalgamating firms before take-over for two reasons. If the acquiring firm paid a price for the acquired firm greater than the book value of its assets, it would usually be entered in the books of the former at its purchase price,† thus increasing the relative value of the net assets of the acquiring firm. Also, in a number of cases – especially when there has been a contest – the profits in the year of take-over may be reduced because the new managers will take a very conservative view of the profits of the company which has been acquired (e.g. by putting a low value on stocks). The results of these accounting operations will be an apparent fall in the profitability of the acquiring firm in the year of take-over.

In order to eliminate this bias, we compared the profitability of acquiring firms 2 years after take-over with their profitability in the year of take-over, i.e. at the first appearance of consolidated accounts or the amalgamating firms. The percentage of acquiring firms in all 5 industries which showed a deterioration in their relative profitability records 2 years after take-over, on the basis of this exercise, was 54.3, compared with the corresponding figure of 57.1 % in table 7.3. Thus we conclude that although the latter figure may be biased upward for accounting reasons, the extent of the bias is very small. Even when due allowance is made for this bias, it is still found that more than 50 % of the acquiring firms suffered a decline in their relative profitability after take-over.

The second important reservation concerns the measures of profitability used in this study. It could legitimately be argued that from the shareholders' point of view, the appropriate measure of the acquiring firm's efficiency is growth of earnings per share. It is possible in principle for a firm to sustain a fall in rate of return on net assets, and yet increase earnings per share. As was mentioned in chapter 6, the non-availability

† The difference between the purchase price and the book value is often entered under the heading of goodwill in the accounts of the acquiring firm.

of data has precluded us from using the growth of earnings per share. Therefore at one level, this is an important qualification to the above results, which must stand. There are, however, two points which should be noted in this connection. First, this reservation is inapplicable if the purpose of the exercise is to assess the overall 'efficiency' of the take-over mechanism in the sense discussed in the introduction to this chapter. For this particular purpose, pre-tax profitability on net assets or post-tax profitability on equity assets are more suitable measures of profitability than growth of earnings per share. Secondly, there is some recent evidence which is also not without relevance to this issue. The earnings records of the thirty largest U.K. companies which were involved in one or more important mergers in the 1960s were studied in a survey carried out by the magazine *Management Today*.† It was found that only a small proportion performed well in terms of growth of earnings per share; the majority did not. The authors of this survey concluded that the biggest potential losers are shareholders in bidding companies, who have been ignored in order to provide the expansion which the managers seek.

To sum up, although the more dynamic and 'efficient' firms tend to acquire the relatively weak and inefficient ones, we have found that in at least half the cases there is subsequent retrogression with respect to profitability on either the combined assets of the amalgamating firms, or the assets of the acquiring firms before take-over. This strongly suggests, although it by no means proves, that it is on balance very unlikely that the reshuffling of economic resources which takes place as a result of the take-over process leads to any more profitable utilisation of these resources. The weight of the evidence indicates that the take-over process is at best neutral in this respect. It could, however, be argued that some of the acquiring firms whose relative profitability falls after take-over are sacrificing profits to growth. It is possible that these firms might have been able to maintain their profitability records if they had not indulged in take-overs.

7.4   SUMMARY

In this chapter we have presented a limited empirical analysis of the acquiring firms to complement the analysis in the previous chapters of taken-over firms. For this purpose, the records of the acquiring firms were compared with those of (i) taken-over firms and (ii) non-acquiring firms. In addition, the profitability records of acquiring firms after take-over were examined in order to discover whether the take-over

† *Management Today*, May 1970.

process leads to a better overall utilisation of the existing assets of firms.

The following main points emerge from the analysis. There are large differences between the characteristics of the acquiring and acquired firms on both a univariate and a multivariate basis. If one were given a list of equal numbers of acquiring and acquired firms, it would be possible to allocate these firms to their respective groups on the basis of their observed characteristics with a fairly high degree of accuracy (more than 80 % of the firms would be correctly allocated). However, the past records of firms would lead to a relatively lower degree of discrimination between the acquiring and the non-acquiring firms, although it would be much greater than on the basis of random allocation. It was also discovered that a more accurate distinction is possible between the characteristics of the acquiring and the non-acquiring firms, than between those of the acquired and the non-acquired firms. The profile of the acquiring firm revealed by the analysis is essentially that of a large, dynamic firm with a very high rate of growth. It is significantly more profitable than the average acquired firm, but not than the average non-acquiring firm. It possesses all the other characteristics one associates with a 'growth-minded' firm, i.e. it retains a greater proportion of profits, is more highly geared and less liquid than the average non-acquiring or the average acquired firm.

The comparison of the profitability records of the acquiring firms after take-over with the combined profitability of amalgamating firms showed that in at least half the cases there is a decline in relative profitability after take-over. It is, therefore, on balance very unlikely that the reorganisation of the firms' assets which takes place through the take-over mechanism leads to a more profitable utilisation of these assets. The evidence indicates that the take-over process is most likely to be neutral in this respect.

BIBLIOGRAPHY

GOVERNMENT PUBLICATIONS

Board of Trade 'Acquisitions and amalgamations of quoted companies, 1954–61', *Economic Trends*, No. 114, April 1963.

Board of Trade 'Non-quoted companies and their finance', *Economic Trends*, No. 136, February 1965.

Board of Trade 'Acquisitions and amalgamations of quoted companies, 1962–63', *Economic Trends*, No. 146, Dec. 1965.

Board of Trade 'Patterns of company finance', *Economic Trends*, No. 169, November 1967.

Central Statistical Office *Annual Abstract of Statistics*.

Ministry of Labour *Statistics on Income, Prices, Employment and Production*, No. 1, April 1962.

OTHER BOOKS AND ARTICLES

Alchian, A. A. [1950] 'Uncertainty, evolution, and economic theory', *Journal of Political Economy*, June 1950.

Alchian, A. A. and Kessel, R. A. [1962] 'Competition, monopoly, and the pursuit of pecuniary gain', *Aspects of Labor Economics*, Conference of the Universities–National Bureau Committee for Economic Research, Princeton, 1962.

Anderson, T. W. [1958] *An Introduction to Multivariate Statistical Analysis*, New York, 1958.

Armstrong, A. and Silberston, A. [1965] 'Size of plant, size of enterprise and concentration in British manufacturing industry, 1935–1958', *Journal of the Royal Statistical Society*, Series A (General), vol. 128, part 3, 1965.

Aspin, A. A. and Welch, B. L. [1949] 'Tables for use in comparisons whose accuracy involves two variances, separately estimated', *Biometrika*, December 1949.

Bain, J. S. [1950] 'The theory of oligopoly: discussion', *American Economic Review*, Papers and Proceedings, May 1950.

Bain, J. S. [1956] *Barriers to New Competition*, Cambridge, Mass., 1956.

Baumol, W. J. [1959] *Business Behavior, Value and Growth*, New York, 1959.

Baumol, W. J. [1962] 'On the theory of the expansion of the firm', *American Economic Review*, December 1962.

Baumol, W. J. [1965] *The Stock Market and Economic Efficiency*, New York, 1965.

Becker, G. S. [1962] 'Irrational behavior and economic theory', *Journal of Political Economy*, February 1962.

Box, G. E. P. [1949] 'A general distribution theory for a class of likelihood criteria', *Biometrika*, December 1949.

Box, G. E. P. [1953] 'Non-normality and tests on variances', *Biometrika*, December 1953.

Bryan, J. G. [1951] 'The generalised discriminant function: mathematical foundation and computational routine', *Harvard Educational Review*, Spring 1951.

Bushnell, J. A. [1961] *Australian Company Mergers, 1916–1959*, Melbourne, 1961.

Caves, R. E. [1968] 'Market organisation, performance, and public policy', *Britain's Economic Prospects*, R. E. Caves and associates, Washington, 1968.

Cochran, W. G. [1964] 'On the performance of the linear discriminant function', *Bulletin of the International Statistics Institute*, Tome 39, Book 2, reprinted in *Technometrics*, May 1964.

Cochran, W. G. and Bliss, C. I. [1948] 'Discriminant functions with covariance', *Annals of Mathematical Statistics*, vol. 19, 1948.

Cook, P. L. and Cohen, R. [1958] *Effects of Mergers*, London, 1958.

Cooley, W. W. and Lhones, P. R. [1962] *Multivariate Procedures for the Behavioral Sciences*, New York, 1962.

Cornfield, J. and Mantel, N. [1950] 'Some new aspects of the application of maximum likelihood to the calculation of the dosage response curve', *Journal of the American Statistical Association*, June 1950.

Cottle, S. and Whitman, T. [1959] *Corporate Earning Power and Market Valuation, 1935–55*, Durham, N. Carolina, 1959.

Cyert, R. M. and March, J. G. [1963] *A Behavioral Theory of the Firm*, Englewood Cliffs, 1963.

Donaldson, G. [1961] *Corporate Debt Capacity*, Boston, 1961.

Eckstein, O. [1961] 'A survey of the theory of public expenditure criteria, reply', *Public Finance: Needs, Sources and Utilization*, Conference of the Universities–National Bureau Committee for Economic Research, Princeton, 1961.

Farrell, M. J. [1962] 'On the structure of the capital market', *Economic Journal*, December 1962.

Financial Times [1961] 'Behind the wave of mergers', 30 March 1961.

Finney, D. J. [1952] *Probit Analysis*, 2nd ed., Cambridge, 1952.

Fisher, R. A. [1936] 'The use of multiple measurements in taxonomic problems', *Annals of Eugenics*, vol. vii, 1936.

Fisher, R. A. [1938] 'The statistical utilisation of multiple measurements', *Annals of Eugenics*, vol. viii, 1938.

Frank, R. E., Massy, W. F. and Morrison, G. D. [1965] 'Bias in multiple discriminant analysis', *Journal of Marketing Research*, August 1965.

Friedman, M. [1953] *Essays in Positive Economics*, Chicago, 1953.

Galbraith, J. K. [1967] 'A review of a review'. *The Public Interest*, Fall 1967.

Goldberger, A. [1964] *Econometric Theory*, New York, 1964.

Gort, M. [1969] 'An economic disturbance theory of mergers', *Quarterly Journal of Economics*, November 1969.

Gutman, W. [1963] 'Book value–market value patterns' in E. M. Lerner (ed.), *Readings in Financial Analysis and Investment Management*, Homewood, Ill., 1963.

Harcourt, G. C. [1965] 'The accountant in the golden age', *Oxford Economic Papers*, March 1965.

Hart, P. E. and Prais, S. J. [1956] 'The analysis of business concentration: a statistical approach', *Journal of the Royal Statistical Society*, Series A (General), vol. 119, part 2, 1956.

Hills, M. [1966] 'Allocation rules and their error rates', *Journal of the Royal Statistical Society*, Series B (Methodological), vol. 28, no. 1, 1966.

Hindley, B. [1969] 'Capitalism and the corporation', *Economica*, November 1969.

Hoel, P. G. [1962] *Introduction to Mathematical Statistics*, 3rd ed., New York, 1962.

Hunter, A. [1969] 'Mergers and industry concentration in Britain', *Banco Nazionale del Lavoro Quarterly Review*, December 1969.

Ito, K. and Schull, W. J. [1964] 'On the robustness of the T_0^2 test in multivariate analysis of variance when variance covariance matrices are not equal', *Biometrika*, June 1964.

Johnson, H. G. [1968] 'The economic approach to social questions', *Economica*, February 1968.

Kaldor, N. [1966] 'Marginal productivity and the macroeconomic theories of distribution', *Review of Economic Studies*, 1966.

Kendall, M. G. [1966] 'Discrimination and classification' in P. R. Krishnaiah (ed.), *Multivariate Analysis*, New York, 1966.

Kendall, M. G. [1968] *A Course in Multivariate Analysis*, 4th imp., London, 1968.

Kendall, M. G. and Stuart, A. [1966] *The Advanced Theory of Statistics*, vol. III, London, 1966.

Koopmans, T. C. [1957] *Three Essays on the State of Economic Science*, New York, 1957.

Lee, Maw Lin [1964] 'Income, income change and durable goods demand', *Journal of the American Statistical Association*, December 1964.

Levene, H. [1960] 'Robust tests for equality of variances', *Contributions to Probability and Statistics*, Palo Alto, 1960.

Lewellen, W. G. [1968] *Executive Compensation in Large Corporations*, New York, 1968.

Ma, R. [1958] 'Composition of the corporate sector: II – a comparison of public and private companies', *Accounting Research*, October 1958.

Ma, R. [1960] 'Births and deaths in the quoted public company sector in the United Kingdom, 1949–1953', *Yorkshire Bulletin of Economic and Social Research*, November 1960.

Machlup, F. [1967] 'Theories of the firm: marginalist, behavioral, managerial', *American Economic Review*, March 1967.

Management Today [1970] March 1970.

Manne, H. G. [1965] 'Mergers and the market for corporate control', *Journal of Political Economy*, 1965.

Markham, J. W. [1955] 'Survey of the evidence and findings on mergers', *Business Concentration and Price Policy*, Conference of the Universities–National Bureau Committee for Economic Research, Princeton, 1955.

Marris, R. L. [1964] *The Economic Theory of 'Managerial' Capitalism*, London, 1964.

Marris, R. L. [1967] 'Profitability and growth in the individual firm', *Business Ratios*, Spring 1967.

Marris, R. L. [1968] 'Galbraith, Solow and the truth about corporations', *The Public Interest*, Spring 1968.

Marris, R. L. [1968b] 'Review of J. K. Galbraith: *The New Industrial State*', *American Economic Review*, 1968.

Marris, R. L. and Singh, A. [1966] 'A measure of a firm's average share price', *Journal of the Royal Statistical Society*, Series A (General), vol. 129, part 1, 1966.

McGowan, J. J. [1965] 'The effects of alternative merger policies on size distribution of firms', *Yale Economic Essays*, Fall 1965.

Meade, J. E. [1968] 'Is "the new industrial state" inevitable?', *Economic Journal*, June 1968.

Mennel, W. [1962] *Take-over: the Growth of Monopoly in Britain, 1951–61*, London, 1962.

Modigliani, F. and Miller, M. H. [1958] 'The cost of capital, corporation finance and the theory of investment', *American Economic Review*, June 1958.

Monsen, R. J., Jr. and Downs, A. [1965] 'A theory of large managerial firms', *Journal of Political Economy*, June 1965.

Moon, R. W. [1968] *Business Mergers and Take-over Bids*, 3rd ed., London, 1968.

Morrison, D. F. [1967] *Multivariate Statistical Methods*, New York, 1967.

Nelson, R. L. [1959] *Merger Movements in American Industry, 1895–1956*, Princeton, 1959.

Nerlove, M. [1968] 'Factors affecting differences among rates of return on investments in individual common stocks', *Review of Economics and Statistics*, August 1968.

Netter, J. and Beaver, W. [1967] discussion on 'Financial ratios as predictors of failure', *Empirical Research in Accounting: Selected Studies, 1966*, Chicago, 1967.

Orcutt, G. H., Greenberger, M., Korbel, J. and Rivilin, A. M. [1961] *Microanalysis of Socioeconomic Systems: a Simulation Study*, New York, 1961.

Papandreou, A. G. [1952] 'Some basic problems in the theory of the firm' in B. F. Haley (ed.), *A Survey of Contemporary Economics*, vol. II, Homewood, Ill., 1952.

Penrose, E. [1959] *The Theory of the Growth of the Firm*, Oxford, 1959.

Rao, C. R. [1952] *Advanced Statistical Methods in Biometric Research*, New York, 1952.

Rao, C. R. [1965] *Linear Statistical Inference and its Application*, New York, 1965.

Reyment, R. A. [1962] 'Observations on homogeneity of covariance matrices in paleontologic biometry', *Biometrics*, March 1962.

Rose, H. B. and Newbould, G. D. [1967] 'The 1967 take-over boom', *Moorgate and Wall Street*, Autumn 1967.

Rubner, A. [1966] *The ensnared Shareholder*, Harmondsworth, 1966.

Shepherd, W. G. [1966] 'Changes in British industrial concentration, 1951–1958', *Oxford Economic Papers*, March 1966.

Simon, H. A. and Samuelson, P. A. [1963] 'Problems of methodology: discussion', *American Economic Review*, Papers and Proceedings, May 1963.

Singh, A. [1963] 'Preliminary notes on a theory of take-overs', unpublished paper, Cambridge, 1963.

Singh, A. [1970] *Take-overs, the Capital Market and the Theory of the Firm: An inter-firm study of industrial acquisitions and mergers in the U.K.*, unpublished Ph.D. dissertation, University of California, Berkeley, 1970.

Singh, A. and Whittington, G. [1968] *Growth, Profitability and Valuation*, Cambridge, 1968.

Smith, C. A. B. 'Some examples of discrimination' *Annals of Eugenics*, vol. XIII, 1947.

Snedecor, G. W. and Cochran, W. G. [1967] *Statistical Methods*, 6th ed., Ames, Iowa, 1967.

Solow, R. [1968] 'The truth further refined: a comment on Marris', *The Public Interest*, Spring 1968.

Stigler, G. J. [1950] 'Monopoly and oligopoly by merger', *American Economic Review*, Supplement, May 1950.

Weston, J. F. [1953] *The Role of Mergers in the Growth of Large Firms*, Berkeley, 1953.

Wilks, S. S. [1960] 'Multi-dimensional statistical scatter' in Ingram, Olkin *et al.* (eds.) *Contributions to Probability and Statistics: Essays in honor of Harold Hotelling*, Palo Alto, 1960.

Williamson, O. [1964] *The Economics of Discretionary Behavior: Managerial Objectives in a Theory of the Firm*, Englewood Cliffs, 1964.

Winter, S. G., Jr. [1964] 'Economic "natural selection" and the theory of the firm', *Yale Economic Essays*, Spring 1964.

Wright, J. F. [1962] 'The capital market and the finance of industry' in G. D. N. Worswick and P. H. Ady (eds.), *The British Economy in the Nineteen-fifties*, Oxford, 1962.

Wright Mills, C. [1959] *The Power Elite*, New York, 1959.

INDEX